The Domestication
of Critical Theory

The Domestication of Critical Theory

Michael J. Thompson

ROWMAN &
LITTLEFIELD
———— INTERNATIONAL

London • New York

Published by Rowman & Littlefield International, Ltd.
Unit A, Whitacre Mews, 26–34 Stannary Street, London SE11 4AB
www.rowmaninternational.com

Rowman & Littlefield International, Ltd. is an affiliate of Rowman & Littlefield
4501 Forbes Boulevard, Suite 200, Lanham, Maryland 20706, USA
With additional offices in Boulder, New York, Toronto (Canada), and Plymouth (UK)
www.rowman.com

British Library Cataloguing in Publication Data
A catalogue record for this book is available from the British Library

ISBN: HB 978-1-78348-430-0
     PB 978-1-78348-431-7

Library of Congress Cataloging-in-Publication Data
Names: Thompson, Michael, 1973– author.
Title: The domestication of critical theory / Michael J. Thompson.
Description: Lanham : Rowman & Littlefield International, 2016. |
   Includes bibliographical references and index.
Identifiers: LCCN 2015044181 (print) | LCCN 2015048350 (ebook) |
   ISBN 9781783484300 (cloth : alk. paper) | ISBN 9781783484317 (pbk. : alk. paper) |
   ISBN 9781783484324 (electronic)
Subjects: LCSH: Critical theory—History—20th century. | Social sciences—Research—
   History—20th century.
Classification: LCC HM480 .T46 2016 (print) | LCC HM480 (ebook) |
   DDC 300.72—dc23
LC record available at https://lccn.loc.gov/2015044181

♾™ The paper used in this publication meets the minimum requirements of American
National Standard for Information Sciences—Permanence of Paper for Printed Library
Materials, ANSI/NISO Z39.48-1992.

Printed in the United States of America

for Stephen Eric Bronner,
who taught the deeper meaning of the phrase
hic Rhodus, hic saltus

Contents

Preface

This book is put forward as a prelude to a more general project of retrieval and reconstruction of critical theory. It is essentially driven by the notion that critical theory's continued relevance can only be sustained if it is to regain its essentially *critical* character—critical in the sense that it fundamentally calls into question the prevailing norms, values, and social institutions that govern society. Ever since the time of Socrates, this has been the express aim of reasoned thought oriented toward public concerns, and it seems to me that any confrontation with the affairs of modern, late capitalist societies must be informed by the kind of questions and forms of thinking that critical theory has at its core. These are needed now more than ever. The fundamental currents of postindustrial society now confront us with the prospect of an ever-growing integration of cultural and psychological patterns of the individual to the prevailing system. Conformity as well as political docility are the dominant features of our political and cultural reality. However one chooses to characterize the politics and culture of the present, there can be little doubt that it has become increasingly submissive to elite interests as well as complicit in an affirmative culture that cements the legitimacy of an irrational, destructive, and unjust social order. To be sure, the growing forces of cultural and social conformity, the submission of large swaths of the world's population to norms and institutions governed by capital, and the increasing analytic and technical nature of contemporary philosophy and the social sciences do not inspire confidence that a new wave of critical consciousness and social change in any enlightened, progressive sense is on the horizon.

With this in mind, I believe it is crucial for critical theory to rethink its foundations and its aims. I want to urge the reader to reconsider the academicized path that has driven critical theory into what I call here a "domesticated" state. I want to suggest a critique of a kind of critical theory that

ix

has marginalized the more radical aims that motivated the first generation
of critical theorists, who saw Marx—no less than Hegel, Weber, Nietzsche,
and Freud—as a central figure in comprehending the dynamics of modernity,
particularly the nature of power, domination, culture, and consciousness
in the modern age. This is precisely what the newer generation of critical
theorists has tirelessly worked against. They have elaborated new paradigms
of thought that have marginalized Marxian ideas, and, as a result, they have
made critical theory impotent in the face of capital and its increasing influence. What I present in the following pages is therefore meant to open a
crevice in the edifice of social and political philosophy more generally as
well as critical theory more specifically. This book makes no pretension at
being systematic in any sense of the word—that will be the aim of subsequent
work. For now, it is important to call into question the critical *bona fides* of
contemporary trends in critical theory and to reconstruct some of the basic
aspects of what I think we should consider critical theory's distinctive logic
(in addition to reconstructing in some sense its deeper, core aim of social
transformation and the kinds of social pathologies that block and frustrate
that essential human drive).

Such an enterprise only has value to the extent that it can help clarify
the ideas of oppositional forms of thinking that are fused to a rationalist,
Enlightenment conception of a rational society organized around the common interest of its members. As Hegel and Marx knew all too well, this
means combatting the forces of reaction as well as the degenerate elements
that have created and maintain a defective form of modernity. Critical theory
persists, it can be said, only because modernity still holds out for us its own
potentiality for a deeper, more satisfying form of social solidarity and individual development than our present reality can provide. The political core
of this kind of critique has always been to see that the perversions of culture,
of society and polity, were the result of structural inequalities of social power
that enabled elite groups to reprogram those domains according to their own
interests. As a social system with such a logic, capitalism must therefore be
at the center of critical theory's concerns. The commodification of consciousness and the reconciliation of modern culture and politics to the prevailing
system have affected a pervasive sense of conformity. It can perhaps even be
said that modern culture is suffering from a severe conservatism in its basic
self-understanding. No longer are we permitted, as were German Idealists,
democratic socialists, avant-garde artists, and the like before us, to look at
our culture as perverting the potentialities for a better, more rational form
of society. No longer is there a sense of the possibility for an alternative,
different course for modern society other than the present. Such a restrained
mentality cannot be the animating spirit of critical theory. It is rather the stuff
of a culture that can only feebly "paint its gray on gray." To restore color to

our world and regenerate a vision for social transformation requires a rehabilitation of the political dimension of critical theory. Reconstructing it along more humanistic, more explicitly radical lines is therefore the primary aim of this book.

Some of the following chapters are drawn from papers presented at different academic conferences and symposia over the past several years at institutions such as Columbia University; New York University; the University of Tennessee, Knoxville; Iowa State University; Uppsala University, Sweden; the John Felice Center in Rome, Italy; the School of Oriental and African Studies, University of London; Cambridge University; the Graduate Center of the City University of New York; and the Department of Philosophy at Stony Brook University. I developed some of the ideas in this book in *Current Perspectives in Social Theory* and *Situations*. Chapter 3 is based on an earlier version of a paper published in *Philosophy and Social Criticism* 40, no. 8 (2014): 779–97, and an earlier version of chapter 6 initially appeared in the volume *Reclaiming the Sane Society: Essays on Erich Fromm's Thought*, edited by Seyed Miri, Robert Lake, and Tricia Kress (Rotterdam: Sense Publishers, 2014), 37–58. I am grateful to these publishers for allowing me to use material initially published there in this book.

My conversations and debates with others on the various ideas presented here have been invaluable to me and helped shape my ideas. Friends and interlocutors who have commented on the ideas that follow include Kevin Anderson, Bob Antonio, Stanley Aronowitz, Marshall Berman, Jim Block, Stephen Eric Bronner, Harry Dahms, Allegra DeLaurentiis, Arnold Farr, Andrew Feenberg, David Harvey, Christoph Henning, Axel Honneth, Dick Howard, Daniel Krier, Todd Kruger, Geoff Kurtz, Lauren Langman, Christian Lotz, Eduardo Mendieta, Patrick Murray, Robespierre de Oliveira, Jeanne Schuler, Tony Smith, Mark Worrell, and Greg Zucker, among others. None of these people can be held accountable for any mistakes that may follow, but they were important in helping me focus and shape many of the ideas developed in this book. Of course, it goes without saying that all errors are my own.

Introduction

How Critical Theory Was Domesticated

Critical theory was initially conceived as a philosophical and social scientific doctrine that called into question the most fundamental sources of social domination in advanced capitalist societies. Its focus was on the various ways that instrumental reason, channeled and harnessed by the pressures of capital and the pulse of market exchange value, had the capacity to deform the cognitive powers of subjects and weaken their ability to critique the prevailing norms and institutions that secured power over them. The withering of critical agency was therefore the central concern of the early critical theorists who saw the dominant forms of theoretical self-understanding as reflecting and reproducing those same forms of power and sought to promote a new kind of theory that would be able to overcome the reification of consciousness. In so doing, they extended and deepened the traditions of western Marxism, the sociological theories of Max Weber, and saw their linkages with the personality and the psyche in their turn to psychoanalysis and social psychology. But at the heart of their program was the thesis that societies based on hierarchy and dominance had adverse, pathological effects upon consciousness and culture. What was essential in the process of critique was the unification of *reason* with *resistance*; with "the power to resist established opinions and, one and the same, also to resist existing institutions, to resist everything that is merely posited, that justifies itself with its existence."[1] Critique is therefore always *in tension* with the given reality and the practices and concepts that it made ambient in a world increasingly riven with reification and dehumanization.

Critique, in the sense that it was taken up by the Frankfurt School in the mid-twentieth century, was also centrally concerned with the confrontation of the very model of society shaped by capital, exchange value, and the increasing power of commodification to shape the nature of consciousness and the personality of modern subjects. Critical theorists therefore saw that the problem of a new form of rationality—one shaped by the harnessing of new forms of social production and technology—was eroding the critical consciousness of modern subjects. At the core of their project was an interdisciplinary theory of modern society that would take as its primary task the articulation of a theory of society that was immune and insurgent to the reified forms of thinking and practice that was infected by capitalist social relations.

But today a new paradigm of critical theory has risen from the ashes of the old. What I am calling here the "domestication" of critical theory therefore refers to the ways that the linguistic, procedural, and recognitive turn in critical theory that was initiated in the 1970s and 1980s by figures such as Jürgen Habermas, Axel Honneth, and others has receded from the confrontation with the primary source of social domination and the disfiguration of human culture: capitalist market society. In essence, the domestication of critical theory implies that it has been effectively emptied of radical political content. The theories of discourse, of recognition, or of justification that contemporary critical theory has elaborated speak more to the concerns of mainstream political philosophy than to a radical challenge to its systemic imperatives and structures of power and domination; they play more into the very rhythms of the predominant social reality than seek any kind of social transformation. To retrieve critical theory is to make it accountable to these structures once again and to show that both Idealist and materialist themes are dialectically related in any kind of theory construction.

With this in mind, the extent to which critical theory remains essentially *critical*—by which I mean oppositional to and explanatory of the concrete forms of social power that shape consciousness, social relations, culture, and the contours of modernity—is today an open question. Once a paradigm of thought that sought to expose the power relations of modernity rooted in capitalist social relations, it seems to have lost its critical edge. What was once a research program into the ideational structures of consciousness and its relation to the structures and functions of capitalist modernity has become a philosophical discourse critical in name only. Today, critical theorists have become accustomed to asking questions about the nature of discourse, of mutual understanding, respect, and recognition, and concerns about justification and human rights. Even as they have embraced the early Enlightenment conception of reason and rationality that was once under sharp attack from both the reactionary forces of fascism and the right, on the one hand, and the reactionary forces of the left under the guise of postmodernism, on the other, they have jettisoned the later enlightened critiques of the Enlightenment, such as Hegel and Marx, who sought to use its general premises to go deeper into the foundations of human sociality and freedom. The project of reconstructing a conception of human reason that could underwrite not only human action but also the institutional structure of democratic society was therefore of great interest and, to be sure, a grand intellectual achievement. But the question remains: Does this transformation of the tradition render critical theory *uncritical*; has the move away from the concerns of Marx and the centrality of the critique of capitalism as a social force and a unique form of social power rooted the tradition in a new set of concerns that are no longer oppositional to the kinds of power that initially inspired the first generation of critical theorists?

I submit that the answer to this question is affirmative, that the dominant trends in critical theory have abandoned the search for the real mechanisms and sources of social power and instead place at the center of their research program a neo-Idealist search for the kinds of reasoning that they believe will create the conditions for democratic politics. The dominant trends in critical theory are domesticated in that they now seek not a confrontation with the forms of organized power that reproduce social pathologies, but rather to articulate an academicized political philosophy sealed off from the realities that affect and deform critical subjectivity. Safe in their respective philosophical systems, they search for an emancipatory theory within the striations of everyday life. More crucially, they seek to ground critical theory in the innate powers of reason, communication, and recognitive relations that they see as untouched by the reificatory and mutilating powers of capitalist society. As a result, they have made the crucial error of positing *the rationality of subjects at the expense of the concrete power relations that socialize and pervert that very same rationality in and through social processes shaped by the imperatives of economic power and interests*. The crucial flaw in contemporary critical theory, the major drawback of what I will call its neo-Idealist premises, is that it *detaches itself from a theory of socialization that is actually fused to the concrete structures of social power and its capacity to shape consciousness and cognition*. More particularly, it ceases to perceive the ways that social power rooted in economic imperatives informed by capital shape and routinize institutionalization and socialization and defective forms of subjectivity. Perhaps more to the point, it ceases to make domination an intrinsic facet of intersubjective relations and the structures of consciousness that are embedded in the practices of everyday life. Rather, it sees intersubjective forms of social action as essentially creative and empowering and overinvests them with the potential for cultivating critical cognition and critical rationality more broadly.

Material structures of power are not, it should be emphasized, to be reduced to economic phenomena in some crude sense. Rather, I will argue that we need to see social power and domination as a social fact that is embedded in social structures, but that these structures and forms of power are social facts produced by the routinization of consciousness to think along the lines of specific cognitive rule-sets, norms, and value-orientations. We should not see power as something merely *external* to us, but rather see ourselves as *constituent subjects and objects of it.* Capital, in this sense, is not simply an empirical phenomenon of production, consumption, and accumulation; it is the social process that is made possible because it has been able to establish cognitive rules, norms, and value-orientations that have become so basic to the modern personality, consciousness, and culture that it has been able to establish itself as the dominant reality—it has become our social reality because it has authority over our cognitive rule-following, our values, and the norms we see as valid. The source of these norms, rules, and so on is, of course, the unequal control over resources, but the essence of the story is that it has been able to shape the culture and ideas that make capital what it is as a process, as a social fact. It is the result of a shared kind of reasoning that infects the deepest structures of the self and consciousness.

Capital is therefore an ontological reality, not a physically material one: we cannot see it, touch it, smell it. It achieves its realization because we follow norms and rules of cognition that we internalize from the institutions we participate in and which socialize us. Uprooting it therefore requires that we posit a new kind of understanding of the social world and its potential— that we articulate a form of reasoning that will look for the deeper, rational structures of what social reality is and judge it by the rational formations that its currently existing pathological forms actively negate. What is required, I contend, is a reconstructed, critical form of cognition and subjectivity, one invested with a critical form of reasoning and willing. Consequently, it is not a postmetaphysical turn that we should embrace, but we should rather seek to construct a *critical metaphysics* understood as an attempt to grasp the nature of social reality in a critical, comprehensive sense as well as grant the individual cognitive access to a more rational form of sociation in order to define the higher purposes and ends that social life can yield for the development of the individual and the collective interest of the community as a whole.

Too much has been made of the supposed antithesis between Hegel and Marx. What is crucial is grasping that both sought to understand social institutions as objectifications of social practices and that these practices were themselves accompanied by specific kinds of thinking about the world and thinking in the world. The key for any critical theory is to look for the correct, objectively valid form of life and set of concepts that can explode the reified forms of life that capitalist modernity secretes. We make a crucial theoretical error, therefore, if we seek to separate capital and economic relations—indeed, the dominant organizing power of modern society—from our social epistemology and practices. The turn to intersubjectivity in critical theory is artificially cleansed of the ways that material bases of social power are able to shape and exert influence on the shape of consciousness as well as the personality system of the individual. Neo-Idealist critical theory proposes a theory of social action that focuses on the kinds of practices that will be able to enhance critical consciousness external to the kinds of pathologies that early critical theory saw as basic. But neo-Idealism differs from Idealism proper by placing the intersubjective over the subjective. Whereas there is no question that the intersubjective turn has opened up much in terms of the ways that socialization processes operate, it seems to me that viewing it as the source for normative claims is mistaken. For one thing, there is no way to secure the pathologies of social reality from seeping into the structures of intersubjectivity. What is needed is to show how a critical subjectivity can be created, one that has in view the concrete social world as the framework for critical judgments. Idealism always sought after this kind of deeper, richer form of subjectivity, one that would be capable of grasping objectively valid reasons for our sociality. Neo-Idealists, however, eschew the advances made by thinkers such as Marx and others who have been consistent in showing how concrete social structures and the mechanisms that hold them together exert formative pressures on socialization and consciousness. Indeed, if we view social domination as I think we should—as a structural-functional phenomenon in which hierarchical forms of social structure are held together by norms, values, and forms of legitimate authority internalized by subjects—then the neo-Idealist premise lacks critical potential as a social theory and a moral-philosophical system.

Of course, this argument should not be construed as implying that the theories of communication, of intersubjective recognition and so on are devoid of relevance or moral-political salience. Habermas's basic claim that a widening of the public sphere, the expansion of communicative forms of rationality, and that limits must be placed on the commercialization of communication and public forms of discourse and deliberation are desirable goals. Similarly, Honneth's thesis that recognitive relations be placed at the center of any kind of humanistically based society and culture are also laudable. But these are projects that presume that modern subjects seek these ends or that the capacity to embrace them results from everyday practices and that struggles against the kinds of reification of consciousness that prevent these kinds of reforms and cultural shifts are already in place. They assume, put simply, that everyday practices, phylogenetically developed by modern institutions and when properly channeled by them, are sufficient to cultivate and generate critical consciousness against unjust social arrangements. They fall into what I will call in this book a neo-Idealist fallacy in that they posit modern subjects with powers of rationality that modern capitalist society, with all of its various mechanisms for producing pathologies of reason, cognition, and self-formation, simply cannot possess. In a theoretical sense, they place the cart before the horse and fail to see that the real need is to shatter the forms of reification and acritical, affirmative, or alienated consciousness that gives support and legitimacy to the social order.

Critical theory was always skeptical of the inevitability of social change and conflict. The "iron cage" of modernity was taken to mean that culture and consciousness were being transformed by the administered society. Against this pessimistic idea, contemporary critical theorists who follow the path of intersubjectivity, recognition, and discourse posit that critique can take place without a confrontation with the organizing pull of economic life. Their theories posit the existence of subjects capable of and looking for a critical, democratic, and progressive confrontation with their society and culture. But the opposite is the case. We now see the lack of large-scale struggle against the integrating system of administered life as well as the increasingly deleterious and de-democratizing effects of the expansion of inequalities of wealth. The question needs to be posed to those who advocate such theories: To what extent do you presuppose a kind of subjectivity that has not been shaped and formed by defective social relations and institutions? If there is a way out of this dialectic between structure and consciousness, I propose that it must take the form of theory helping us to view the inner potentialities of what a rational social order can provide, what modernity can become if it were to be organized according to the rational framework of a free community. To this end, we must examine the ontological properties of social life to understand how to examine the false forms of social structure and consciousness that pervades our world. We must derive our categories of critique from the very purposes immanent within social life and ensure that they are governed by the rational principles of individual self-development no less than those of collective need. We must seek to create the kind of cognition that will lay a foundation for a critical form of judgment.

But contemporary critical theory has moved away from such questions. Now we are asked to look toward the formal practices of discourse, justification, or recognition as resources for emancipatory critique. But the basic problem remains that neo-Idealist theory falls into the trap of abstraction in that it sidesteps the dilemma of perverted subject-formation—and that this perverted subject-formation is largely a function of the kind of political economy that pervades late modernity. Their search for a formalist, procedural understanding of sociation entails a logical misstep in that, as Hegel knew all too well, form and content cannot be separated without doing violence to our rational grasp of reality.[2] In essence, even though these models of human action and the kind of moral philosophy to which they give rise possess some normative attraction, they have telescoped the project of critical theory to a point where the processes of social pathologies have already been overcome within certain basic capacities of the subject. The domestication of critical theory is expressed in the ways that these theories and models are asserted outside of the real-world pressures of capitalist modernity. Moving toward a paradigm in which social action could be separated from the pressures of capitalist economic life was a crucial step in moving critical theory away from a radical critique of society. Axel Honneth makes this move explicitly. For him, the problem that plagues earlier variants of critical theory was a dependence on the paradigm of social labor as the only form of social action relevant for analysis. "Because no other type of social action is conceded alongside societal labor," Honneth writes, "Horkheimer can only take the instrumental forms of societal practice systematically into account on the level of his theory of society, and thus loses sight of that dimension of everyday practice in which socialized subjects generate and creatively develop common action-orientations in a communicative manner."[3]

The severing of forms of social action from the unequal control of social resources and the kinds of social-cultural forms of legitimacy that it entails paves the way for the domestication of critical theory in that now the theoretical mind is free to create moral and philosophical systems that are cleansed of the forces of concrete power. Critical theorists such as Horkheimer, Adorno, Fromm, and Marcuse subscribed to an implicit model of modern society in which the kind of power needed to coordinate economic production, consumption, and the hierarchies generated by these new forms of social life had to permeate into noneconomic spheres of the society, polity, and culture. They took the problem of reification elaborated earlier by Georg Lukács as a central pathology of consciousness that was itself dialectically related to the structural-functional processes that pulsed beneath the appearance of everyday life. Power and domination were no longer exerted by state power but rather embedded in the normative order of rationalized institutions that were increasingly tethered to the dynamic logic of capital's expansion and preservation. Behind even this was the basic problem initially pointed out by Rousseau, that concrete forms of social power—of extraction, of exploitation—require cultural and psychological forms of control and subordination—a shaping of consciousness, norms, culture, and so on—in order to stabilize the system and make legitimate an irrational form of reality. What they saw was that the convulsive nature of nineteenth-century political and social life was now being eclipsed by a society of acquiescence and a new form of rationalized legitimacy.

One way I seek to make sense of the limits of these contemporary currents of critical theory and also uncover the deeper logic of the distinctiveness of what critical theory is about and what it has to offer is through a concept of power I develop and call *constitutive power*. As I see it, this is the kind of social power that results from the ways that socialization occurs within social-structural and institutional contexts and the way this socialization shapes and structures the attitudes, values, consciousness, and cognitive powers of subjects. In a basic sense, I derive the idea from Rousseau, who was concerned with the ways that norms and customs within civil society conditioned the individual to accept and actively to endorse and participate in an unjust, corrupt society of inequality and domination. This captures the essence of what early critical theorists saw as an essential aspect of modern forms of social power: namely, that it has the capacity to shape the subject and his rational, emotive, and evaluative powers. Following Hegel and Marx, critical theory must therefore be concerned with the ways that concrete forms of social power possess the capacity to shape the kinds of social reality that is then used to sustain those same structures of power. What is relevant here is that this kind of power shapes the personality of the individual as well as his cognitive and evaluative powers. To assume that language, recognition, or some other social-relational form of social action can resist this kind of power, I contend, allows for the infiltration of power into the very kinds of social action that contemporary critical theorists see as emancipatory and democratic. The domestication of critical theory results, then, when critique abandons the premise of constitutive power and seeks to invest critical power in forms of social action that are taken to be untouched by the pressing forces of social power—that is, of communication, recognition, and so on. Indeed, the main task of critical theory must remain the unmasking of the social forms of consciousness that hide from view the true sources of social power and domination. Making critical theory radical means rethinking the ethical goal of what a rational society ought to be able to make manifest.

Indeed, in this sense, we could say that the initial premise that gave coherence to critical theory was derived from the base-superstructure hypothesis of Marx. It was in the notion that there are particular forms of thought, of cognition, that were conditioned by the concrete processes of rationalized, commodified, industrial society. By no means was this a simple process of consciousness being mapped by the prevailing economic system. Rather, what resulted was a widespread surface legitimacy of the systemic imperatives of capitalist economic life as well as the widespread problem of social pathologies that emerged from the sublimation of the contradictions that it entailed. The studies in the social psychology of authority, Fromm's analysis of "sadistic" and "masochistic" personality types, and the general problem of one-dimensional thought, no less than the attack on positivism and the culture industry, still retain their importance. One reason is because these arguments took modern society as a whole as its analysis—there could be no crude separation of political economy from the processes of socialization, of communication, of the family, of any of the forms of social action that contemporary critical theory takes as central resources for an "intramundane" critique of society.[4] Rather, the first generation of critical theorists sought to unmask the ways that the basic, foundational structural-functional processes of social life come to affect, to shape, and to distort forms of thought, the personality system, and the basic drives of human subjects. The basic idea was that ideas, politics, law, the state, religion, were all shaped or in some sense guided by the base economic institutions and practices that emerge from the ways that human society organizes its basic production and reproduction. Under capitalism, this means the articulation of new forms of ideological constraint that orient subjects toward compliance with social systems that do not serve their interest, the interests of the community as a whole. With the intensification of capitalist crisis and development, the realm of culture and ideology became paramount: organizing a common consciousness to oppose the imperatives of capitalist interests was seen as a central means of overthrowing the structures of capitalism and moving toward a radical transformation of society.

But the new currents in critical theory look to a different set of intellectual and philosophical resources to articulate their ideas. Ever since the rise of analytic moral and political philosophy, associated with the success of the work of John Rawls, the basic trend has been to create ideal models of moral argument that can be used to regulate political and social life. A separation between the real and the ideal underlies this effort and a fall back into formalism—which Hegel saw as problematic in Kant—returns as a central theme in domesticated critical theory. A central feature of this domesticated theory is a return to pre-Marxian forms of Idealism (primarily Kant and Hegel) as resources for social philosophy. Hence, Rainer Forst can argue that, in his attempt to construct a "critical theory of justice," that "[t]he principles and right that result from moral constructivism form the normative core of what I call political constructivism (again I use a concept from Rawls but differently). This means that the collective and discursive 'construction' and establishment of a basic social structure for a political community—whether in a single state or across borders—is, speaking ideally, an autonomous achievement of the members themselves."[5] The move back to Kant, however, raises more issues than it solves. For one thing—and this is the central thesis that I want to develop in the pages that follow—the task of critical theory must be to call into question the innate, formal capacity of individuals to construct ideal principles and institutional contexts such as those that Forst suggests.

The appeal of this kind of thinking should be of little surprise. With the collapse of Marxism throughout the 1970s and 1980s and the reconciliation of major political parties in western democracies to the capitalist system, the search for a theory of critique that could be found in everyday life has an obvious appeal. Indeed, since thinkers such as Adorno and Horkheimer had led critical theory into a kind of philosophical cul de sac with their emphasis on a radical, negative subjectivity, critical theory had few places to turn. In the end, the turn that was made has created a domesticated critical theory that no longer calls into question the perverting mechanisms of liberal, industrial (and postindustrial) capitalism, but seeks to articulate theories of justice and democracy as if those mechanisms have no effect on society and subject-formation more broadly. Indeed, recent expressions of this kind of critical theory such as Axel Honneth's work have even sought to argue that the structures of market capitalism possess inherent norms of recognition and freedom.[6] Its conception of reason purportedly exists outside of the forms and structure of power that pervert it. Although they recognize the power of the market and, at times, the kind of exploitation distinctive of capitalist relations, they wrongly assume that these are the only forces that shape the dynamics of subject-formation. They instead invest intersubjective practices with a form of cognition that can oppose the forces of modern forms of social integration and to articulate theories of democracy that are essentially outside of economic concerns. But as I will show, this is to mistake the real aim of critical philosophy, which is to explode the reified forms of thought through the vantage point of theoretical reflection.

The decoupling of thinkers such as Kant and Hegel from Marx is perhaps the central means of domestication because now theory follows Idealist premises and forms of thought. What is troubling, however, is that this theoretical shift is occurring at the same time as a massive integration of social life along neoliberal lines. Now, the culture industry, commodified forms of technology, the ideological legitimation of the goals of capitalist economic life, right-wing reaction, and the quietism of social conflict and critique— themes that were in view for the classical generation of critical theorists— once again saturate our age. Any attempt to see moral constructivism, recognition, discourse ethics, and so on as operating outside of the pressures and forces of the kind of deformed subject-formation that this kind of social order produces must therefore be called into question. The divide between the idealized forms of praxis and cognition these theorists espouse and the actual mechanisms of the real world could not be greater—indeed, could not be more alienated from one another. Critical theory must, in this sense, insist on its own auto-critique. Habermas, Honneth, and their followers have forged a theoretical apparatus that seeks to articulate procedural norms, or to isolate aspects of social relations (such as recognitive relations) that can then be used to understand the whole of social life. But this makes the fundamental error posed by Hegel of defining the whole through one of its moments.

In contrast to this neo-Idealist kind of theory construction, a critical-dialectical approach places cognition not only within the social structures of actual living relations, as Hegel proposed, but also, along with Marx, sees that these social structures are no longer autonomous from the integrative power of economic imperatives. This does not mean we cannot achieve an objective, critical perspective; it merely implies that we cannot achieve this perspective from within the intramundane practices that pervade the prevailing reality.

This approach to political economy should not be misconstrued as simply a specific logic or distinctive form of rationality, it is also, and indeed primarily, a structural way of understanding the power relations that actively constitute social relations. The kind of cognition needed for critical thought must embrace the historically situated theory of capital that Marx describes as well as the kind of normative ontology that Hegel elaborates in his critical metaphysics. The root of the Hegelian-Marxist viewpoint therefore is not only methodological but also ontological: it proposes that critical knowledge of the world is knowledge of process as well as knowledge of internal relations. The essential structure of human social life is one of processual development as well as social relatedness. For modernity to fulfill its inner potential, for it to be able to truly liberate human life, its internal contradictions must be overcome.

This critical-ontological view is distinct from the neo-Idealist view in that it does not see intersubjective life alone as constituting what Hegel and Marx meant by sociality or society in general. The neo-Idealist sees intersubjectivity as a basically cognitive-practical reality, rooted in either communicative or recognitive terms. But this return to Kantian and Hegelian Idealism, respectively, no longer allows a critique of the political dimensions of social power rooted in material life that then deform those same powers of communication and recognition. None of this is meant to take away from the important achievement of this intersubjective paradigm in overcoming the sterility of the liberal-individualist view. But in doing so, they now see the material-structural realities of capitalism as, at best, vestigial concerns. This has defanged the political potential of critical theory. In what follows, I will therefore seek to show the limits of this turn in critical theory and to revisit what I see to be a more fruitful way of understanding the logic of critical theory. It is my hope that a renewed interest in constructing a critical form of cognition can aid in struggles for social justice and progressive, enlightened social transformation.

NOTES

1. T. W. Adorno, *Critical Models: Interventions and Catchwords* (New York: Columbia University Press, 1998), 281–82.

2. See the discussion by Konstantinos Kavoulakos, "Back to History? Reinterpreting Lukács' Early Marxist Work in Light of the Antinomies of Contemporary Critical Theory," in M. Thompson (ed.), *Georg Lukács Reconsidered: Critical Essays in Politics, Philosophy and Aesthetics* (New York: Continuum, 2011), 151–71.

3. Axel Honneth, *The Fragmented World of the Social: Essays in Social and Political Philosophy* (Albany, NY: SUNY Press, 1995), 71–72.

4. See the important critique of Habermas and his neglect of political economy for his theory of discourse by Tom Rockmore, "Habermas, Critical Theory and Political Economy," in G. Smulewicz-Zucker and M. Thompson (eds.), *Radical Intellectuals and the Subversion of Progressive Politics: The Betrayal of Politics* (New York: Palgrave Macmillan, 2015), 191–210.

5. Rainer Forst, *The Right to Justification: Elements of a Constructivist Theory of Justice* (New York: Columbia University Press, 2012), 6.

6. See Axel Honneth, *Das Recht der Freiheit. Grundriß einer demokratischen Sittlichkeit* (Frankfurt: Suhrkamp, 2011), 317–470.

Part I

THE PRESENT STATE
OF CRITICAL THEORY

Chapter 1

The Rise of Neo-Idealist Critical Theory

I. INTRODUCTION

In what follows, I would like to identify and critique a paradigm shift in contemporary critical theory defined by a move away from the Marxian and Weberian themes that animated classical critical theory and toward Idealist themes of cognition and intersubjectivity that I will here call "neo-Idealist." By neo-Idealist I mean that these thinkers proceed from the premise that there is a self-sufficiency to the powers of intersubjective reason, discourse, structures of justification, and recognition. Their theories stem from an account of reason, of social practices and noumenal capacities that are divorced from the distorting potency of social power, rooted in the material organization of social life, to shape norms, values, and cognition. This paradigm shift in critical theory asks us to consider the ways that communication, justification, and recognition all possess an autonomous power to provide a critical theory of society. What they actively evade, I suggest, are the various ways that capitalist social relations and the kinds of power that stem from them shape subjectivity and the kind of capacities that they see as the nucleus for emancipatory critique. I submit that this transformation of critical theory has essentially *domesticated* it by rendering it unable to critique the actual mechanisms of social domination and power in modern societies, placing philosophical discourse external to the essential forms of domination and unfreedom that persist under modern capitalist society. Unwittingly, they have created intricate theories that have the potential to reproduce the power relations that govern the existent reality. Indeed, although the new critical theory has been made palatable to mainstream academic debates about language, ethics, and democratic theory, it has abandoned its critical stance toward the kinds of domination characteristic of late capitalism.

The neo-Idealist view holds that noneconomic types of action and power should be privileged over the "technicist" forms of power expressed by capitalist social relations of production and exchange as well as the bureaucratic forms of rationalization that pervade the formal institutions of modernity. But my argument here will not be one that looks backward. Rather, my thesis concerns the ways that the sphere of values and norms is in fact deeply entwined with the institutions of economic and social power. That the attempt to approach a critical theory of society from the point of view of intersubjective forms of praxis derived from the insights of pragmatism is deeply flawed. Neo-Idealism is the result of a reaction against Marxism and the Marxian roots of critical theory, and it is characterized by an inflated assessment of the powers of human communication and recognitive relations that, wrongly, invests such practices with critical and emancipatory potential. It has adopted an approach inspired by pragmatism that places emphasis on forms of thought and social practices that supposedly constitute a critical theory of society.

The object of neo-Idealism is therefore radically different from that of classical critical theory: in place of a critique of consciousness that was tethered to the mechanisms of social structures and functions, neo-Idealism sees consciousness as the result of intersubjectivity and discourse. Its object is not the critique of capitalism and the kind of social order it engenders, but rather the means by which subjects will come to mutual understanding through rational discourse, or "struggle for recognition." But the problem with this new paradigm of critical theory is not its intentions but its inability to perform what I deem a basic task of critical theory—namely, exposing the social processes responsible for promoting a *homogeneity of values and norms that are capable of coordinating and legitimating capitalist social institutions and social relations*. The Marxian twist on the Idealist notion of critique was to show that ideas were shaped—indeed, *determined*—by social structure, that objective social processes shape subjective processes (psychological, cognitive, affective, evaluative, etc.). Power was inherent in the social relations that crystallize around resource extraction, and the realm of ideas, of consciousness, was a function of this form of power. It is not that material forms of power simply map themselves onto consciousness, but that new forms of legitimacy, new norms, and new values come to pervade the social world, making everyday life an adjunct to securing domination-relations, not a fertile ground for evoking an "intramundane" critical praxis.

But neo-Idealist critical theory adopts just this point of view. Its emphasis on forms of human action and thought at the expense of the objective and material domain of social structure renders it essentially uncritical of the forms of power that continue to shape and dominate modern societies. Neo-Idealist thinkers have effectively made critical theory an academic discipline sealed off from the realities of real politics and concrete relations of social power within society. By moving away from the structural-functional mechanisms of capitalist social formations, neo-Idealism promises a liberated form of theory; what it provides, however, is one that no longer has in view the true source of social power and dominance. Capitalist modernity was a central concern for critical theorists because they were able to grasp that it was the central organizing principle of modern societies and that the concepts of alienation, reification, and domination were endemic to it. Domesticated critical theory does not so much drop these categories of analysis as much as recast them in a meta-social light. Despite their claims that they have overcome the metaphysical elements of classical critical theory by resolving the tension between subject and object through the synthesis of consciousness and intersubjective praxis, they have eliminated the essence of the Marxian element of critical theory: that a relation between base and superstructure is a fundamental aspect of social pathologies restraining critical consciousness and sustaining modern forms of rational domination.

II. TWO PARADIGMS OF CRITICAL THEORY

The move away form the Hegelian and Marxian roots of critical theory can be seen as a shift from the concerns of how social relations and structures constitute consciousness to one in which the intersubjective relations between agents constitutes consciousness. This is by no means a subtle shift in emphasis, but a paradigm shift where concerns about the relationship of the subjective world, of consciousness itself, and the objective world—nature, social structure, and so on—are transposed. I want to suggest here that the paradigm shift in critical theory has moved from one based on a Marx-Weber paradigm to one based on an Idealist-pragmatist paradigm. At the core of the Marx-Weber paradigm of critical theory is the premise that forms of socialization and social integration are shaped and affected by concrete forms of extractive dominance that pervade not only economic relationships but also rationalized social relations of noneconomic spheres of life and consciousness that provide a nonrational (but nevertheless *rationalized*) basis for the willing acceptance of authority and the generation of social and personal pathologies. In essence, to the extent that economic forms of production are the basis for forms of social power, value systems will emerge to legitimate those processes of production and consumption. The values of elites will become the values of the community as a whole.[1] This includes the kinds of cultural and psychological structures that pervade modern societies. The Idealist-pragmatist paradigm, by contrast, places emphasis on the epistemic and symbolic forms of action and dimensions of social integration and sees these as constitutive of consciousness. It seeks to reveal within social action

the capacities for critique and to identify social pathologies without reference
to the fundamental role played by economic relations. For critical theorists
of this strain, the core element of critique is to be found in the ways that ego
development is shaped by noneconomic social relations. Social relations are
not seen as embedded in economic power, in the exchange relations that
dominate modern capitalism, but are conceived as a nexus of symbolic and
moral relations that are oriented toward social solidarity.

The basic distinction between these two paradigms concerns the
nature of *constitution*: Do forms of power and relations with social
structures and institutions constitute subjectivity and consciousness, or
do epistemic and symbolically mediated forms of social action constitute
consciousness and subjectivity? For those attracted to the Marx-Weber paradigm, the constitution of the self (as well as of community, culture, institutions, and so on) occurs through the nexus of power relations rooted in capital
and in the kinds of rationalized social institutions that are shaped by it for the
realization of its ends. But this process is not simple or mechanistic. Rather,
it occurs through a process of what I will call below *constitutive domination*,
where the very forms of social action that neo-Idealists privilege are colonized
by authority structures, thereby rendering their capacity for critique minimal
at best. For those attracted to the Idealist-pragmatic paradigm, individuals
construct their lifeworlds through symbolic and linguistically mediated forms
of social integration as well as through forms of mutual recognition, justification, and understanding. Cognitive capacities are split from the pressures and
forces of material social organization, not unlike the classical Kantian dualism of "noumena" and "phenomena." Indeed, the critique of such a dualism
was premised, at least in Marx, by the thesis that forms of social power have
a formative effect on the mental states of subjects. But for neo-Idealists, the
noumenal realm is elevated above the social phenomena in which power,
hierarchy, and dominance are essential features. They view economic power
as a marginal concern, either relegating it to a different level of social action
(Habermas) or seeking to absorb it into a theory of markets without the realities of capital (Honneth). My thesis here is that the shift from the former to
the latter describes the state of contemporary critical theory. My second thesis
is that this shift is responsible for a *domestication of critical theory*, which
means that it is rendered unable to critique the fundamental forms of social
power that distort consciousness and therefore is unable to serve as a means
of elucidating an emancipatory consciousness for social critique.

It should be said that the Marx-Weber paradigm in critical theory was at
least partly responsible for its own self-destruction. Marxism's theoretical
growth led in a direction that was overly mechanistic and simplistic, and
Weber's thesis of the "iron cage" of modernity was in fact too pessimistic.
Indeed, the reason for the neo-Idealist turn in critical theory is not without

warrant. The Frankfurt School's early interdisciplinary project was to investigate the structures of consciousness that accompanied advanced industrial society. It sought to understand the ways that consciousness under the forces of modernity—itself rooted in mass industrial capitalism—was shaped and the ways that it was able to constrain critical consciousness. Reification was the key concept, variously interpreted, that became the touchstone for their research. It brought together the various ideas of Marx, Weber, and Freud in an attempt to construct a research program for a modern, advanced, industrial capitalist society. But the rise of fascism and the postwar years saw a different direction take shape. Adorno and Horkheimer came to see the Enlightenment as leading to its dialectical opposite: into mass deception, the dominance of instrumental rationality, and the bureaucratic state. Marcuse emphasized the importance of negation as a central philosophical concern, and Adorno's later philosophy saw as fundamental the need for not only negation but also a return to the defense of a radical subjectivity in a world so infected by reification that a negative dialectic was the only means of preserving subjective critical consciousness. In effect, Adorno advanced an interpretation of subjectivity as a last refuge—in particular in his aesthetic theory—that led him into a kind of cul de sac: the social world was so riven by reification that the subject stood alone and his central task was to negate the totality that was the administered world. It was clear, to anyone entering critical theory at the time, that there was no way to move forward.

Habermas's reconstruction of critical theory during the 1970s needs to be seen in this context. The most important shift here was a project in which he would purge critical theory of its Marxian and Hegelian elements and replace them with a new, pragmatist-inspired conception of social action. Habermas's critique of Marx centered on the thesis that communicative action follows a logic that is independent of the force of social systems. He pulls from Durkheim to show that there is an autonomous form of social action and social cognition—specifically in the realm of values and norms—that can ultimately be expressed in language, in communication.[2] Habermas separates what he sees to be the Marxian thesis that social action is organized by technically useful knowledge that is oriented by the mode of production and counterposes to it the cognitive dimension of moral-practical knowledge inherent in structures of communicative interaction.[3] Now the concept of social action is cleaved in two: the Marxian understanding is relegated to the dimension of technical reason, and communicative action dwells in the dimension of moral cognition, a kind of reasoning that possesses its own logic and is separate from the structural-functional concerns.[4] The critique of Marxism was initiated by showing its limitations in terms of a theory of social rationality. For Habermas, Marxian theories of social action construed human beings as constrained to act within the confines of technological and instrumental rationality. Economic imperatives under capitalist forms of production were therefore seen to be responsible for an isomorphism between the social norms and practices determined by capitalist economic life and forms of subjective consciousness. But Habermas's move against this was to see that social integration takes place not only through the material reproduction of the species but also through the discourse concerning the validity of values that are raised in the context of everyday communication.

Here, a Durkheimian move is made in that the concept of social integration is seen as occurring at the level of value consensus and modes of normative agreement that serve as the foundation for socialization itself. Habermas's starting point is the hermeneutic concept of the "lifeworld," which he comes to see as separate from the pathological effects of capital and economic/ instrumental imperatives.[5] This model of socialization is distinct from the Marx-Weber paradigm that sees institutional structures as causal in the process of social integration as well as ego and self-formation. There is also an element of pragmatism here that stresses the intersubjective action of individuals to come to some form of agreement about the forms of life and values that undergird social life. The Kantian layer of this argument is that cognition essentially occurs at the level of the subject's capacity to reason through the arguments presented in discourse. But the same is true with the neo-Idealist appropriation of Hegel in the work of Axel Honneth. Honneth's project of a theory of socialization shaped by recognitive relations asserts that norms, the ideal norms of the community, are the Ideal structures that shape socialization processes. The ends of the family, of the modern economy, and of law should be seen as operating according to the norms of what the modern community views as rational and as valid ends. Norms become the crucible of progress and potential freedom in that recognitive relations should alter social norms that govern social interactions and mechanisms that produce misrecognition.[6] In a neo-Hegelian move, Honneth moves socialization back to norms and evades the question of material power and its impact on socialization and consciousness.

Most problematic was the move away from a perspective that emphasized the constitutive power of objective social structure and function on the contours of consciousness and subjective capacities for cognition. Habermas was able to outflank the questions of objective social structure and function and its constitutive power on subjects by pointing to the "links between the symbolically structured lifeworld, communicative action, and discourse."[7] Intersubjective praxis is therefore a means of transposing the nature of social action in order to overcome the traditional philosophy of consciousness as well as the "productivist" paradigm that reduces social action to labor. But this move should also be construed as neo-Idealist in the sense that it sees norms as being essentially detached from material forms of social power and the structural-functional social logics that support patterns of social power that result from resource control.[8] But the basic insight of the Marx-Weber paradigm is that the focus of critical theory must be to reveal the mechanisms that prevent and erode the critical capacities of subjects, to isolate and bring to consciousness those forms of material and resource power (specifically conveyed by the theory of capital outlined by Marxist theory) that serve to shape culture and consciousness and sustain and reproduce that power. One way this is achieved is through the production and maintenance of value-orientations and value-patterns that can create structures of legitimate, rational authority relations.

III. SOCIAL ACTION WITHOUT SOCIAL STRUCTURE: THE NEO-IDEALIST PREMISE

Since neo-Idealist critical theory places at the center of its concerns symbolically and linguistically mediated modes of social action, the economic embeddedness of social relations is displaced and subjects are now seen as capable of constructing critical reasons and sensibilities outside of the structural-functional pressures of administered economic life. The constitution of the self, of morality, of critical reason, is located within an intersubjective mode of praxis that is oriented toward mutual agreement and the codification of valid norms and values. It therefore takes as its basis the thesis that the symbolic and cognitive elements of social action are causally and empirically distinct from the material structures of social life. Indeed, as Karl-Otto Apel argued, paving a path toward this vantage point, "The ethically relevant question which is raised by the reference to conventions is whether it is possible to state and justify a basic ethical norm that makes it a duty for all individuals to strive, in principle, for a binding agreement with other people in all practical questions and furthermore to subsequently adhere to this agreement."[9] Apel's project aimed to rid ethical philosophy of any kind of scientific ground, one that was in any way dependent on ontological claims about the world and the nature of things. In its place, a hermeneutic of mutual understanding and agreement about binding norms would take its place. But here we see a first move toward neo-Idealism in that the ideas about normative values are to be grounded in discourse and not a critical grasp of the structures of reality itself. Second, there is the added, second-order problem of how values cannot be disembedded from the structural-functional context within which subjects encounter them as part of their socialization. The normative structures of meaning that individuals use are themselves rooted in and, in part, expressions of the material organization of power in which they are embedded. Simply separating them from social

structure and transposing them into intersubjective forms of action and justification pretends that we can rationally create norms and values external to
those power structures.

This move is therefore neo-Idealist in the sense that it severs the structures
of consciousness and social action from the structural-functional logics of
social systems and, as a result, creates a sphere of social activity that is no
longer shaped and influenced by social processes that are rooted in the centripetal coordinating forces of capital, but merely those of consciousness,
language, and intersubjective praxis. This leads to two claims that I see as
particularly problematic. First, *critical consciousness, critique itself, is to
be cultivated immanently within social practices.* This can be through communication, intersubjective processes of recognition, or any form of social
action in which one comes to seek some sort of justification for the norms
to which they are subjected. Second, as a result of this, neo-Idealist theory
is unable *to expose the ways that the content and form of consciousness is
shaped and determined by structural-functional logics that come to distort
and orient value-patterns and epistemic powers toward elite interests and
concerns.* What initially seems appealing is the idea that social practices can
be freed from the clenches of materialism and structuralism. But this is in
fact the point at which valid critique becomes compromised: by detaching
the sphere of social practices and cognition from the structural-functional
domain of social life, neo-Idealism pens us into a sphere of consciousness that
is abstract in that it is unable to secure objectively valid political and ethical
claims. It separates the sphere of thought from the material organization of
the social world and the kinds of power inherent to those forms of organization. In the end, we are left with no objective point from which to judge the
norms and values that are inscribed in social action. Second, and perhaps
more important, neo-Idealism naively assumes that the powers of intersubjectivity are able to resist and overcome the strong pull of reification that results
from rationalized social institutions that seek compliance with norms that
are ultimately rooted in economic efficiency and extractive social relations.
But even more, the thesis that reification is an expression of technical and
instrumental rationality should also be questioned. Indeed, for Lukács, the
basic idea was that reification was a pathology of cognition in the sense that
the object literally becomes unrecognizable by the subject. In social theoretic
terms, it means that subjects are unable to grasp the mechanisms of the social
world *as it is* and that are responsible for their own domination.

But in neo-Idealism, what results is a theoretical tradition that places its
emphasis not on the objective foundations of social structure and the force
it exerts on subjective consciousness, but on the *attributes of subjective and
social life that are linked to it.* Habermas laid this basic dichotomy out in
Knowledge and Human Interests when he argued:

Empirical analysis discloses reality from the viewpoint of possible technical control over objectified processes of nature, while hermeneutics maintains the intersubjectivity of possible action-orienting mutual understanding. . . . The rigorously empirical sciences are subject to the transcendental conditions of instrumental action, while the hermeneutic sciences proceed on the level of communicative action.[10]

Since empirical science can only offer us an instrumental form of reasoning and, hence, lead us to positivism, Habermas suggests that hermeneutics can offer us a separate means by which critical theory can be oriented, which is toward the theory of communicative action and discourse ethics. But this breaks the crucial dialectic that Marx sought to bridge in terms of the ways that economic relations shape social institutions and, in the end, the consciousness of subjects. Lukács's concept of reification was a means of expressing more clearly in philosophical terms the cognitive pathology that results from the penetration of market and exchange relations throughout social life and culture. Indeed, for Lukács, the basic issue was that the cognition of subjects comes to be fused to the commodity form. Reification, in this sense, is not simply a cultural problem of how we tend to view human subjects as means rather than ends, as petrified objects rather than vital ones. It is, more importantly and more correctly, a thesis regarding what happens to the processes of consciousness itself. Reification can also be the result of *the kinds of norms and values that individuals adopt and which in turn shape their cognitive powers of judgment and thought*. In this sense, it is not simply restricted to the dimension of technical rationality, but it also explains the ways that individuals come to accept norms and values that legitimate the dominant forces within a given social order. Reification, therefore, can infect communicative action and discourse ethics, neutralizing their supposed power to shape critical consciousness and mutual understanding. And even more, reification in these terms is a direct result of the kind of functional forces that modern institutions require for socialization into a system dominated by economic logics of accumulation and consumption.

In this sense, the central issue becomes the extent to which communicative forms of reasoning—or any intersubjective relations *tout court*—can be immunized against the powers of reification. Indeed, one of the central weaknesses of neo-Idealist critical theory is the assumption that reification is not a concept anchored in economic functionalism.[11] Rather, it has been cast, by Axel Honneth among others, as a "forgetting" of the relations of recognition and as a pathology of social practices. Similarly with the concept of "alienation," which is now to be seen, in the words of Rahel Jaeggi, as an inability to "appropriate" (*Aneignung*) the world, an inability to be at home in one's own world.[12] The abstractness of these approaches—and, to be sure, their lack of usefulness in social research—attests to the power of neo-Idealism to transform the basic thought categories that have been at the bedrock of critical social theory. And this means that critical theory can only remain relevant in a political sense once it returns to a theory of society and socialization that emphasizes the structural-functional powers of social relations to shape and produce forms of consciousness and cognition. What needs to be kept in view is the extent to which reification remains a central pathology of consciousness to such an extent that it is able to undermine the thesis that a critical form of reason is grounded in the intersubjective construction of binding norms. Recall that, for Habermas, the capacity to reach mutual understanding (or his principle of "U") is dependent on the power of discourse alone—that is, on the power of language to be able to structure a justificatory framework for normative agreement. The problem remains, however, that the power of class-based societies—that is, those that are structured around extractive social relations and commodity consumption as their primary social goals—requires the inclusion of almost all basic social institutions in order to maximize its efficiency. As a consequence, the forms of rationality developed by subjects cannot be properly grasped external to those processes since they are braided with the cognitive, epistemic, evaluative, and even cathectic dimensions of self-formation. This is the basic thrust of the Marx-Weber thesis: that epistemological processes are dialectically linked to socialization processes infected by rationalized value-orientations rooted in the logic of capital agglomeration. To claim otherwise is to commit the neo-Idealist fallacy.

Here we can see how the central problem becomes one of *constitution*. In the Marx-Weber paradigm, as I have been describing and defending it, the problem of constitution is one that occurs at the level of the personality system of individuals. It is the result of socialization where specific value-orientations—which are themselves functionally dependent on and necessary to the logics of economic interests and purposes—are routinized, rationalized, and internalized by subjects. The terminus of this process is the production of an implicit, and at times explicit, consensus around internally valid values capable of coordinating macro-social action (production, consumption, efficiency, toleration of contradictions, etc.). But this itself produces a reification of consciousness in the sense that subjects begin to take the norms and values that make up their world as largely valid on their face, learning to live within them rather than to question them. They come to shape the basic normative worldview that they see as normal and legitimate. Hence, attempts to posit principles of justice that exist outside of this nexus of socialized value-consensus must be Idealist in the sense that they look for the actors themselves to critique the value-orientations they have already internalized. Consider, as an example, Rainer Forst's argument that a critical conception of politics construes the basic question of legitimate rule as a question of just—and that means justified, non-arbitrary, and non-dominating—rule and it offers a recursive reconstruction of the in part procedural and in part substantive norms which make such a justification possible. Here justice is not only what counts as just in a society but what could hold in it in a reciprocal and general manner if those subject to the norms were their free and equal authors.[13]

Here we are confronted with a double dose of neo-Idealism. The positing of a legitimate conception of rule in these terms does nothing to help us understand how dominant power relations are able to rob individuals of the capacity to seek justification for the basic norms into which they are socialized. Forst does little more than posit the procedural and ideal-typical formulation that subjects view norms as if they were "their free and equal authors." But there is no discussion of the pathologies of consciousness that disable such a recognition. Nor is there a discussion about the ways in which the norms that are accepted do not gain legitimacy in this fashion; that their legitimacy comes from routinization, rationalization, and internalization. The central blind spot here—one that is an expression of the neo-Idealist position—is that socialization processes cultivate certain forms of value-consensus without which the institutions of power would no longer be able to operate. If subjects accept as valid the prevailing institutions of their community, they will tend to see them already as "just" in some basic sense and will not be able to operate in a space that is critical to those institutions. Forst's theory of justification has the real danger of *simply reproducing the basic validity of the social reality that already exists*. We are asked to consider a critical theory of politics not from the *actual*, the *real basis* of social life, but from an ideal-typical understanding of social action and rationality.

This raises the issue of judgment. If agents involved in an intersubjective social act seeking mutual agreement seek justifications, how are the subjects seeking the justifications to know whether these are valid in any objective sense? Even more, how are they to know if the premises about which they argue and seek to justify are themselves not rooted in values and ideas that are expressive of the prevailing power structure of reality? If the dominant values of the economic system are so deeply ingrained within politics, culture, consciousness, and law, where is the objective referent to make judgments? Forst presents us with a neat picture (an *Idealist* picture, to be sure) of how justification ought to work, but there is no real sense that this will produce a critical attitude or consciousness of political power. Forst's is a noncritical theory because it is unable to call into question the power relations inherent within the reified structures of consciousness. There is no reason to assume that discourse can explode the reified layers of consciousness since power is able to shape forms of cognition as well as the value-orientations of subjects. Indeed,

critical theory is in play once it is recognized that a modern, rationalized form
of power operates at the level of the *shaping of norms*, not at the level of
obstructing justification. In this sense, once norms are shaped, routinized, and
internalized by subjects, justification ceases to be a major concern since the
validity of norms is no longer sought. Forst assumes, as do all neo-Idealists,
that the subject's rationality is a variable external to the social processes that
shape it. It is, for him, an *a priori* capacity that is translated into everyday practices and capacities. This wrong turn, however, is plagued by the problem of
folding us back into everyday life and consciousness, of lacking the capacity to
separate subjects cognitively from the prevailing thought categories and value-
orientations that pervade their world. Indeed, the power of critical theory is the
capacity of alternate forms of consciousness (derived from art, philosophy, and
so on) to be able to mediate consciousness of the "inverted world" of capitalist
society. We must be asked not to look into the very folds of our reality but to
approach it with a kind of cognition that reveals it negatively.

Here we can begin to grasp why the neo-Idealist move away from the dialectical relation between consciousness and social structure—the basic standpoint of Western Marxism—and the move toward the symbolic-cognitive is
so problematic. From a theoretical point of view, it is weak because it fails
to capture the ways that social pathologies are rooted in social forces that
are predominantly grounded in economic logics, and it is normatively weak
because it places emphasis on norms of social action that cannot possibly
maintain their rationality under the pressures of reification. Almost the entire
direction of critical theory since this move by Habermas can be seen as taking place within the confines of this paradigm. Idealist concerns come to take
center stage in that we are concerned with forms of consciousness on their
own and not with the material forms of social power that shape them.

This leads me back to my basic thesis: namely, that the moral-cognitive
dimension of thought and the intersubjective dimension of social action—
both of which, in varying forms, make up the basis of neo-Idealism—cannot
be separated from the structural-functional logics of capitalist social institutions. Moreover, these modes of thought and action continue to be infected
by pathologies of consciousness and rationality and are unable to be effective
as a general critical theory of society. The domestication of critical theory,
as I am using the term here, results from the fact that the object of critique
has been shifted from the dialectic between subjectivity and social structural
forms to a research program that pursues the forms of praxis that can cultivate
critical consciousness absent the material concerns over the power to shape
institutional power and the kinds of power that institutions have over subject-
formation. Now, it is assumed that the intersubjective paradigm is sufficient
to overcome the forms of reification and injustice that pervade modern
society. It is domesticated in the sense that it no longer sees the basic concepts

of critical theory—such as alienation, reification, domination ideology, and so on—as rooted in material forms of social life and power but as properties of discourse, recognition, or some other philosophical concern.

But this communicative turn in critical theory has, in my view, weakened and debased the tradition of its more radical, more immanently critical power. It has returned critical theory to an Idealist set of concerns by placing emphasis on the epistemic and cognitive capacities for reason and by isolating social practices from the material-structural forms of power that shape them and orient them. This communicative turn has therefore domesticated critical theory: it has sealed off the structural realm of socialization from the forms of communicative and discursive practices that it takes as central to the will-formation of individuals. Whether it takes the form of Habermas's "discourse ethics" or Axel Honneth's premise of an "ethics of recognition," and other attempts at what can be termed a neoconstructivist theory of judgment and justice, the bulk of this theoretical tradition works within a neo-Idealist framework that has become blind to the true source of social and psychological pathologies that make the very foundations of the theory itself unworkable.

Neo-Idealism, therefore, is problematic because it conceives of social action as intersubjective and cognitive *outside* of the pressures and forces of social structure and function. It is concerned with questions of epistemology and theories of democracy torn from the questions of social structure and its ability to shape and structure forms of consciousness, culture, and subjective ego and will formation. Of primary importance is the ways that moral cognition is distorted by the socialization processes of hierarchical social relations or domination and control that characterize capitalist society. The kind of intersubjectivist epistemology that is relied upon by these thinkers is assumed outside of the structural-functional forces that shape the personality structure and moral-cognitive processes of modern subjects. My thesis is that by turning away from the structural-functionalist paradigm in social theory, these thinkers have turned the discourse of critical theory away from a confrontation with the distorting effects of capitalism on the patterns of culture and social psychology that can lead to a more effective form of social praxis.

IV. CONSTITUTIVE POWER AND THE SHAPING OF NORMS

What, then, can we say is the mechanism that prevents the neo-Idealist theories from becoming valid descriptive and normative accounts of social life? As I have argued above, the neo-Idealist paradigm is strongly grounded in an understanding of social life, praxis, and cognition that is detached from Marxian concepts of social power and their ability to shape social and subjective life. Democratic and humane forms of life are to be understood as stemming from the unleashing of rational forces that are intrinsic to the norms of communication or recognition or justification that modern rationality makes possible. But as I have shown above, this evades the crucial problem of subject constitution that is endemic to administrative-capitalist societies. I stress this because it seems to me that the shift away from the Marxian foundations of critical theory dissolved the genuine critical force from critical theory. Marx's thesis about the nature of capitalist society was such that the infrastructural basis of social life—its reproduction and sustenance based on particular economic formations—was causally related to the superstructural dimensions of culture, law, state, and, we must emphasize, consciousness itself. However, Marx was unable to elaborate or to defend this hypothesis with any degree of satisfaction according to the standards of contemporary social science. Marx's thesis, however, can be successfully defended once we grasp that modern capitalist social relations and goals—which rest on the expansion of production and consumption as well as the maintenance of efficient productive and consumptive practices and behaviors—themselves *require a specific cognitive and evaluative orientation to the world*. This orientation must be able to achieve the ends of efficiency in the above relations and practices but also, in addition, to hide or at least legitimate the nature of extractive domination that is constitutive of the relations and practices of the social order as well. In short, the theme of the reification of consciousness again enters into the picture once we realize that the Marxian and Weberian elements of critical theory create a unified *explanans* for the currents of modernity that fuses the domains of material and resource power operative in the economic domain of society with the value-orientations and socialization processes that take place within the cultural domain. Hence, we are left with the problem of resolving these two approaches in order to construct a critical theory of consciousness that problematizes the neo-Idealist premises of contemporary critical theory.

    In light of this, what I would like to propose now is an alternative understanding of social power and its mechanisms that bridges the two elements of material power or resource control rooted in economic dominance and the processes of social integration and subject-formation in order to provide a critique of the neo-Idealist philosophy of social action according to purely intersubjective-cognitive mechanisms. According to the thesis I am developing here, forms of resource and social power affect the values, norms, and conventions of social institutions, thereby enabling them to shape and mold forms of cognition and subjectivity. Marx's insight about the nature of capitalist social relations and their ability to forge structural and institutional formations must be brought into line with Weber's analysis of value-orientations and their ability to orient cognitive and evaluative frames of mind. Indeed, although neither of them made space for the dimension of intersubjective action, this can be easily provided by showing that values serve to underlie the frames of cognitive and intersubjective frames of thought and action and that many of the most crucial value-orientations are not achieved through rational forms of intersubjective action but, quite to the contrary, through highly rationalized and heteronomous forms of institutional inculcation.

In order to provide the foundation for this approach, I will use Rousseau's understanding of social norms and conventions (*moeurs*) and the particular form of social domination that he sees as fundamental to extend and complete the Marx-Weber paradigm of critical theory. What I have in view here is the thesis that material forms of social power and their coordination for broader social goals, made possible by the rationalization of bureaucratic structures and the kinds of social integration they privilege, undercuts the basic tenets of the neo-Idealist current in contemporary critical theory and its emphasis on intersubjective-cognitive social practices as a means of building critical consciousness and an emancipatory interest. Rousseau begins his critique of civil society, which he views as the fundamental basis for the domination of man by man, by arguing that the basic processes of society are such that social power is expressed and sustained through the shaping and the formation of forms of subjectivity that accept, willingly, the predominant configurations of power and domination. In contrast to the static theories of mind that were dominant in the seventeenth- and eighteenth-century models of epistemology, Rousseau's thesis posited a dynamic, processual understanding of cognition that was shaped diachronically by conventions, practices, and institutional social formations that impress themselves upon the subjective attributes of individuals.

In his *Discours sur l'origine et les fondements de l'inégalité parmi les hommes*, Rousseau proposes a theory about the development of social relations premised on the view that material inequalities within society must rest upon certain "metaphysical" inequalities wherein individuals accept the legitimacy of the power of others and their authority over things and people. This begins with the formation of private property: "The first person who, having enclosed a plot of land, called it his, and found people simple enough to believe him was the true founder of civil society."[14] For Rousseau, the domination of man by man was made possible by the impulse to self-aggrandize at the expense of others. But what at first looks like a psychological thesis immediately turns into a sociological one since it is followed by "the need to mold and manipulate others to comply with the subjugated role required from them."[15] What Rousseau sees as central to his critique of modern civilization is the problem that domination and asymmetrical power relations are not only structured objectively in the realms of law and property but, more crucially, also embedded in the system of norms and conventions that pervade the culture and, *ex hypothesi*, the psychology of the individual.

But Rousseau seems to go further than this. He is aware that there are certain psychological tendencies within individuals, but he establishes the thesis that the minds of men within society are shaped and molded by social power relations; that these power relations will create and deploy norms and conventions that will be in the service of that power. And if this is the case, it becomes deeply entrenched in the feelings, sentiments, and ideas that we carry with us and that we actively reproduce in everyday life. We can perhaps say that Rousseau is positing a hypothesis that can explain the ways that consciousness and thought itself becomes dependent on the kinds of norms that are rooted in these structural power relations. Even more, if this is the case, then we can see that this provides us with a crucial way to understand the limits of the neo-Idealist approach: intersubjective-cognitive processes and action alone—whether in the form of communication, recognition, or justification—are unable to work out for us an emancipatory interest to serve as the impulse and groundwork for critical consciousness. Rousseau is outlining a form of power that is able to mold the subjective orientations of individuals themselves, to structure and order the relation between value-orientations and the social-cognitive faculties.

I call the kind of social power that Rousseau describes *constitutive power* and define it more formally as *the capacity of any agent or institution to form, shape, or constitute the values, norms, cognitive capacities, and frames of any subject to the extent that said subject internalizes them into his own personality system and pattern of cognition.* Constitutive power is a means by which the subjectivity of the subject is equipped with value-patterns that have their sense of validity already fused within them, what I will call here the *internal validity of norms and values.* In this sense, the rational subject can come to accept norms as legitimate that support structures of domination. It also suggests that the capacity to have constitutive power at all, in particular in modern societies, is through the ability to control resources. Power over resources is linked to the power over institutions that themselves provide socialization for members of society. Indeed, the more power over resources is concentrated and organized, the more likely that it will be able to shape institutional goals for the benefit of its members. Marx's thesis about the concentration of capital and the interests of the capitalist class meld with Weber's insight about routinization of authority and its rationalization through institutionalization and bureaucratization. In this sense, what we see is that Weber's ideas about authority, when wedded to Marx's thesis about the base-superstructure model of society as well as the thesis concerning the centralization of capital and its control over various reproductive aspects of social life, gives us a model of social power in which the domination of material resources also grants—and indeed necessitates—domination over the processes of socialization. Value-orientations need to be deployed and made ambient in all elements of social life that legitimate the practices and norms that reproduce the community.

Indeed, Durkheim's understanding of social facts as consisting of an essentially coercive force impelling subjects to obey and conform to them is in line with Rousseau's ideas. Although Durkheim seeks to use it for the purposes of methodological concerns, the thesis is that social facts consist of "the power of external coercion which it exercises or is capable of exercising over individuals, and the presence of this power may be recognized in its turn either by the existence of some specific sanction or by the resistance offered against every individual effort that tends to violate it."[16] What this means is that the basic normative structure of the value-system of constitutive social dominance is able to imbricate itself into the norms of everyday life, creating doxic forms of thought and practice that not only cement social-relational forms of power but also orient the cognitive and evaluative powers of subjects. Indeed, in his critical discussion of pragmatism, Durkheim also insists that it is unable to explain social action fully, since it "claims to explain truth psychologically and subjectively."[17] Durkheim was aware of the limits of any conception of social action that is dissolved into epistemic constructs. But even he was nevertheless unaware of the ways that social forms of power are active in shaping cognition and norms. Still, the neo-Idealists make a move toward constructivism (Kant) and recognition (Hegel) as roots for a different paradigm of practical reason. Now, social theory is made into the servant of moral philosophy: social practices, rendered explicit by social-theoretic arguments, are the crucible for normative claims themselves. But nowhere is it seen that the limitations of the Idealist position was always that it assumed a kind of cognition that was sealed off from the mechanisms of social power.

This means that the neo-Idealist approach to the question of values needs to be rethought. Recall that for Habermas, the crucial element of communicative action is the proposal that the act of making an assertoric or normative validity claim can be challenged. For Habermas, the key is that norms that are considered sacred become linguistified and, as a result, migrate from the realm of the sacred and uncriticizable to a case where, because of the illocutionary force of the speech acts that constitute it, the norm now becomes open to questioning and in need of justification.[18] If it is the case, as the neo-Idealists all seem to suggest, that only social practices (communication, discourse, recognition, justification, or whatever) detached from material power configurations can be free to create the requisite capacities for critical consciousness, we must, as about the extent to which constitutive domination of subjects allows such an approach to be meaningful. Indeed, processes of communication, of recognition, of the capacities needed for "justification," all can be colonized by the constitutive domination. But constitutive power is not simply something anyone can express or possess. It requires the shaping of social norms and values that are in some sense predominant throughout the society. In order for broad forms of social action to be coordinated in even the most basic sense, these values must be so ambient within the community that it is also routinized and internalized by subjects.

Even further, since constitutive power is concerned with the value systems and value patterns that are mapped onto the personality, it also shapes the cognitive capacities of subjects in that their rational faculties are colonized with the normative beliefs that the value-pattern provides. Hence, language also possesses the properties of social structure itself, since it is not only the values that undergird semantic concepts but also the structural forms of language that are adapted to specific functional ends and value-consensus that is also of concern. Constitutive power is therefore contrasted with the forms of moral obligation outlined by Kant. For Kant, the subject reflects rationally on the validity of any norm before accepting it as a basis for thought and action. Similarly, in deliberative understandings of moral cognitivism, we are asked rationally to scrutinize the validity claims inherent in moral utterances. We are asked, as Rainer Forst proposes, to consider a conception of critical cognition where "moral persons have a fundamental *right to justification*, and a corresponding unconditional *duty to justify* morally relevant actions."[19] But this simply sidesteps the entire problematic that critical theory placed at the center of social theory: the extent to which the reification of consciousness renders subjects acritical to the extent to which the socialization into a value-system that possesses the internal validity ready-made can predispose subjects to forms of cognitive pathologies such that their ability to call for justifications and critique wither.

The power of domination therefore lies in the extent to which subjects are rendered unable or even unwilling to call into question the forms of authority that pervade their lives. Forst seems to assume that these pathologies of consciousness and cognition are of little (if any) consequence—that individuals possess an *a priori* right to justification and the capacity for calling for it. But this is simply absurd: the practices that call for the justification of norms need to be claimed, not simply assumed. Even though he is broadly correct that subjects ought to call for justification, there is no sense that what stands between that ought and the actual realities that prevent that capacity among individuals from being cultivated is what has concerned true critical theory from the beginning. Indeed, they would have rightly characterized such assumptions as harking back to a form of Idealism in which the material organization of society, authority, and legitimate forms of domination and their reificatory effects on consciousness were not considered. Forst's arguments, no less than those of Honneth, bring us full circle: now the Ideals of the norms of justification and recognition should be enough to overcome all forms of domination and help us create a more humane, democratic ethical life.

V. NEO-IDEALIST THEORY AND THE
PERSISTENCE OF SOCIAL DOMINATION

One reason this development in critical theory remains problematic is that it is unable to appreciate how power and domination work in modern societies. Because of this blind spot, it has been successful not only in redrawing the parameters of critical theory but also in domesticating it. Indeed, the next thesis I would like to explore is that neo-Idealism in fact allows for the persistence of social domination and is unable to counteract its effects on social, cultural, and political life. Since the thesis of constitutive domination, as I laid it out above, concerns the shaping and structuring of norms at both collective and subjective levels, I can now move to the heart of my critique of neo-Idealist critical theory by showing how this kind of domination allows for (1) the persistence of psychological and cultural mechanisms for social domination and (2) an inability for communicative, recognitive, and discursive forms of social action and praxis to provide for the requisite critical capacities against it.

The central weakness of the neo-Idealists is their core assumption—drawn largely from Mead and reinforced by Habermas—that *sociation* rather than social *domination* is the central characteristic of socialization and social relations.[20] For Mead, the basic nucleus of modern human societies lies in the fact that they are composed of social relations and roles that are interdependent and that mutually affect each other. Central to his social theory is the notion that dominance, a characteristic of premodern societies, has been displaced by what he calls "sociality." This means that the hierarchical forms of social relations that were once premised on unequal forms of social power have shifted to a form of social relations in which individuals are differentiated into different roles, but essentially cooperate for the attainment of common ends. In so doing, he expunges domination from his theory of socialization. However, Mead's framework for sociation—adopted as a backbone position by neo-Idealists—does not involve the ways in which structures of domination are in fact the formal shape, the concrete framework within which sociation occurs. As Lonnie Athens correctly observes, "For, at least, all complex human social actions, human domination makes super-ordination and sub-ordination integral, whereas human sociality does not make them integral to the construction of these social actions, no matter how complex that they may be."[21] Athens's critique of Mead can be extended into a critique of the neo-Idealists in the sense that they, too, view sociation outside of domination relations. Although they recognize the importance of *conflict*, as does Mead, they seem to think domination is of little importance with respect to the ways that sociation occurs.

What needs to be recognized is that domination and conflict are not the same phenomenon. The former conveys a sense of power over that which is secure and legitimate, or at least made so, through the shaping of values, institutions, norms, and ideas reifying the power structure that exists in real terms. It is rendered legitimate as a result of the ways that cognitive processes are oriented toward the goals of those who dominate and possess material power. Self-determination is therefore recircuited to place the interests of others within the domain of the interests of the self—the imperatives of alter become the forms of legitimate action and behavior of ego. Domination in the modern sense—indeed, in the sense that critical theory has in view—is therefore not something that can be comprehended within the context of the social practices shaped by this kind of power. These in fact become the very vehicles of domination and power, not the crucible for emancipation. This, in the end, is the fatal flaw of neo-Idealist theory leading to the domestication of critical theory as an enterprise. As I have been suggesting here, however, this is the primary area of concern for any valid critical social theory since it is in the ways that constitutive power is welded to concrete forms of extractive power that presents us with the pathologies of consciousness (i.e., of reification, alienation, and so on). This is because social domination is a structural-functional phenomenon in which the hierarchical structures of power use the functional nature of norms and value-orientations to secure that power and to shape consciousness toward its legitimacy. The pragmatist elements of neo-Idealist theory therefore promote social conformity rather than encourage its critical examination and contestation.[22]

Social power is the capacity to be able to achieve some end through directing the resources or capacities (natural or human) of another. Social power is therefore the ability to orient the capacities of another(s) in order to obtain some surplus for oneself or to realize one's self-interest at the expense of another or through the efforts of another. Social power becomes social domination once a subset of any community is able to achieve their ends or goals by using the capacities of others and there exists a structural inequality between the agents using the capacities and those from whom the capacities are extracted. Any time that this structural form of superordination and subordination becomes stable over time, this is achieved through social integration around a value consensus in which such structural relations of domination and superordination/subordination are made legitimate in some basic sense. Hence, the material power of certain individuals or groups to extract benefits from others requires a normative force in the realm of social facts, which, in turn, must affect the cognitive and evaluative capacities of the subject.

Otherwise, no one would voluntarily submit to the domination-relations. This is a rudimentary definition, but we can see that for such a structurally unequal relation of power, it can only be stable over time once there exists some kind of legitimate authority for the domination. In this sense, what above I termed *constitutive domination* exists alongside the kind of extractive domination that is at the base of social relations of unequal power. Once the legitimacy of certain social practices and structures becomes embedded within the institutions that socialize agents, it becomes a concrete social formation that unites the material basis for domination (extraction) as well as the cultural, psychological, and cognitive (constitutive) mode of domination as well. The linking element in this model is the extent to which norms and values are pressed into the service of the first kind of domination by the second. Indeed, this is not a static but a dynamic process. Norms and values that at one time were not acceptable, or were seen as tyrannical or dominating, can at another time be accepted as legitimate and "natural." We can think of the rise of wage labor in the consciousness of working people in the early nineteenth century as an example of how the norm of wage labor—initially seen as a kind of servitude to masters and lords—became an acceptable and normal part of industrial society.

But the real kernel of the argument consists in the fact that norms and value-orientations are functionally dependent, within administrative societies, on the concrete aspects of the social order. This means that norms are put into service that render legitimate large-scale forms of production, exploitation, extraction, self-alienation, and consumption that are structured by the aims and goals of elites. Certain values and norms can indeed come into conflict with those of elites, but over time, if the system is to be stable, they will have to be absorbed by and translated into the norms that codify the social order.[23] Unlike Durkheim, who conceived of social integration as a process of articulating normative orders of social life, the Marx-Weber thesis postulates that norms and values will hinge on the concrete nature of power inherent in the social order and that these norms will be structured in the service of the goals of concrete power relations. The symbolic domains of life—that of consciousness, of language, of value-orientations, and so on—will be pulled toward the power centers of the community. As Marshall Sahlins insightfully remarks, "In bourgeois society, material production is the dominant locus of symbolic production."[24] Industrial and postindustrial societies require the absorption of large segments of the population to accept certain values as basic and that orient their ways of thinking and acting in the world.

At the root of the neo-Idealist premise, however, is the assumption that intersubjective relations can freely shape and transform consciousness, that social norms can be scrutinized according to rational practices that seek their justification. But if we accept the thesis of constitutive dominance that I sketched above, we see that there is a problem with this program, since constitution is seen as occurring at the level of functional systems and subsystems that, if they are successful in socializing agents, are capable of providing a basic normative framework from which they derive their subjective value-systems. But perhaps even more, the kind of conceptual development that is encouraged by societies grounded in commodity production and consumption also become constricted and narrow, rendering thought processes barren of richer forms of understanding. The neo-Idealist failing here is that norms shape the cognitive capacities of individuals, the very capacities upon which they rely for their theories of social action and critical consciousness. What neo-Idealism abandons is a dialectical conception of consciousness that is able to grasp the actual source of norms: their attachment to functionalist properties of hierarchical social systems and goals. Lacking this, we are not really working with a critical theory of society at all, but a social philosophy hermetically sealed off from the concrete nature of power and its rootedness in economic power and organization.

NOTES

1. This is not, however, only a viewpoint rooted in Marxism. Cf. the insightful discussion by John Kenneth Galbraith, *The New Industrial State* (Boston: Houghton Mifflin, 1967), 388ff.

2. Habermas specifically argues that "by social integration I understand, with Durkheim, securing the unity of a social life-world through values and norms." Jürgen Habermas, *Zur Rekonstruktion des Historischen Materialismus* (Frankfurt: Suhrkamp, 1976), 159. This shift toward a theory of socialization is based on a move toward discursive understanding of social integration and socialization, where the real basis of socialization processes consist in the mutual agreement about binding norms and values that serve as the basis of the social order. Hence, the move away from Marx is effected where norms are no longer rooted in concrete forms of power but rather in the fluidity of norms and individuation.

3. "The species learns not only in the dimension of technically useful knowledge decisive for the development of productive forces but also in the dimension of moral-practical consciousness decisive for structures of interaction. The rules of communicative action do develop in reaction to changes in the domain of instrumental and strategic action; but in doing so they follow *their own logic*." Ibid., 163.

4. Axel Honneth has written on this theme that "today, social theory based on Marx can regain its critical potential only if the functionalist prioritizing of the economic sphere is dropped and the weight of the other domains of action are brought to bear: an analysis in which the achievements of all remaining spheres had been investigated as contributing to the one systemic aim of material production must give way to a research program that investigates the historically specific interrelationships of independent spheres of action." *The Fragmented World of the Social: Essays in Social and Political Philosophy* (Albany, NY: SUNY Press, 1995), 5.

5. Cf. the discussion by Herbert Schnädelbach, "Transformation der Kritischen Theorie," in Axel Honneth and Hans Joas (eds.), *Kommunikatives Handeln. Beiträge zu* Jürgen Habermas' *»Theorie des kommunikativen Handelns«* (Frankfurt: Suhrkamp, 1986), 28ff. Although Habermas does admit to the problem of the "colonization of the lifeworld" in his earlier theory of communication, this is later dropped in favor of a purer theory of communication and language that no longer suffers from the social distortions of reified consciousness.

6. See Axel Honneth, *Das Recht der Freiheit: Grundriß einer demokratischen Sittlichkeit* (Frankfurt: Suhrkamp, 2011), 58ff. as well as 81ff.

7. Jürgen Habermas, *Postmetaphysical Thinking: Philosophical Essays* (Cambridge, MA: MIT Press, 1993), 9.

8. In this sense, Habermas's critique of Parsons led critical theory away from the concerns of how values and norms are connected with more concrete forms of social power. See the discussion by John Holmwood, "From 1968 to 1951: How Habermas Transformed Marx into Parsons," *Czech Sociological Review* 69, no. 5 (2008): 923–43.

9. Karl-Otto Apel, *Towards a Transformation of Philosophy* (London: Routledge and Kegan Paul, 1980), 238–39. Also see the discussion by Eduardo Mendieta, *The Adventures of Transcendental Philosophy* (Lanham, MD: Rowman & Littlefield, 2002), 141ff.

10. Jürgen Habermas, *Knowledge and Human Interests* (Boston: Beacon Press, 1971), 191.

11. Axel Honneth attempted to make this move in his study *Reification: A New Look at an Old Idea* (New York: Oxford University Press, 2008). What is missed here is the ways that reification refers not to a "forgetting of recognition," but rather to the distortion of ethical capacities and cognitive faculties and capacities more broadly. See the excellent discussion by Rüdiger Dannemann, *Das Prinzip Verdinglichung. Studie zur Philosophie Georg Lukács* (Frankfurt: Sendler Verlag, 1987), 131ff. Also see the important discussion by Andrew Feenberg, *The Philosophy of Praxis: Marx, Lukács and the Frankfurt School* (London: Verso, 2014), 61ff.

12. Rahel Jaeggi argues that alienation should be seen as a loss of the ability to "appropriate" (*Aneignung*) the world as one's own; it is a *Beziehung der Beziehungslosigkeit. Entfremdung. Zur Aktualität eines sozialphilosophischen Problems* (Frankfurt: Campus Verlag, 2005), 19 and *passim*. Again, this is formulated outside the systems of social production and the value-systems that internally validate them. For a competing approach to this theory of alienation, see my paper "Alienation as Atrophied Moral Cognition and Its Implications for Political Behavior," *Journal for the Theory of Social Behaviour* 43, no. 3 (2013): 301–21.

13. Rainer Forst, *Justification and Critique: Toward a Critical Theory of Politics* (Cambridge: Polity Press, 2014), 5.

14. Jean-Jacques Rousseau, *Discours sur l'origine et les fondements de l'inégalité parmi les hommes*, in Bernard Gagnebin and Marcel Raymond (eds.), *Œuvres Complètes*, vol. 3 (Paris: Éditions Gallimard, 1964).

15. Nicholas Dent, *Rousseau: An Introduction to His Psychological, Social and Political Theory* (Oxford: Basil Blackwell, 1988), 61. Also see the important discussion by Zev M. Trachtenberg, *Making Citizens: Rousseau's Political Theory of Culture* (New York: Routledge, 1993), 144–74.

16. Emile Durkheim, *The Rules of Sociological Method* (New York: Free Press, 1938), 76.

17. Emile Durkheim, *Pragmatism and Sociology* (Cambridge: Cambridge University Press, 1983), 83 and *passim*.

18. Habermas suggests that assertoric statements that take the form of "It is right that *a* in *s*," and its metalinguistic form "It is the case (is true) that *p*," "express the validity claim *itself*, in one case as a normative validity claim in the other as an assertoric validity claim." *The Theory of Communicative Action*, vol. 2, trans. Thomas McCarthy (Boston: Beacon Press, 1987), 69. From this, Habermas maintains that all norms can be expressed linguistically, and as a result, all linguistified norms express a validity claim and can be challenged or criticized. No norms can be protected from critique by sacralization once they become rationalized by language. I elaborate a critique of this basic idea in the next chapter.

19. Rainer Forst, *The Right to Justification: Elements of a Constructivist Theory of Justice* (New York: Columbia University Press, 2012), 21.

20. See Lonnie Athens and his critique of Mead along these very same lines. "Mead's Analysis of Social Conflict: A Radical Interactionist's Critique," *The American Sociologist* 43 (2012): 428–47 as well as his "'Domination': The Blind Spot in Mead's Analysis of the Social Act," *Journal of Classical Sociology* 2 (2002): 25–42.

21. Athens, "Mead's Analysis of Social Conflict," 436.

22. This critique has been leveled also against Dewey, no less than Meade. For a critique of Dewey's pragmatism along the lines of encouraging social conformism, see James Block, *A Nation of Agents: The American Path to a Modern Self and Society* (Cambridge, MA: Harvard University Press, 2002), 537ff.

23. Robert Park notes on this aspect of domination that "the fundamental function of dominance seems to be everywhere the same. It is to stabilize, to maintain order, and to permit the growth of structure in which that order and the corresponding functions are embedded." Robert Park, "Dominance," in Everett Hughes (ed.), *Human Communities* (New York: Free Press, 1952 [1934]), 159–64, 163.

24. Marshall Sahlins, *Culture and Practical Reason* (Chicago: University of Chicago Press, 1976), 212.

Chapter 2

One-Dimensional Rationality and the Limits of Pragmatist Reason

I. INTRODUCTION

Significant currents in contemporary social, moral, and political philosophy have fallen under the spell of pragmatism. The attraction is not totally unjustified. At its base, pragmatism—as a philosophical method as well as an approach to ethics—is a philosophy that seeks to embrace the power of cooperation, interaction, and an implicitly democratic path to meaning and knowledge. It rejects forms of ready-made truth, seeks rational justification for ideas typically seen as "foundational" and absolute, and takes fallibalism and doubt as the basic starting point for philosophy.[1] It places emphasis on inquiry over foundational truths and forces epistemological concerns out from their subjective limits and into the realm of intersubjectivity. Since Habermas, critical theory has also been deeply shaped by the impact of pragmatism and its search for a post-foundational form of reasoned inquiry. The paradigm shift toward communication, discourse, language, and intersubjective recognition is rooted firmly in the pragmatist doctrines of social action and supposedly critical inquiry. But what I would like to suggest here is that this view is mistaken. My thesis is that this paradigm shift has overlooked one of the core organizing principles of critical theory—namely, that the desiccation of consciousness is a basic consequence of the structural and functional dynamics of modern, administered, capitalist society. Further, we need to see that the pragmatist insistence on socially embedded forms of inquiry and the reliance on language as a means of fostering critical inquiry instead leads us to reproduce forms of power and, instead of exposing them to meaningful critical inquiry, entrenches their legitimacy.[2]

To open a path for this critique of pragmatism, I will explore Herbert Marcuse's thesis of one-dimensional consciousness and its relation to language and discourse. For Marcuse, the condition of one-dimensionality is characterized by a deep reification of consciousness that constrains, even disables, the critical capacities of subjects, making them willful participants in exploitive relations that dominate their lives. The basis of this thesis is that the cognitive capacity of subjects to evaluate their social world and its legitimacy is actively undermined by the functional forces of highly rationalized and tightly administered forms of socialization. Whereas in previous eras of the history of religion, political *mythoi* of sacred power, status, or some other social variable served as the legitimating mechanism of the social order and worked to imbue the state and law as well as consciousness with the values needed for hierarchical forms of power; modernity is coordinated according to a liberation of identities even as the organization of society as a whole fulfills the interests and needs of a single class. What is needed for any form of organized power to exert itself and be effective as well as efficient is the willing participation of all members of the community toward its ends. What is needed is that all individuals become, to a greater or lesser extent, constituent of the dominant forms of power that pervade the community. Marcuse's thesis is that one-dimensional consciousness is a key aspect of this kind of constituent power. It is a deformed mode of thought and consciousness that can be seen as disabling the critical-cognitive faculties of individuals, leaving them with an immediate relation to the mechanisms of social power and the purposes of social life. Creative, *critical* forms of thought become subordinated to a technicist and instrumental rationality that adapts drives and goals to its own imperatives.

The nature of this kind of one-dimensional consciousness is marked by the inability of subjects to cognize autonomously their own worldviews and to force them to accept—as a result of strong forms of socialization due to isomorphically constituted social institutions—the value-patterns and forms of cognition that help cement the power of the prevailing social order. This entails an acceptance of not only the legitimacy of the institutions that pervade one's social world but also—as Max Weber intimated—the patterns of thought and value-orientations that are required for those institutions to function in any socially meaningful way. Critical theorists of the first generation explored consistently this conception of modern forms of power and domination. It remained a central problematic that gave critical theory its distinctive sense of social inquiry and normative power. However, contemporary critical theory largely works under the premise of a postmetaphysical understanding of human action that posits a pragmatist understanding of human meaning and critique. This paradigm shift in critical theory has moved the emphasis and focus of critical theory toward discursive and deliberative forms of social action as the nexus of theory and praxis, as the very expression and activity of social critique. It maintains that the very structure of language and forms of intersubjectivity constitute patterns of socialization and practical reasoning that escape and counter the centripetal force of institutionalization.

Further, according to this view, an emancipatory form of social action is inherent in the language games and recognitive relations of intersubjective social practices. These views see the thesis of power and domination as colonizing subjective, cognitive, and personality systems, as vestigial and no longer a viable hypothesis for understanding modernity.

In challenging this claim, it is important to expose the ways that the particular kinds of social power that characterize technical, rational, capitalist societies and institutions deforms and corrupts the linguistic and, by extension, cognitive powers of individuals. In chapter 4 of *One-Dimensional Man*, Marcuse suggests that the problem of one-dimensional thinking infects the very nature of discourse and thought. He suggests that the manipulation of language by technocratic elites for the purposes of consumption and war creates a conformism through the medium of language. What I would like to do here is expand on Marcuse's thesis to outline a critique of the rationalist presuppositions of discourse ethics and to show the limits of the pragmatist paradigm in critical theory. What Marcuse takes as basic in his analysis in *One-Dimensional Man* is that there exists a complex but resilient causal connection between the functional logics of the social system as a whole and the cognitive processes of subjects in particular. And this relation is of such a nature that the shapes of consciousness that result are unable to generate critical forms of reason on their own, especially because, as Marcuse argues, the structure of language and communication is deeply affected by the kinds of concepts used in communication and thought.

What Marcuse's analysis provides is a crucial counterargument to the communicative turn in critical theory. His analysis of the closing of the universe of discourse holds that a reified public sphere, engineered by the interests of capital, occurs along a technicist line where individuals come to flatten out the concepts that they use to make cognitive sense of their world. The thesis I propose, therefore, is the following: that Marcuse's analysis of the effects of one-dimensionality on language and communication in *One-Dimensional Man* holds that discourse alone is incapable of serving as an emancipatory form of social action since it, too, is imbued by the pathological effects of reified structures of thought. Linguistic mechanisms are shaped by one-dimensional discourse, and we are faced with the premise that subjects are rendered unable to escape the confines of one-dimensionality through communicative action or discourse ethics. Marcuse effectively anticipates the move taken by Jürgen Habermas—and now seen as a paradigm shift in critical theory—toward the communicative turn, but opposes such a theory on the grounds that language is prone to fall victim to one-dimensionality, to the problem that conceptual thought can be gutted by the means of communication and discourse typical of administrative-capitalist societies. Before developing this thesis into a broader critique of pragmatic forms of reasoning and discourse-theoretic approaches to critical theory, we should examine the details of Marcuse's critique of one-dimensional discourse.

II. ONE-DIMENSIONAL DISCOURSE

Marcuse sees the public manipulation of discourse as a crucial, if not central, mechanism for the creation and cultivation of one-dimensional conscious-ness. He begins his discussion by asserting a causal relation between the sphere of public discourse and the ways that this is able to shape the cognitive faculties of subjects. As Marcuse writes:

> [P]ublicity agents shape the universe of communication in which the one-dimensional behavior expresses itself. Its language testifies to identification and unification, to the systematic promotion of positive thinking and doing, to the concerted attack on transcendent, critical notions. In the prevailing modes of speech, the contrast appears between two-dimensional, dialectical modes of thought and technological behavior or social "habits of thought."[3]

What is crucial is the role that identification and unification plays in the "closing of the universe of discourse." These terms—identification and uni-fication—convey the problem of flattening consciousness and conceptual thought, rendering thinking a merely mechanical process that mirrors the pre-dominant social reality uncritically. Opposed to this is a kind of cognition that seeks mediations, to grasp conceptually the mechanisms and value systems that give the predominant social reality its coherence. If this can be done, then we would be moving in a space of critical reasons as opposed simply to a space of reasons themselves; we would be working with concepts that mediate by tying our cognitive content with the actual structures of reality. A critical space of reasons, as I will argue below, is one that requires us to leave the realm of discourse alone and the structure of language and the kind of mental acts that it entails, and instead to move toward a way of thinking that ties concepts, words, and cognition itself to existing social processes and to inquire into the full conceptualization of their essence. What makes this kind of critical thinking impossible is the de-conceptualization of conscious-ness, of the capacity for social norms, institutions, and the constitutive power of social formations to render thought immediate by eliding the content of thought with the functioning of empirical objects.

Marcuse's term for this is *operationalization*, where the names and mean-ings of things are collapsed into their functions. The style of thinking that emerges as a result of this process is one that fuses thought to what is exis-tent—that is, to the given reality that predominates. This is done through language, through the manipulation of language, through its simplification and rationalization: "It is the word that orders and organizes, that induces people to do, to buy, and to accept. It is transmitted in a style which is a veritable linguistic creation; a syntax in which the structure of the sentence is abridged and condensed in such a way that no tension, no 'space' is left between the parts of the sentence. This linguistic form militates against a development of meaning."[4] Communication is therefore affected in a specific way, and at the level of the syntactic structure of the sentence itself. The central concern here is the *closing* or *constriction* of meaning, which signifies a narrowing not only of the nature of public discourse (and by extension intersubjective relations in general) but also of cognition itself. This goes to the heart of Marcuse's thesis: namely, that the techniques used by public relations experts in the fields of politics as well as the management of consumer society take on the characteristics of scientific-technical language in which the semantic field of words are sharpened in order to name discrete entities, whereas, in critical discourse, there is the need to expand the semantic field, to enlarge the sphere of meaning that words can have, in order to not only name what is given *empirically* but also understand the alternative possibilities that lay dormant in the prevailing modes of thinking. Objects and social reality are dynamic realities, not static ones. They possess potentialities and essences, purposes that are not always—indeed, rarely—recognized by consciousness. In this sense, the importance of contrasting the deeper purposes and functionings, the dynamic potentialities that are thwarted by industrial and postindustrial forms of life and culture, can only be brought out through the dialectical mode of consciousness. But in one-dimensional thought and discourse, negativity becomes neutralized, and dialectics disintegrates into analytics.

Language, as thought and as communication, is deeply affected by this breakdown of dialectical thinking. Marcuse's thesis is that linguistic structure itself—in both semantic and syntactic terms—becomes a rigid framework for expression as well as thought. The one-dimensionality of language occurs through the ways that the lexical content of words becomes riveted to predefined cultural concepts that frame meaning. Violating the narrow confines of semantic meaning therefore means the violation of norms of thought and conduct: "Transgression of the discourse beyond the closed analytical structure is incorrect or propaganda, although the means of enforcing the truth and the degree of punishment are very different. In this universe of public discourse, speech moves in synonyms and tautologies."[5] One-dimensional reality, therefore, has the power to shape the cognitive powers of individuals. "Here, the functionalization of language," Marcuse writes, "expresses an abridgement of meaning which has a political connotation. The names of things are not only 'indicative of their manner of functioning,' but their (actual) manner of functioning also defines and 'closes' the meaning of the thing, excluding other manners of functioning."[6] The "noun governs the sentence in an authoritarian and totalitarian fashion,"[7] meaning that the semantic fields of nouns refer to stable concepts—democracy, capitalism, success, happiness, and so on—that are themselves meant to secure compliance to particular value-orientations and particular forms of established reality. Since the legitimacy of the system is dependent on subjective values being oriented toward needs and desires that are themselves satisfied by that system, it is essential that the semantic meaning of words—that is, their descriptive content—be rooted in the particular values that are most likely to produce institutional efficiency. Hence, there is, underlying the *descriptive* valence of words, a *normative* valence that orients the values and cognitive thought processes of the subject. *Democracy* is not simply a noun *describing* a particular mode of social and political power—it also becomes *normatively* associated with what is familiar to the subject, to what is "his" in some basic sense, to what is "good" versus "bad," to what is safe versus what is threatening, and so on; it becomes a constitutive rule of a language game that routinizes particular value-concepts into the worldviews of those embedded in the discourse.[8] What it cannot be is a word that describes a rich field of meaning, specifically one that contradicts the social facts that constitute the world that the subject is meant to accept as legitimate. It cannot come into conflict with or render dissonant the values that undergird the prevailing social order and that shape its purposes and logic.

One-dimensional discourse, therefore, has multiple layers. Since it is managed by elites, it seeks to modify the semantic and lexical fields of meaning that words take. It also, and more important, becomes a central tool in socialization by shaping the cognitive and evaluative powers and capacities of subjects. The *operationalization* of words and their meanings constricts the ways that individuals can think through the world by tying their meanings to particular descriptive and normative referents. In so doing, it creates certain norms of thinking and communicating; norms that ultimately root themselves in the *sensus communis* that is cultivated by what can be called *administered discourse*. I think this idea is what is behind Marcuse's argument that "[t]he analytic structure insulates the governing noun from those of its contents which would invalidate or at least disturb the accepted use of the noun in statements of policy and public opinion. The ritualized concept is made immune against contradiction."[9] Ritualization here refers to the kind of power that is made possible by the *routinization (Veralltäglichung)* of norms, practices, and meanings that become internalized by subjects and woven into a kind of basic conception of the world. Words and their meanings, through this process of routinization, become fused to particular significations and even forms of collective intentionality, where the cognitive practices and capacities of subjects become oriented by the strong pull of functional forms of socialization that impose normative strictures on accepted forms of meaning, and, by implication, accepted forms of social practice.[10]

Speaking and hearing become activities that braid the ways that subjects think about the world and how they evaluate it as well. In this sense, Marcuse's thesis implies a connection between speech and thought; it is a connection that is also echoed in modern analytic philosophy where language is seen as not only a form of communication but also capturing forms of thought itself. As Wilfred Sellars insightfully argues on this problem, "We must resolutely put aside the temptation to draw the kind of distinction between *thought* and its *expression* which this formulation implies and continue with the intriguing idea that an uttering of 'p' which is a primary expression of a belief that-p is not merely an *expression* of a thinking that-p, but is itself a *thinking*, i.e., a thinking-out-loud that-p."[11] However, for Marcuse, thinking and expressing, language, thought, and communication do not occur in a philosophic vacuum, but rather within a framework of social power that is concrete and institutionalized, rationalized and patterned, exerting formative pressures on the cognitive capacities of subjects. As a result, communication and thought are deeply affected and shaped by the contours of social power that operate within and orient social institutions.

What we are faced with is the notion that material forms of power shape and determine forms of consciousness in specific ways. For Marcuse, this kind of consciousness is the product of an "authoritarian character" of language—a kind of language characterized by the rigid semantic fields that have been fused to value-concepts that are fitted to institutional logics.[12] What results is "a telescoping and abridgment of syntax which cuts off development of meaning by creating fixed images which impose themselves with an overwhelming and petrified concreteness."[13] Language, not only as action or the activity of thought but also, as Hegel noted, as the vehicle of thought, therefore becomes of primary concern for Marcuse.[14] The basic problem is social as well as psychological and epistemic: one-dimensional discourse controls the stable legitimacy of the social order by imposing new normative standards of meaning and thought that constrict information or ideas that transgress the boundaries imposed by the discourse.[15] Dialectical thought is therefore negated by the force and imposition of analytic reasoning.

As I interpret it, Marcuse posits a concrete relation between three dimensions or levels of linguistic action and social cognition. First, there is the *social level*, which refers to the ways in which language is shaped and created by socialization processes and institutions (media, schools, technological forms of reason, and so on). Second, there is the *relation between the syntactic and semantic layers of language* and the forms of logic that are dominant in social facts. Third, there is the relation between these syntactic and semantic logics and the *workings of consciousness*—that is, of the *content of conceptual thought itself*. I will now turn to elaborate each of these levels of linguistic action before considering their effects on critical theory after its linguistic and intersubjectivist turn.

Recall that the process of *operationalization* is central for Marcuse's discussion of one-dimensional discourse. It is a process of reification, of making immediate what should be mediated—it is a process of de-conceptualizing the world for the subject (it is the "thing identified with its function"). "This language," writes Marcuse, "which constantly imposes *images*, militates against the development and expression of *concepts*. In its immediacy and directness, it impedes conceptual thinking; thus, it impedes thinking. For the concept does *not* identify the thing and its function."[16] One-dimensional discourse therefore simplifies and reifies thought by replacing concepts with images; with the act of making the act of thinking one of *identification*. Thought ceases to be reflective in any complex way and turns to immediacy: the generalized semantic reference of a given word no longer functions as a concept, but as a schematic of thought, orienting consciousness for the purpose of coordinating social actions to predesigned purposes. Subjective thought therefore comes to mirror the logics imposed by socialization and anchored in the logic of the prevailing system that together "dissolve the concepts in operations and exclude the conceptual intent which is opposed to such dissolution. Prior to its operational usage, the concept *denies* the identification of the thing with its function; it distinguishes that which the thing is from the contingent functions of the thing in the established reality."[17] One-dimensional discourse, therefore, forces thought into the sphere of *Verstand* as opposed to that of *Vernunft*: it is the essence of reification itself.

What rationalized institutions therefore seek to promote—in order to secure mass consumption, macro-sociological forms of social coordination and legitimacy, and so on—is a kind of mental activity among subjects that restricts consciousness to the specific operational and empirical fields needed for institutional functionality.[18] In Marcuse's sense, it is not conceptual activity but a kind of mental activity that is shot through with mental "images" as opposed to a rational grasp of objective reality. This distinction is important, for it registers a degradation of mental capacity and thereby of the kinds of social cohesion—as opposed to conflict—that results from it. Again, it is important to point out that the mechanism for this process is essentially *linguistic* in that socialization pressures act to constrict semantic fields to purely instrumental ends or ends that comply with the imperatives and functionings of the prevalent reality rather than the range of potentialities to which objects and concepts give rise in critical thought. This results in the syntactic (or grammatical) shift in which the semantic meanings of words are gutted of concepts and replaced by images that function to mesh word and function, thought and reality.[19] Marcuse refers to this as an "abridgment of thought" and of meaning in which the words used in discourse come to be identified with the dominant reality principle. But this occurs through syntactic as well as semantic means: "I have alluded to the philosophy of grammar in order to illuminate the extent to which the linguistic abridgments indicate an abridgment of thought which they in turn fortify and promote. Insistence on the philosophical elements in grammar, on the link between the grammatical, logical, and ontological 'subject,' points up the contents which are suppressed in the functional language, barred from expression and communication."[20] In this context, the question to consider next is to what extent the reliance on discourse, communication, and intersubjective reason giving is for critical theory. The thesis I will therefore turn to is that Marcuse's analysis of one-dimensional discourse vitiates this program in critical theory and beckons a return to a conception of critical cognition based on the relation of concepts and reason with the ontological structure of reality.

III. ONE-DIMENSIONAL DISCOURSE AND THE CRITIQUE OF THE PRAGMATIC TURN IN CRITICAL THEORY

Marcuse's analysis of the closure of discourse in the administered society implies that the conception of a communicative and discursive critical theory is in some basic sense problematic. One reason is that if, as the pragmatist argues, we develop reasons and forms of justification through discourse with others, there is no way to guarantee that the discourse within which anyone is situated will be able to get them outside of the dominating value-fields that are established by the dominant discourse. Since values are a synthesis of conceptual (and therefore cognitive) and affective and normative domains of consciousness, they have a particular force on the power of language to be able to serve as an objective context within which individuals can communicate. The structure of language, therefore, ought not to be seen, as Habermas suggests, to be a means of escaping the problem of reification and one-dimensionality. This is because the problem of one-dimensionality is essentially a problem of *concept formation* and not one of *syntactic structure*. For Habermas, the key issue is that the linguistification of norms opens up the possibility for the rational critique of all previously sacred or socially accepted norms and values, allowing for a conception of critical reason that is accountable to forms of social action that are intrinsically reflexive. Hence, Habermas's thesis is that the pragmatics of language are capable of supplying subjects with the requisite capacities for critical cognition. But his discussion of this is reliant on the thesis that the propositional form of speech acts renders statements as validity claims rather than as merely locutionary statements. Recall that Habermas builds this thesis from the fact that statements such as (*a*) It is right that *a* in *s*.

as well as

(*b*) It is the case (is true) that *p*.

express a speech act in which a validity claim is being raised. "Unlike the illocutionary components of standard speech acts which express the fact that the speaker is raising a validity claim, (*a*) and (*b*) express the validity claim *itself*, in one case as a normative validity claim, in the other as an assertoric validity claim."[21]

But the problem here is that, as my reconstruction of Marcuse's thesis would suggest, the propositional structure of language is not where the validity of the values reside. Indeed, the deeper problem that affects reified forms of consciousness is the extent to which the concepts that underpin the semantic units of any sentence are themselves rational/critical or whether they are reified and merely reflect the given reality back at them. In this sense, reification is the problem of the ways that routinized and rationalized forms of value-orientations become fused to power structures and relations and get reflected in consciousness. And these power relations themselves, although they do not sacralize power in some premodern sense, nevertheless make many of these value-patterns conventional by tying values to particular institutional roles and actions. The dominant concepts of "success," "freedom," of "right" and "just," are themselves given their particular shape by the values that undergird them. It is the conceptual nature of these semantic units that concern us, not the syntactic means by which they are expressed. Indeed, even if we accept Habermas's thesis about the critical nature of communication and discourse, we are still not done with the problem of *moral semantics* and, on a deeper level, of the problem of *conceptual cognition*. One-dimensional rationality therefore does not affect the syntactic structure of assertoric or normative validity claims; rather, it affects the *conceptual content of the very words used to describe and understand it.*

What this means is that the validity of the value-orientation is more importantly located in the *semantic content of the concepts* uttered than in the propositional content of the syntactic structure of the utterance itself. Habermas, following the theoretical structure of the philosophy of language, sees semantics as fixed to the meaning of sentences as a whole, and not as a matter of the concepts used in cognition.[22] This formal-pragmatic approach that Habermas employs therefore steps over the problem Marcuse raises since the meaning of sentences for speakers and for hearers are constituted by the cognitive frames they bring to any communicative encounter, thereby inherently shaping the nature of communication itself. What this means is that the issue underpinning the nature of critical versus reified forms of consciousness is the extent to which the concepts used to make sense of semantic meaning are themselves constrained by value-orientations that the speaker/hearer has imbibed and which he uses as the basis for understanding utterances as well as the general structure of the world itself. This follows on Gunnar Myrdal's thesis that all forms of social cognition are the mixture of beliefs and valuations, the former expressing knowledge about how the world works and the latter on the "right/wrongness" of things, or how the world ought to work. In this sense, objectivity is the status of isolating the values from the beliefs in order to verify their truth-status.[23] What this raises is the problem of how values shape knowledge and cognition; it brings up the question of whether it is possible for pragmatic theories of language to serve as an adequate basis for genuine critical thought.

Indeed, Marcuse's thesis suggests that the socialization process that occurs under the auspices of rationalized administrative societies that operate on a capitalist productive-consumptive basis are prone to socialize agents with value-orientations already fashioned with what we might call "internal validity."[24] In this sense, the concepts that underpin cognition become flattened and fail to grasp the complexity of the object of consciousness. Instead, we are left with the prefabricated cognitive image of what a word "means," and we fail to delve into critical knowledge, which is to apprehend the processual and dynamic essence of any thing. But Habermas proposes that the *structure of language itself* provides the ground for the critique of validity claims. If we turn back to Habermas's argument, we can see how this problem becomes apparent. First, if we take (*a*) and give it semantic content, we could see that

> (*a'*) It is right to do as your boss commands.

or again that

> (*b'*) It is true (is the case) that bosses should be listened to.

The problem clearly is that the syntactic structure of the sentences is not where the problem of critical consciousness lies. It is rather in the semantic units that possess conceptual content. The conceptual content here is both *descriptive* and *normative*: to know what a boss is is also to know why a boss's role should be relevant to you. As a result, the fact of a boss and the role a boss ought to play are both expressed by the word *boss*. We can take another example that conforms to the same syntactic structure as (*a*):

> (*a''*) It is not right for homosexuals to marry.

and also that

> (*b″*) It is true that it is not right for homosexuals to marry.

Now, in both (*a″*) and (*b″*) we see that all that will be open to the hearer to do is to question the validity of the statement. But the illocutionary statement itself is not enough to open up the meaning expressed in the utterance to be critically questioned since it necessitates a meta-linguistic question of the value-status of homosexuality as well as what it actually means for something "to be right" or "to be not-right."[25] The analytic conception of syntactic meaning therefore is too narrow to capture the value-orientations and their effect on semantic meaning. Values, shaped and internalized by socialization processes, underwrite semantic meaning and therefore cannot be uprooted through the syntactic features of language. Hence, we are left with the thesis that communicative action does not open for us the rational critique of statements, but rather *the acceptance or rejection of statements, the normative substance to which our own cultural or social values predispose us.*

Indeed, we should take Marcuse's argument to a new level. His analysis centered on the scientific-technical manipulation of language and consciousness, but it should also be seen that, in addition to this force, there are the added problems of how language meshes with value-orientations and renders subjective thought acritical with respect to prevailing social norms and institutions. Nevertheless, the basic thesis he advances retains its salience: the closing of discourse, the flattening of its power to enlighten and to serve as a space of critical reasons results from the force to conform to the sovereign meanings deployed within the culture. Concepts, no less than the words *democracy, freedom*, or whatever, become narrow fields of semantic reference. They no longer become attached to deeper understandings about the nature of the world, but become riveted to the predominant forms of institutional behaviors and actions that have fashioned (or refashioned) them in order to coordinate institutional action. The key to one-dimensionality is that it closes off the capacity for thinking external to the dominant values, concepts, and system of discourse. Pragmatic forms of rationality seek, however, to develop a critical form of inquiry from within these very structures. But the exchange of reasons that occurs within this kind of context can only lead us to conformity to the predominant reality.

Habermas does consider the extent to which a speech act is "institutionally bound" or not, but this raises the sociological question against the philosophical claims derived from the philosophy of language: What would a truly non-institutionally bound speech act look like? In reality, everyday speech could be a candidate, that of asking for things, warning people, and so on. But forms of meaning and concepts that are in some way shaped by institutional concerns always touch utterances that are involved with issues of normative significance. In fact, all issues of genuine social power concern and involve concepts that are constitutive of that power. There is no way, under the conditions of modernity, for me to have power over you or for an institution to have power over you unless I have imbibed the requisite norms that allow for the efficiency of social action. But this means that we should consider the thesis that the power over discourse is also the power over the capacity to shape cognition and subjective forms of experience. Marcuse is expressing a concern that goes back to the Marxian thesis that a relation exists between base and superstructure; that there is a necessary dependence of language and thought on the forms of socialization and institutional power that congeal within societies. Marcuse's suggestion is that language and thought cannot be autonomous from these processes, that the dependence of linguistic action on socialization is in part rooted in the ways that semantic meaning is shaped and deployed as conventions of meaning. These conventions of meaning are therefore constitutive of power relations since the structure of such relations require the acceptance of norms for them to be sustained. These norms are codified by value-patterns and belief-disbelief systems that shape the cognition of subjects. We cannot simply escape the problem of questioning norms through the structure of language itself since there exist cognitive complexes of meaning and even cathectic value-investment that communicative action cannot penetrate critically.

IV. THE LOGIC OF CONSTITUTIVE DOMINATION AND THE IMPOTENCE OF PRAGMATISM

This is merely a prelude to a broader critique of discourse ethics. But it should suffice to show that the theory of critical reason proposed by Habermas and others within the pragmatic turn in critical theory ignore the pathology of consciousness and cognition that Marcuse suggests in his critique of one-dimensional discourse. In fact, I believe that it points us in a different direction, one where a particular form of power can be conceived where the cognitive powers and content of subjects are shaped and fashioned. If we consider this proposition, then we can see that institutions have what I referred to in chapter 1 as *constitutive power* over individuals in the sense that they socialize subjects toward the compliance of dominant powers and interests. As I argued earlier, if agent A has constitutive power over agent B, then A has the capacity to shape the norms, values, and rules that govern the subjective as well as objective life of B. A therefore has a unique form of power over B in that A can *shape the very values and norms that will operate within B as subject and not merely as object.* B's consciousness, patterns of belief, capacities for cognition, and so on, are mapped by A to the extent that B acts in ways that are fitted to the interests of *A*. Constitutive power, therefore, is deeply linked to material forms of power or resources that grant *A power over* institutions and forms of social life since it is through this kind of power that institutions (agents of socialization and the very crucibles of subject-constitution) can be organized and shaped. The values that serve as the basis for subjective and structural forms of integration can be shaped, in societies where power relations concentrate unevenly into mass and elite, in order to serve the interests of that elite. Since institutions can only function with the consent, compliance, and legitimacy of their members, the ability to constitute the subjectivity of subjects should be seen as a distinct form of power in that it is not simply a power over an agent by another, but rather power over the norms and values that shape subjectivity. In this sense, constitutive power is different from other forms of power such as coercion, arbitrary interference, or power over resources, even though they are or at least can be linked to it. Rather, constitutive power is a kind of power to shape the values and forms of thought that individuals take as basic, which form the patterns of life of the community as a whole.

If we grant the ability of constitutive power to be able to shape the rules of thought, this can only be done by orienting thought toward established reality and not toward the actual reality that is extant in the world. This occurs at the level of values since they are able to organize and orient semantic meaning so that the cognitive development of subjects are directed by the kinds of values that are deployed during socialization processes. The constitutive power of institutions is effective to the extent that *compliance to authority and norms is accomplished without need for rational justification.* Norms do not refer simply to behaviors but also to forms of thought: the norms of thinking can be shaped by organizing the rules that underlie collective forms of intentionality. In this sense, material forms of power and the subjectivity of mental states are brought together to show that one-dimensional thinking is the expression of specific forms of socialization and the structure and function of capitalist economic life, on the one hand, and a pathology of cognition that renders pragmatic critical theory unable to serve as an adequate foundation for critical theory, on the other. Now it remains for me to show what a critical theory does require and what kind of research program is appropriate for the development of critical social theory and critical social philosophy.

V. RECONSTRUCTING CRITICAL THEORY
AND CRITICAL COGNITION

Marcuse's argument suggests that socialization forces within capitalist societies are too powerful to allow for discursive forms of social praxis to serve as a sufficient form of social critique. The current academic fashion has turned to the philosophy of language and the exchange of reasons as an adequate means of establishing reasons that are rationally optimal. But this current in thought is deeply problematized by Marcuse's suggestion that power relations within society are corrupted by language and subjective (not to mention collective) rationality. What I alluded to earlier in this chapter was the notion that there exists a distinction between what can be called the space of reasons and what I will refer to the *space of critical reasons*. The distinction rests on the way that we conceive of the relation between thought and reality, between subject and object. What is essential to the latter is the notion that cognitive concepts are critical—that is, truly rational—when they are able to grasp objects in their dynamic totality, when they are able to grasp the universal elements within particular phenomena. What is also crucial is that these concepts be in dialectical relation with objective reality and not simply conform to abstract standards of "rationality." In this sense, we cannot restrict ourselves to the formal praxis of discourse without understanding that the propositions we enunciate in speech have some kind of relation to the structure of reality itself. What is critical is not simply the act of asking for justification—it is more centrally concerned with the transformation of the structures of the world that inhibit the rational organization of social life.

This Hegelian move against Kantian conceptions of reason is crucial in that it paves a way toward a foundation for the progression of thought as well as serves to posit a foundation for critical judgment. The problem with Kant's ideas, for Hegel, was that they were trapped in abstraction: they limited themselves to the subjective sphere of cognition without partaking in the objective processes that constitute reality—objective processes that were themselves rational and could be grasped dialectically only through grasping reason as an objective property of mind and world. Pragmatic conceptions of reason that emphasize forms of justification, norms, and conditions of rationality that take as their standard for rationality an intersubjective stance toward other selves and their reasons is clearly insufficient to this task. One reason is that they, too, fall into the same trap that Hegel spotted in Kant's philosophy: that it was centered on the notion of formality. In this sense, the reason is seen to exist within the ways that the mind is exercised rather than about its accountability to the objective structure of the world itself. The pragmatist asks only about the ways we come to knowledge claims, not about the ways that knowledge claims stack up against the objective structure of reality. The key is not simply intersubjective justification; more important, it must ask about the ways in which the structures of the social world disable modern society from realizing its deeper, immanent possibilities, from realizing the universal, common, rational interest of society as a whole.

The pragmatist, however, sees value in the way that we recognize others in social interaction. Robert Brandom makes such a move by placing Hegel within such an abstract space of reasons that, as I will argue below, is essentially uncritical:

> As I read him, Hegel criticizes Kant on just this point. He sees Kant as having been uncharacteristically and culpably uncritical about the origin and nature of the *determinateness* of the contents of empirical concepts. Hegel's principle innovation is his idea that in order to follow through on Kant's fundamental insight into the essentially *normative* character of mind, meaning, and rationality, we need to recognize that normative statuses such as authority and responsibility are at base social statuses. He broadens Kant's account of synthesizing normative individual selves or subjects (unities of apperception) by the activity of *rational integration*, into an account of the simultaneous synthesizing of apperceiving individual selves (subjects of normative statuses) and their communities, by practices of *reciprocal recognition*.[26]

What makes such an approach problematic—and one that fits into the critique that Marcuse has in view—is that conceptual activity is not simply accountable to other selves through recognitive relations. There needs to be a third dimension of critical reason that allows us to have access into the objective structure of social life and its deeper purposes and potentialities. Lacking this, we are lost in a space of reasons; we succumb to the neo-Idealist notion that reasons can themselves explode the constraints placed upon them by social structure and domination. Rather, it is primarily, as Hegel lays it out in his *Logik*, a matter of the ways that *concepts are related and accountable to the structure of reality itself*.[27] This is a crucial point since the main issue is that any rational form of knowledge, one that could be appropriate for critique, is that it be able to serve as the *explanans* for objective reality. When it comes to the realm of social facts, this means inquiring into the ways that our concept about the world are accountable to the essential purposes of social life, not merely the norms that we use in pragmatic communication. This is radically different in focus since, if the thesis of constitutive power is even conditionally accepted, we can see that there is an issue in the ways that reasons cannot be considered rational simply on the basis of being accountable to linguistic and discursive norms but must have as their ground the dynamic reality of objects. Any approach to a critical-cognitive conception of reason therefore requires that we grasp the essential ontology of objects that is to become the very content of conceptual thought itself. If we lose Hegel in the intersubjective and discursive frame that Brandom wants to place him in, we are short-circuiting the critical power of Hegel's ideas as well as cutting off his relation to Marxian concepts of critical theory.

If we take the discursive theories of Habermas and Brandom as a basis for a critical theory, we are mistaking the role of reason in any truly critical sense.

What is central, as Marcuse makes clear, is that the nature of the concept is such that it serves as a dialectic between the subjective sphere of concepts and the objective world of reality itself. The crucial problem that Hegel wants to solve is that of obtaining valid, absolute, and objectively valid truth-claims. These cannot be obtained through a mutual agreement or through intersubjective reasoning and justification. One reason for this is that such reasons would themselves obtain their validity through their relation to other reasons, not to the objective reality of the objects themselves. This would seem to make sense only with respect to material objects, to stones, grass, watches, and so on, but would seem to fail to capture the essence of a coffee cup, the concept of what is "good," or other social facts. But this is not the case: all reality possesses an essential structure that can be known to consciousness. It is this essential structure that the concept seeks to capture, to make into the Idea. The concept is therefore a grasping of the essential purposes and ends of objects, of things; it is the ability to know the essential *telos* of the objects of reality, to know them for what they are on their own terms. It is only once the conceptual scheme that forms the content of consciousness is the same as the rational structure of reality that we can claim to have valid, absolute, knowledge of the world. Without this, we are relying on the understanding, on partial, deficient forms of reasoning to guide the understanding. When we rely only on the "reasons" of others, as Brandom and Habermas would have us, then we are locked into an abstract realm where reality cannot be penetrated, where critique is not able to envelop the reality of the world itself.

This is why Marx's so-called materialist move is so essential to critical theory since it gives a kind of directionality to the Hegelian conceptual schema. Marx's ideas should not be construed as materialist but as ontological. The basic thesis is that objective social structures, generally formed by economic patterns of any given society, have constitutive power over subjective dimensions of the personality and consciousness. Critical knowledge is only genuinely critical once it seeks to understand how the concepts used in abstract thought are related to social phenomena and how the objective social structures and functions actually operate. A truly critical orientation to the world must take into consideration the analysis of the ways in which human reasons are themselves shaped and structured by the institutional power relations that are rooted in economic life. This means that resource power leads to constitutive power; that the shape of the power relations of any society will map themselves onto the forms of life and consciousness of its members. In such a case, how can we rely on discursive reasoning alone to pierce the essential nature of the forms of life that predominate? It is only by abstracting thinking, reasoning, and relating socially away from these concrete forms of power and the processes that sustain and cultivate that power that can allow us to entertain the pragmatist thesis. Otherwise, we would need to take Marcuse's critique seriously that the degradation of discourse means the degradation of subjective cognitive capacities—that the unique form of power, of *constitutive power*, that is prevalent in modern societies is its ability to distort cognition's ability to relate dialectically to reality. To simply be accountable to others, to be in a recognitive relation to others and their reasons and reason giving, fails this test since it is not pegged to a relation to reality, *but only to other abstract reasons.*

Communicative and intersubjective forms of reasoning cannot provide this added step for consciousness since the validity of propositions is not aimed at the concrete actuality of the social world, but only the norms inherent in linguistic behavior. Linguistic statements remain abstract to the extent that is the concepts used in the formulation of utterances remain uninterrogated. The critical move is to understand the rational grounding in the world for the concepts that we use and to erode the socially constituted meanings of words that masquerade as conceptual thought. The cognitive content that is derived from this kind of theoretical vantage point is therefore one in which thought is sealed off from the actual processes that constitute it. The problem is therefore that linguistic conventions and linguistic capacities, although they seem to mirror the structure of thinking itself, or reason, should instead be seen as insufficient and potentially vulnerable to irrational forms of concept formation (or even the danger of what Marcuse seems to see as a de-conceptualization of cognition). The emancipatory function of concepts is therefore found in the structural relation they have to actual objects. A concept properly grasps its object only once it has been able to grasp the processes and ends that make that object what it is. This is the difference between a partial understanding of an object and a rational, conceptual grasp of it.

Thus any concept, φ, bears a relation to an object, X, in such a way that it can capture either the full nature of X or a partial or deformed picture of X; we can denote the latter with an asterisk, X^*. φ^* therefore is the *belief* (*not* the concept) that relates to the distorted picture of the object X^*. Simply using φ^* within the discursive and pragmatic encounters gets us nowhere in actually understanding what X actually is. If the community of speakers and hearers to which I belong generally uses φ^* by uttering the given word, ω, to represent it, then the collective consciousness of that community will misunderstand X as X^* whenever ω is uttered. Similarly, if φ^* is also accompanied by a value, ψ, which is a normative understanding about how the world *ought* to work (in other words, they believe that X is really X *iff* it is X^*, or it is right that ω be understood as X^*), then we can see that the structure of language and communication can simply reproduce the flawed nature of concepts about the world *and remain abstract in nature.* Hence, any time that

$$\omega \rightarrow \begin{cases} \varphi, \\ \psi \end{cases}$$

or when any word possesses both a descriptive belief about the world and a normative denotation of it, we can consider the utterances themselves as resting values and beliefs that cannot capture the essential reality of the world. Critical cognition is thereby upended, and we find ourselves in a condition in which the ontological reality of things and processes, the actual nature of the world, is sealed off from cognition. But, perhaps more dangerous, we are open to the deeper problem in which cognitive processes are colonized by the value-fields and semantic manipulation deployed by culture and institutions of society. This is the very essence of noncritical thinking, and it indicates that there is a strong problem accompanying the linguistic and intersubjective turn in critical theory.

This flaw in thought that I am seeking to isolate here can be understood as a *style of cognition*: a way of thinking that combines beliefs about the world and values about how the object to which the belief refers ought to be. This is not very insightful if we speak about stones, or pencils, or lamps. For it is clear that lamps, to be lamps, must shine light, or pencils be able to be used to write things, and so on. Indeed, the concept of a pencil is only grasped once we realize that the actual nature of the pencil is to have the *telos* as an instrument of writing, just as with lamps to emit light, and so on. What this means is that to know something rationally, to be able to have a true concept of it, is to know what the *activity of the object actually is*.[28] We can go a step further in the social field, as opposed to the field of natural facts, and say that the social practices and institutions we create can have multiple meanings, ends, or purposes. The real key is to ask which are most democratic—which are the purposes and ends toward which we ought to direct our legitimacy. They would not be true concepts if we understood a lamp to function as a paperweight or a pencil as an eating utensil, or whatever. But it does become significant when we talk about concepts such as democracy, society, capitalism, work, freedom, individual, and so on. Not only are these concepts reliant on other concepts that are equally weighted, but they also have values attached to them that blend with the concept in order to form an ideological mental state. In this sense, the accepted view of concepts such as democracy* or free* or just*, or whatever, is taken as valid and true even though it is not a genuine concept in the sense that it does not capture the true end of what these objects or things are supposed to achieve. Generally, as Marcuse seems to be arguing, the reason for defective beliefs about the world, the effects of one-dimensional consciousness itself, is the imposition and internalization of heteronomous beliefs and value-orientations. This forms the substrate for all forms of social action, including that of communication. Although Habermas points out that the lifeworld and system operate according to different forms of action—communicative and purposive rationality, respectively—the connective tissue between the two realms is the value systems that are diffused through socialization in order to secure socially coordinated action that has been increasingly penetrated by commodified and administered forms of life. Cognition and consciousness cannot be decisively separated out from the social integration of systems.

Habermas is therefore mistaken when he argues that we should see this distinction between principles of social integration "between the mechanism of linguistic communication that is oriented to validity claims—a mechanism that emerges in increasing purity from the rationalization of the lifeworld—and those de-linguistified steering media through which systems of success-oriented action are differentiated out."[29] This is because the latter form of social integration itself relies on value-patterns and orientations that also infect communicative action. The values that are embedded in consciousness and cognition rely on the beliefs that are needed for institutionalized success and action and that also de-conceptualize thought. There is no sense given that communication itself can restore what has been lost: conceptual, critical thought. Since the concept of constitutive power is able to impress specific forms of meaning and styles of cognition on subjects—a power that itself is rooted in resource power—we must ask what means there is to escape the potential trap of abstraction that prevails when discursive and pragmatic forms of reasoning are asserted as a rationalist alternative. The conception of a critical space of reasons can now be taken up as the emerging negatively from Marcuse's analysis in the sense that only those concepts can be considered rational that are able to capture objects of consciousness as processual, dynamic, and with certain teleological ends.[30] Indeed, since the linguistic turn in critical theory is problematic, in this sense, because it supposes that language and communicative competence is sufficient as a means to critical consciousness. But this kind of neo-Idealism that calls itself "postmetaphysical" is perhaps, as Marcuse seems to indicate, too isolated from the structural-functional forces exerted upon consciousness by administered-capitalist institutions. The deep impress of rationalized, routinized forms of social life that come to affect the forms of consciousness and cognition are so severe that the necessary preconditions for a critical-cognitive consciousness is lacking.

In the end, a critical space of reasons can only be achieved once we are forced to inquire about the objectivity of the concepts that are used in thought and in communication. The flaw of de-conceptualized thought—a result of one-dimensional, reified thinking—is that cognition does not rely on concepts in the rational, full sense, but rather on images of what the world actually is, on beliefs that are not critically examined and that nevertheless serve as the mechanisms for legitimate forms of authority in modern societies. It also relies on heteronomous value-patterns that give shape to social cognition. Although the pragmatic-oriented theorists who have sought to retool critical theory have been successful at elaborating a framework, it does not seem convincing that they have provided a means of escaping the forces responsible for the reification of consciousness. If anything, they have sidestepped the matter; because of this, it is of great value to return to Marcuse's thesis about the nature of one-dimensionality in order to see how the impulses and trends of contemporary theory are still limited by the same problematics that gave rise to the task of critical theory in the first place. I believe that only through a return to concepts that are secured through their ontological validity can we place critical theory in play with the kinds of power that pervade modern society. Only by cultivating a form of thought that uses concrete concepts of objects, that has in view the ways that objective, material forms of social structure and power are able to shape consciousness, can we begin to talk about the revival of critical theory and critical thought.

NOTES

1. For an important overview of the basic doctrines of pragmatism and their relevance for contemporary philosophy, see Richard J. Bernstein, *The New Constellation: The Ethical-Political Horizons of Modernity/Postmodernity* (Cambridge, MA: MIT Press, 1991), 323ff., as well as his more extended discussion in *The Pragmatic Turn* (Cambridge: Polity Press, 2010).

2. This thesis has also been explored, via a study of educational practices, by James Block, *The Crucible of Consent* (Cambridge, MA: Harvard University Press, 2012).

3. Herbert Marcuse, *One-Dimensional Man: Studies in the Ideology of Advanced Industrial Society* (Boston: Beacon Press, 1964), 85.

4. Ibid., 86.

5. Ibid., 88.

6. Ibid., 87.

7. Ibid.

8. In this sense, Wittgenstein notes in his discussion of language games that it "is meant to bring into prominence the fact that the speaking of language is part of an activity, or of a form of life (*Lebensform*)." *Philosophical Investigations*, I §23. For Marcuse, however, such a language game would require that the personality system of the subject is impressed with the particular cognitive, affective, and evaluative rules that are promulgated by rationalized institutional powers that socialize agents. Language games do not, and indeed cannot, operate outside of the fields of social power and, consequently, must be seen as embedded in power relations. Marcuse, therefore, sees that these forms of linguistic action are tied to deeper forms of capacities for power relations to constitute consciousness.

9. Marcuse, *One-Dimensional Man*, 88.

10. Elsewhere I have elaborated this insight into a broader theory of social domination. See my paper "A Functionalist Theory of Social Domination," *Journal of Political Power* 6, no. 2 (2013): 179–99.

11. Wilfred Sellars, "Language as Thought and as Communication," in *In the Space of Reasons: Selected Essays of Wilfred Sellars* (Cambridge, MA: Harvard University Press, 2007), 70.

12. One can see a process like this at work in the ways that certain words have been taken over time are whittled of their originary meaning. The Greek word λόγος, which has a broad field of conceptual content in classical Greek—meaning culture, reason, language, truth—becomes reduced to "study of" or "knowledge of" in words such as bio*logy*, psycho*logy*, anthropo*logy*, and so on such that the words' originary meanings are fitted to new, more constricted, and narrow requirements.

13. Marcuse, *One-Dimensional Man*, 91.

14. Marcuse references the discussion of the "speculative sentence" in Hegel's *Phänomenologie*, which marks a distinction between the sentence as a means of conveying an idea and a deeper way that the sentence can be perceived as opening up conceptual content itself. They are two different, but not mutually exclusive, uses of a given sentence. See the discussion by Jere Paul Surber, "Hegel's Speculative Sentence," *Hegel-Studien* 10 (1975): 210–30, as well as Chong-Fuk Lau, "Language and Metaphysics: The Dialectics of Hegel's Speculative Proposition," in Jere O'Neill Surber (ed.), *Hegel and Language* (Albany, NY: SUNY Press, 2006), 55–74. Rüdiger Bubner has also argued, "In contrast to current perspectives strongly oriented to the theory of communicative interaction, Hegel does not regard the linguistically constituted community as the final word of reason, but rather as its mere *semblance*. For the more actuality is replaced by language, the more it forfeits its own semblance." *The Innovations of Idealism* (New York: Cambridge University Press, 2003), 153.

15. The notion that new norms of meaning are created by the dominant discourse has overlap with contemporary philosophies of language and mind. Sellars points to this when he argues that "to be a being capable of conceptual activity, is to be a being which acts, which recognizes norms and standards and engages in practical reasoning. It is, as Kant pointed out, one and the same reason which is in some of its activities 'theoretical,' and in some of its activities 'practical.' Of course, if one gives to 'practical' the specific meaning *ethical* then a fairly sharp separation of these activities can be maintained. But if one means by 'practical' pertaining to norms, then so-called theoretical reason is as larded with the practical as is practical reasoning itself." "Language as Thought and as Communication," 62. Also see the discussion by Robert B. Brandom, *Reason in Philosophy: Animating Ideas* (Cambridge, MA: Harvard University Press, 2009), 27ff. These ideas are limited by the fact that they possess no sense of social power and its ability to shape and affect the content of norms, something Marcuse has in view in his discussion.

16. Marcuse, *One-Dimensional Man*, 95.

17. Ibid.

18. Marcuse argues on this point that "if the linguistic behavior blocks conceptual development, if it militates against abstraction and mediation, if it surrenders to the immediate facts, it repels recognition of the factors behind the facts, and thus repels recognition of the facts, and of their historical content. In and for the society, this organization of functional discourse is of vital importance; it serves as a vehicle of coordination and subordination." Ibid., 97.

19. Marcuse therefore sees conceptual thought, in Hegelian fashion, as inherently explosive to static forms of reality and understanding. Marcuse rightly argues that "all cognitive concepts have a transitive meaning: they go beyond descriptive reference to particular facts. And if the facts are those of society, the cognitive concepts also go beyond any particular context of facts—into the processes and conditions on which the respective society rests, and which enter into all particular facts, making, sustaining, and destroying the society." Ibid., 106.

20. Ibid., 96.

21. Jürgen Habermas, *The Theory of Communicative Action*, vol. 2, trans. Thomas McCarthy (Boston: Beacon Press, 1987), 69.

22. Habermas argues that "the pragmatic level of agreement that is effective for coordination connects the semantic level of understanding meaning with the empirical level of developing further—in a manner dependent on the context—the accord relevant to the sequel of interaction." *The Theory of Communicative Action*, vol. 1, trans. Thomas McCarthy (Boston: Beacon Press, 1984), 297.

23. See Gunnar Myrdal, *Objectivity in Social Research* (New York: Random House, 1969).

24. Talcott Parsons makes a similar argument when he states that society presents us with value-patterns where "moral problems are treated by the actor as solved." See Talcott Parsons and Edward Shils, *Toward a General Theory of Action* (Cambridge, MA: Harvard University Press, 1951), 166 and *passim*.

25. I have elaborated on this thesis in more detail in my paper "The Wrath of Thrasymachus: Value Irrationality and the Failures of Deliberative Democracy," *Theoria: A Journal of Social and Political Theory* 62, no. 2 (2015): 33–58.

26. Brandom, *Reason in Philosophy*, 66.

27. For a critique of Brandom's reading of Hegel from this point of view, see Stephen Houlgate, "Phenomenology and *De Re* Interpretation: A Critique of Brandom's Reading of Hegel," *International Journal of Philosophical Studies* 17, no. 1 (2009): 29–47.

28. In his recent essay on Aristotle's metaphysical doctrine, Aryeh Kosman argues that we should see Aristotle's idea of ἐνέργεια as an activity that means that his notion of ontology is one in which things realize their capacity (δυνάμις) to act in the ways that are intrinsic to that thing. See his *The Activity of Being: An Essay on Aristotle's Ontology* (Cambridge, MA: Harvard University Press, 2013). I believe this can and should be extended to Hegel's logical doctrine and metaphysics, and it informs implicitly the way I am using the term *concept* here in that the proper (i.e., rational) concept of any object is one that grasps the realized capacities of the thing that make it act as it does.

29. Habermas, *Theory of Communicative Action*, vol. 1, 342.

30. Elsewhere, I have elaborated on the relation of concepts in this dynamic, teleological sense with normative and cognitive forms of reasoning in my paper "Philosophical Foundations for a Marxian Ethics," in M. Thompson (ed.), *Constructing Marxist Ethics: Critique, Normativity, Praxis* (Leiden: Brill, 2015): 235–65.

Chapter 3

The Insufficiency of Recognition

A Critique of Axel Honneth's Concept of Critical Theory

I. ASCENDANCE OF THE RECOGNITION PARADIGM

The theory of recognition proposes a social-theoretic argument about the nature of socialization and the development of subjects, as well as a normative, moral-philosophical claim concerning the pathologies of modern societies. In this sense, it ostensibly fits well within the tradition of critical theory in that it seeks to sublate the distinction between facts and values and also continues the postmetaphysical project that has become the hallmark for what counts as modern theory. The theory of recognition, therefore, seeks to combine the normative concerns of moral philosophy with a social-theoretic account of socialization and subject-formation. But I would like to suggest that there is a core flaw in the theory of recognition. Whereas anyone would be hard-pressed to argue against recognition as a moral good or even a human need that is in some sense basic, I want to argue here that recognition cannot serve as a means of understanding properly either the nature and processes of human socialization, especially in modern societies, nor can it serve as a foundation for a critical theory of society. In what follows, I will confine my critical remarks to addressing the question of whether recognition can serve as a sufficient paradigm for a critical theory of society that is able to diagnose social and personal pathologies, as well as provide a valid normative theory to establish a theory of justice.

As I see it, the attempt to construct a critical theory of society grounded in a theory of recognition is flawed because it cannot show that relations of mutual recognition are able to produce a critical cognition of the structures of social power that permeate modern societies. This is because the problem of identity formation is linked to the reproduction of forms of economic power to the extent that ego and self-development do not come into conflict with the hierarchical and oligarchical relations of social power that steer collective forms of social life and, more important, the processes of socialization that shape the personality systems of individuals. The premise of recognition is that critical consciousness can be cultivated through the struggles that occur at different levels of identity formation. But this seems unlikely to lead to any sense of critical cognition with respect to the organization of legal-rational authority and institutions that pervade and distort cognitive capacities. The theory of recognition is therefore insufficient to deal with the problems of concrete forms of social power and inequality mainly because of the ability for these forms of power to mediate the very "practical relations to self" that undergird those recognitive relations that are supposed to provide a developed sense of self and moral autonomy. Quite to the contrary, I believe that by placing emphasis on the symbolic dimension of intersubjective relations and detaching itself from the concrete foundations of social power nested in economic life, the theoretical apparatus of recognition minimizes the formative effects of power relations to such an extent that it cannot serve as a valid empirical account of socialization processes, nor can it serve as a compelling moral philosophy against the structures of social power that constitute modern societies. This is because the power relations rooted in capitalist forms of economic life structure the deeper socialization processes that shape the cognitive and evaluative dimensions of the personalities of subjects. Recognition can, in this sense, even serve to promote and cement the power relations that already exist rather than necessarily call them into question. But in the end, my thesis here will be that recognition, as theorized by Honneth, is misconstrued from its Hegelian source and detached from the larger metaphysical project in which Hegel embeds it.

The theory of recognition may strike us as being a compelling moral philosophy, but the empirical resources needed for its normative claims to serve as a foundation for a critical theory of society seem to me to be lacking. If my basic thesis is even conditionally accepted, then it seems to me that the claim for founding an "intramundane possibility for emancipation,"[1] or an immanent critique of society, is unwarranted and the theory of recognition collapses into a neo-Idealist moral philosophy—one that suffers from the separation of normative arguments and values from the matrix of social relations shaped by material forms of power. The reason for this is that economic (material) forms of power under capitalism are framed by a nexus of norms and forms of thinking that constitute the world of social facts. Recognition, as a system of intersubjective processes of self-formation, is infected by these concepts and norms. The kind of self that is formed by reification is affirmed by recognition, at least to a significant extent that it is disabled as a central means of providing a paradigm for a critical theory of society. The atomization of modern social life therefore constitutes fragmented, particularist forms of identity that can then be inserted into the recognition paradigm. As a result, it produces a political theory of identity rather than a critical theory of modern domination.

In light of this, recognition as a philosophical and empirically informed theoretical project fails as a critical theory of society because it emphasizes social action at the expense of the distorting influence of social structure and function. It is plagued by a kind of abstraction in that it fails to take seriously the core impulse that classical critical theory had always placed at its center: namely, the ways in which forms of consciousness are shaped and perverted to accept and even legitimize rationalized forms of domination and control—especially within capitalist market economies. This affects the theory of recognition in that Honneth and his followers suppose that we can somehow achieve a process of self-formation that is cleansed of the roles, values, and concepts that are already ambient in society. Recognition, therefore, serves more as a kind of metaphorical hall of mirrors for the self where we are asked to "recognize" selves that are pathologically shaped culture. Even though we can agree that recognition is a crucial aspect of healthy socialization, it cannot serve, on its own, as a critical theory of society, as it is too easily co-opted by the pathologies of the dominant socialization regimes. Even more, by severing the connection between the unequal control over social resources, on the one hand, and its effects on the cultural forms of life and cognitive patterns and attitudes of subjects, on the other, the theory of recognition seems to me to be unable to serve as an emancipatory theory of society and morality, let alone a satisfying descriptive account of social action and consciousness.

II. HONNETH'S RECONSTRUCTION OF RECOGNITION

At the core of the theory of recognition is the idea that intersubjective relations are the context within which individuals realize themselves as autonomous beings. Individuality is based on a mutual form of recognition in which each respects the other's basic needs and identities. As Honneth has argued, "Subjects encounter each other within the parameters of the reciprocal expectation that they be given recognition as moral persons and for their social achievements."[2] The opposite of recognition is nonrecognition or misrecognition (*Mißachtung*), a situation in which one is not accorded the reciprocal recognition that is expected as part of the process of socialization. Misrecognition, in the words of Charles Taylor, "can inflict harm, can be a form of oppression, imprisoning someone in a false, distorted, and reduced mode of being."[3] The identities that individuals construct for themselves are seen to have their genesis in the social nexus of intersubjective relations—but relations that build and support a stable and confident sense of self that can serve as the foundation for robust moral autonomy.[4] These relations are responsible for the specific kinds of ego formation and individualization that literally produce individuals. Recognition moves to the center of concern once we see that it is not only a vital need but also a basic property of the species. The denial of recognition therefore becomes an issue of social justice, as Honneth claims when he argues that "moral injustice is at hand whenever, contrary to their expectations, human subjects are denied the recognition they feel they deserve."[5]

The basis for this argument is rooted in the process of ego development that, according to Honneth, is the result of three spheres of intersubjective recognition. The first is that of family or love, where subjects as children acquire "via the continuous experience of 'maternal' care, the basic self-confidence to assert their needs in an unforced manner."[6] This is followed by the sphere of legal recognition, of rights, where "adult subjects acquire, via the experience of legal recognition, the possibility of seeing their actions as the universally respected expression of their own autonomy."[7] Finally, this is followed by the need for social esteem, where each individual is granted recognition of their identities, unique traits, and abilities. A just society is therefore one that will promote to the fullest extent within the institutions of society each of these levels of the model.

At each phase of this recognitive process of ego formation, the self develops through mutual relations of respect, and one sees that one's own self is dependent on the recognition of others. But the insufficiency of recognition stems from the fact that these very spheres of intersubjectivity and socialization are themselves deeply shaped by structural and functional power relations that are routinized by the prerogatives and goals of social systems. Economic logics are therefore deterministic in the basic sense that they are able to place limits on the kinds of rules, norms, and logics of noneconomic institutions. Recognition therefore grants us not a way out of the problems of social domination and injustice, but a domesticated moral philosophy bereft of the cognitive resources needed for critical judgment. A central reason for this lies in the various ways in which social structures and processes—particularly within capitalist societies—are able to adapt individuals to purposes and projects that are not their own. This occurs through the adaptation of subjects to the value-orientations and norms that are structured and sanctioned by market imperatives, rationalized administrative institutions, and the production-consumption patterns for which they are coordinated.[8] But at a more basic level, the theory of recognition as expounded by Honneth is insufficient as a critical theory of society because we cannot obtain rational, critical cognition about the world without the aid of a theoretical dimension that is able to provide us with some form of theoretical distance or conceptual mediation from the object of inquiry. We cannot, I will argue here, promulgate a critical theory from the actual processes of everyday life itself.

The basic premise that underlies classical critical theory was always to unmask the mechanisms of self-formation that were fused to the class-based forms of power that constitute modern capitalist societies. The theory of recognition abandons this premise. My challenge to theorists of recognition therefore asks: Can recognition mitigate the gravitational pull of the functionalist nature of modern institutions, particularly those rooted in capitalist forms of accumulation and oligarchic wealth defense and their concomitant impact on socialization and ego formation? Further, can it provide an antidote to the defective forms of subjectivity that emerge from these socialization processes, and their power to shape and orient the cognitive and affective dimensions of the personality system?

III. RECOGNITION AND THE PATHOLOGIES OF SOCIALIZATION

Since the theory of recognition places emphasis on the autonomy of social action and praxis and away from that of the structural-functional forces that constitute modern society, I believe the answer to the above questions is no. As Honneth himself has claimed, "Critical social theory must shift its attention from the self-generated independence of systems to the damage and distortion of social relations of recognition."[9] For Honneth, this is part of a larger project of moving critical theory away from its Marxian foundations.[10] When I speak of the functional elements of socialization, I mean the ways in which the symbolic domain of culture more generally and the cognition of subjects more particularly are shaped by the role expectations of social institutions— social institutions that, in modern integrated market economies dominated by capital, increasingly have as their central goal the maximization of economic efficiency. The functional element of socialization occurs through the ways structural forms of power relations shape and organize the symbolic means by which we come to code our social world. To put this another way, it is a question of *subject-constitution*: the extent to which individuals are constituted by the social formations that they inhabit and which affect their norms, values, and cognitive patterns of thought. The functional impulse of institutions is able, on this view, to rationalize, routinize, and have subjects internalize the particular symbolic codes and value-orientations that are needed for the very sustenance and stability of those institutions. The extent to which the rationalization and routinization of these institutions occurs is also the extent to which relations of recognition will be stamped by the imperatives of those roles and role expectations rather than by a seemingly natural process of intersubjective relations somehow occurring outside of these systemic and functional forces.[11] What is of importance here is the ways in which class

domination over social institutions and processes has the capacity to orient
and shape the personality system of individuals, the ways that the organizational structure of society and its various forms of reproduction are affected
by power relations and how this reality deforms the symbolic realm within
which recognition takes place.[12]

Initial focus needs to be placed on the *formative development of individuals*
and the ways that economic forces mold socialization process. But according
to the neo-Idealist interpretation of socialization, these processes of self-
development and ego formation occur externally to these forces. According
to Honneth, this begins with the "primary affectional relationships" found in
the processes of early child development in which "affectional attachment to
other persons is revealed to be a process whose success is dependent on the
mutual maintenance of a tension between symbiotic self-sacrifice and individual self-assertion."[13] For Honneth, object relations theory provides us with
an insight into the pattern of mutual recognition oriented toward the development of self, since "[i]t systematically takes into account the increased insight
into the psychological status of interactive experiences of early childhood by
supplementing the organization of libidinal drives with affective relationships
to other persons as a second component of the maturational process."[14] Here
we begin to glimpse how the decoupling of systemic social processes and
self-development processes causes problems. Since social systems operate
through an organized network of roles and role expectations, their logics will
come to orient processes of socialization, or at least put pressure on different
socialization spheres to orient them in specific ways.

Honneth's thesis indicates that these primary affectional relations are to
serve as the ground for a moral epistemology rooted in recognitive relations.
But this argument sidesteps the problems inherent in subject-formation in
modern culture, especially under the pressures of capitalist forms of economic life. There is a curious simplicity to this model that obscures one of
the central theses to come from the critical theory literature—namely, that of
the relation between the family and authority relations in modern societies.
According this thesis, ego development in late-capitalist societies is marked
by the eclipse of the family as a substantive and autonomous mechanism
for the formation of the self. At the core of this theory, as Marcuse claims,
is the "subjection of previously private, asocial dimensions of existence to
methodical indoctrination, manipulation, control."[15] The implication of this
view is that the family can no longer serve as the context for the development of the critical ego. Marcuse's thesis is that the family itself has become
absorbed into the general social structure, and the spheres of socialization
that were previously circumscribed by the family unit are now absorbed by
the larger processes of socialization that homogenize thought and values.
Honneth's view of the family is therefore largely anachronistic in the sense

that we now see social norms and values as being that of acquiescence to the social system and not in opposition toward it.

What Marcuse had in mind was the Freudian notion that the development of the ego in the bourgeois family was typically subjected to pressures of struggle that are now glossed over. In place of a struggle for identity, for recognition, we now have egos that seek acceptance in terms of the dominant ideational and value structure that society makes ambient. The question of how to engender a critical consciousness, however, which should be the real aim of critical theory, is lost here. The family now becomes merely a conduit for the dominant value-system of capitalist modernity, for conformity, and for the acceptance of the status quo. In particular, it is through the family that values of consumption, ideas, and values about gender, of race, and class and other value-orientations, are introduced and routinized, forming a pattern of moral cognition that can, and many times is, sustained into adulthood. And if this is the case, we are forced to confront the ways that the family—not to mention the market—are, rather than potential resources for critical consciousness, instead mechanisms for the *reproduction* of social domination.

One core way that this happens is that the relation between the nascent ego and alters within family life become infected by the problem of a direct identification of the ego with various alters throughout the child-development process. This is in the form of the relation of child with parents, as well as the other extrafamilial cultural forces that affect and shape nascent cultural value-orientations. It is not only the parents who are the source of socialization but also the ways that parents themselves see their roles, the ways that economic life dominates and shapes the value-orientations inculcated within the ego-development process. Add to this the transmission of hegemonic value-orientations through various media outlets such as television, radio, electronic media, as well as the peer groups with which children identify. The fact that children are socialized not simply by their parents but also by the dominant value-systems and orientations that their parents have internalized, is nothing new. But it does point to an empirical reality about the nature of the family overlooked by Honneth's model. The recognitive relations at the inchoate stage of ego development are therefore inseparable from the dominant value spheres that are required by capitalist society. And these processes of socialization infiltrate the relational structures of the family, as well as other domains of the socialization process during youth, such as schools, sports culture, and other spheres.[16] In addition to the *form* of recognition—or love for family members—there is also a recognition of the *content* of the values that family members possess as right or correct, forming the foundations of their moral psychology and their value system and worldview. Recognition, in this sense, not only includes the primary bonds of love and affection that, in some cases, family life can provide but also, and perhaps more fundamentally, serves as the conduit for the dominant value-orientations and role expectations that pervade the culture more broadly. Recognition can therefore serve to reproduce, even legitimate at the most basic libidinal level, the forms of power, the heteronomous value systems that mark our culture.

One way that this occurs is through the process of *identification*. But not simply in the sense that a simple emotional bond comes to be formed, but also that the ego tends to identify with the dominant norms that constitute its conception of self, its own value-orientations. The problem with this kind of identification is that it stunts the growth of subjectivity, reducing the capacities needed for critical forms of cognition.[17] This was also an insight by Parsons, whose theory of socialization has as one of its core components "mechanisms of social control." As social systems become more deeply rationalized, they also become dominated by functional patterns of normative social expectations that in turn shape the notions of deviance and conformity.[18] A set of predefined value-patterns begins to constitute all forms of social interaction, and the more institutional rationalization that has taken place, the more the subject sees the moral problems of the world as already solved. The evaluative, cathectic, and cognitive components of the personality system become structured not by open relations of intersubjectivity, but by the broader systemic imperatives that shape the experiences of everyday life.

In this sense, the roles that are assigned to individuals by the institutional logics they inhabit come to dominate the socialization process, leading to an internalization of value-orientation patterns "through reciprocal attachments, that is, through ego becoming integrated in a reciprocal and complementary role relative to alter which reaches the level of organization and cathectic sensitivity which we call that of attachment and a common value pattern involving loyalty."[19] Or perhaps it is better to say that the intersubjective relations of different spheres of social life become harnessed to the systemic logics of institutional goals—and these constitute part of the basis of different socialization processes. The values that alter are able to instill in ego therefore become coordinated by extrafamilial institutions. Even if we accept the thesis that the family—specifically, the mother-child relation—instills within us "a pattern of interaction whose mature reappearance in adult life is an indication of successful affectional bonds to other people,"[20] this does not negate the fact that the individual also may accept hierarchical authority relations as well, since they, too, are a deep pattern of family life and other forms of early socialization.[21] Indeed, we are dealing here with a formal theory that lacks historical and sociological content: there is no reason to assume that the kind of recognition that is cultivated in a particular family setting may be hierarchical and authoritarian, and yet still grant the ego comfort and a stable identity. Such selves may be more likely to justify such relations than seek to confront or alter them. In fact, there seems no reason to assume that recognition plays a stronger role than identification does, and that the power of the latter is stronger than that of the former.

The social and political consequences of this are far reaching. For one thing, if the developing ego is cultivated in a routinized fashion to see hierarchical relations as valid, or to see specific hegemonic values as legitimate, and so on, then, in some sense, it sinks to the level of second nature, and the mechanism of recognition actually cements those institutional patterns in adult life.[22] For Parsons, this means that intersubjective relations establish between ego and alter "a reciprocal role relationship in which value-patterns are shared. Alter is a model and this is a learning process, because ego did not at the beginning of it possess the values in question."[23] In a society of highly rationalized institutional roles, predefined and reinforced by the imperatives and needs of a highly rationalized and routinized social order organized around the stability and growth of economic ends and imperatives, the identification of the nascent ego with various forms of prefashioned identities (gender, racial, cultural, and so on) as well as, at a more basic level, the acceptance of the value-systems that code the cognitive and evaluative capacities of the subject, infiltrate the intersubjective and recognitive relations between ego and alters, having a strong formative force on the socialization process.[24] Recognition can therefore become a means of legitimating the prevailing power relations rather than serve to undermine or call them into question, as when we "recognize" our role obligations with references to others within a hierarchical social context that has legitimate authority.[25] And it only makes sense that advanced capitalist modernity is able to sustain itself as a result of the efficiency of these socialization processes. The capacity of elites to reproduce a complex, rationalized system of extraction, social waste, and social stratification can be secured only through the formation of subjects that recognize such a system, at least in some basic sense, as legitimate.[26] Even more, the domestication of modern societies to the imperatives of elites is only more entrenched through the process of displacing social struggles away from concrete issues of power toward the symbolic domain of culture and the "recognition" of new forms of identities.

For Marcuse, too, this socialization process explains the ways that ego development can be managed and oriented toward the purposes and functions of the social structure more broadly. The ego ideal, in this sense, orients the nascent ego toward the role expectations that are a best fit for success in the various rule-governed institutions that make up rationalized society. The developing ego sees in the culture the ego ideal that orients a cathexis toward it, and it can be said that this, too, is a process of recognition, although it is not one that has within it an ethical, or in any sense a critical or emancipatory, function. Marcuse's argument is worth looking at in more detail:

The mediation between the self and the other gives way to immediate identification. In the social structure, the individual becomes the conscious and unconscious object of administration and obtains his freedom and satisfaction in his
role as such an object; in the mental structure, the ego shrinks to such an extent
that it seems no longer capable of sustaining itself, as a self, in distinction from
id and superego.[27]

This drive for *identification* displaces, or at least shapes, the supposed
powers of *recognition* in the process of ego formation through the mediation
of the family structure by the social forces that render role expectations as
well as the norms and value-orientations that are required of the broader social
structure. The relation between parents and children, therefore, sheds the
more insulated character that Honneth assumes and becomes more a force of
socialization harnessed to the norms and expectations and value-orientations
of economic life more broadly. This was an insight that was considerably
more prevalent in analyses of the immediate postwar period. One example
of this, Maurice Stein's *Eclipse of Community*, illustrates this phenomenon:

> One of the lessons soon learned by the child is the appreciation of properly dis-
> played property. He begins to feel this as a source of ego-enhancement so that
> new items are always preferred to the old. As the child accumulates property for
> his own room, the advertising theorem that happiness comes from acquisition
> is painlessly inculcated. He watches his mother light up when she gets a shiny
> new kitchen appliance, so that cooking for her, as the advertisers would have
> it, does take on new meaning. But as the appliance ages and loses its capacity
> to bring appreciative responses from the neighbors it has to be quickly replaced
> by another.[28]

What this means is that the material organization of social relations—the
economic imperatives that shape the value-patterns of the community—is
entwined with the forms of recognition that serve as the basis of socialization. But even more, it means that the norms that are necessary for material-
based power are severed from the more flexible norms of self-expression and
identity. Recognition of one's right for sexual, gendered, or other cultural
styles of life now become the key concern rather than the general structures
of power and domination that constitute the social order of capitalism. The
real question is whether recognition provides us with a real theory of social
change that cannot be explained by the expansion of liberal norms. The key
is the issue of the nature of "struggle"—whether recognition is something
that characterizes ego development so that it can provide new psychological,
emotional, and even cognitive resources for critique and social opposition,
or whether it simply falls into the subjective search for legitimating cultural
forms of identity. Indeed, there is no reason to assume that the move toward

the acceptance of difference has the capacity to provide in immanent insight into the deficits of recognition in the sphere of economic life or other aspects of capitalist society. Capital has its own needs and imperatives that shape the normative context of social power, and Honneth seems unable to discover a means of opposing the dominant socialization pressures that enable the system to reproduce itself.

Indeed, I think we can see that recognition cannot occur *external* to these processes and, as a result, can be (and, I would go so far as to say, *must be*) shaped and oriented by them. The influences and patterns of early childhood therefore affect the psychological or mental patterns that guide evaluative and cognitive capacities and beliefs about the world. In this sense, social power is cemented by the routinization of values and their absorption into the personality structure and cognitive patterns of individuals. The relations between individuals within different socialization contexts—family, school, workplace, the market, and so on—therefore become imbued by the logic of economic efficiency, consumption, and other attitudes shared by the group as a whole. In essence, according to this functionalist understanding of domination, individuals are constituted increasingly to possess value-orientations that cement hierarchical forms of social relations. Their symbolic world and interpretive schemes come to be shaped more by the kinds of subordination they experience than an open-ended, equalitarian intersubjectivity.[29] Through processes of socialization that are increasingly steered by economic interests, role expectations are more and more determined by the imperatives of elite interests to the extent that critical subjectivity is thwarted. Not only does the socialization process under administrative-capitalist society short-circuit the ethical potentialities of the Idealist reading of recognition that Honneth puts forth, but it also shows that the actual empirical mechanisms of socialization are unable to support its normative and philosophical claims.[30]

The theory of recognition is therefore an insufficient means of accounting for the process of socialization within modern capitalist societies. The search for an "intramundane" theory of morality cannot, it seems to me, escape the more powerful functional forces that modern administrative institutions exert in a culture permeated by economic rationality and the hierarchical forms of power that characterize it. It does not mean that the functional structures that shape individuals are exclusively and absolutely determining; rather, it means that background conditions significantly shape the interpretative schemes and categorial structures of consciousness that orient subjective action.[31] In short, the very sources of recognition and the kind of moral autonomy that it is supposed to produce are lacking empirically in modern societies. It could be that this is a result of the kind of theorizing that Honneth himself pursues, one stamped by a neo-Idealist concern with human epistemic, emotional, and social life bereft of the deep structures that are the product of concrete power relations.[32] In addition, it seems to me that the theory of recognition can place us in a situation in which identities shaped by a fragmented culture predominate more substantive and more ontologically valid forms of social criticism and critical cognition.

IV. RECOGNITION AS FAILED SOCIAL PHILOSOPHY

The centrality of capitalist social formations and their capacity to deform the critical, even ethical potentialities of recognition requires further discussion. First, Honneth's neo-Idealist reinterpretation of the market is one that sees it as an almost precapitalist phenomenon. He sees Adam Smith as well as Hegel and Durkheim as teasing out certain moral dimensions that underlay market society. Capital as a process of accumulation, as a process of shaping power and social relations, is essentially nonexistent for Honneth. Recognition is looked for everywhere, and found. Once we posit social relations that have some degree of legitimacy and that exist without genuine conflict, we are asked to see them as the result of norms that spring from recognition. But this continues to sidestep the essential problem I have been exploring here: namely, that the mere existence of stable social relations should not permit us to validate those relations. Critique begins not from whether one feels disrespect; it begins from the more central question of whether the relations, practices, norms, and institutions of society are rational in that they promote the universal interests of society. Honneth here falls into a trap: he conceives of the development of individual selves in conjunction with social norms of mutual respect as evident in modern late-capitalist society.

One of the persistent claims of Honneth's neo-Idealism is the compelling critique that Marxist analysis is essentially deterministic and operates under a structural-functionalist logic that is no longer tenable. But as I have been arguing above with respect to the family, the basic problem here is that we need to see structural-functional arguments not in mechanistic terms, but in terms of value-patterns. In this sense, viewing Marx's base-superstructure thesis through the lens of Weber and Parsons, we can glimpse a more complex and nuanced understanding of how social formations are rooted in and shaped by logics of capital. The importance of Marx's insights for critical theory, therefore, should be seen not in his analysis of social labor, but rather in the ways that the nature of the economic structure of society also organizes wider patterns of socialization. Here Weber's notion of legitimate authority must be read in conjunction with the theories of the self beginning with Freud and continuing through Reich, Fromm, Marcuse, and contemporary theories of system-justification and social dominance. According to this reading, domination and power no longer give rise to conflicts between individuals so much as within them. Legitimate authority obtains its deep roots within society through the transformation of the self to be in harmony with the dominant mechanisms of the community. Dominant hierarchies that inscribe norms and values within the self form the subject. Reification is therefore not a matter of the "forgetting of recognition," but a process of cognitive and self-formation that prevents the subject from achieving a critical grasp of the society as a whole—its deeper purposes and its true contours.

If this basic idea is accepted, then the realist description of modern societies must compete with the thesis that modernity is to be read as a kind of expanding sphere of moral progress possessing "normative potentials that are gradually unlocked and become available for groups seeking justice."[33] But this neo-Idealist claim should be read against the backdrop of the ways that a search for justice can be misguided away from the broader power structures of the community and routed toward more manageable, more domesticated forms. So the emergence of the welfare state, according to Honneth's reading, is seen—via T. H. Marshall's interpretation—as an expansion of social rights. But this view is contestable, particularly when we consider the fact that the welfare state was a reform that was meant to insulate capitalism and elites from radical social transformation.[34] The regulation of the poor and working class can be viewed as an expansion of their rights and dignity, but the structural conditions for exploitation, for extraction, for the dominance of the community by elite interests remains.

The contradiction of capitalist modernity is an expression of the kind of pathologies that early critical theorists were able to grasp: subjective forms of recognition may validate personal identities, but they are ineffectual against modern forms of social power rooted in material resources and the powers that institutions have in constituting subjectivity. The disintegration of racist norms, of rigid gender divisions, of new acceptance and toleration for previously excluded sexual identities, and so on, should be seen, on this view, as contradictions with the broader forms of social power that are consolidated by class interests. The fracturing of a more universalist identity, with the republican sentiments that animated radical political ideas and movements during the nineteenth century, are lost as individuals become absorbed in particularistic identities, subjectivity, and ever-expanding narcissistic explorations of self. Recognition of new cultural identities now takes center stage once liberal polities have extended rights to previously oppressed and marginalized groups. Recognition can serve these kinds of projects well, but they are impotent against the material forms of social power—the control over the resources of the community as a whole and the values that support that control and power—and it can be argued that the expansion of cultural recognition, when taken separate from struggles for economic justice, inhibits the kind of solidarity of interests required to challenge precisely those kinds of power.

A more robust conception of justice, one based on the universal, common interest of the whole, is not grasped by the normative impulse of recognition since it is merely a hermeneutic rooted in the particularity of subjects. Honneth does not take the step that Hegel saw was needed: that recognition is a *phenomenological process* that reveals to cognition the ontological structure of human sociality. We discover, through recognition, not simply that the other deserves respect, but rather that I am part of a larger structure of reality; that we-thinking depends upon a certain kind of social relatedness and interdependence that constitutes the essential structure of a social ontology that, when rationally organized, will enable the self-development of each member's individuality as well as provide the requisite collective goods that will enable this kind of social solidarity and individual development and freedom. Hence, universality comes to possess an objective content in that it refers to an actual structure in the world. Indeed, this was something Hegel, too, was able to grasp in his mature work, in which the state, or the objective embodiment of the universal, must stand as the end of a modern conception of right. When Honneth reconstructs Hegel's theory of right as "a normative theory of those spheres of reciprocal recognition that must be preserved intact because they constitute the moral identity of modern societies,"[35] he is missing the deeper dimensions of Hegel's ideas and their potential for a more robust critical theory. For Hegel, recognition had to move beyond the merely intersubjective process of recognition into an insight into a higher structure of sociality, an objective context of socialization and social interdependence, and his early interest in political economy shows that he was looking for just such an ontological structure, not simply the phenomenological process of recognition alone. Recognition *is a means to that fuller cognitive grasp of the essential structure of human social life*, and, as such, we can use this as a foundational understanding of the ways that social life should be structured, social goods distributed, legal codes articulated, and so on. The kind of self-realization that comes from this kind of society, Hegel seems to maintain, would be a progression over the one-sided forms of individuality and society that liberalism sustains.[36]

The comprehension of this social ontology allows modern subjects not only to grasp the interdependent nature of our sociality but also to show that this sociality is dynamic and an essential feature of a rational community. The realization in conceptual thought of this sociality is to become the basis for our concepts of freedom, of individuality, the "good," and to therefore be seen as universal in nature since they are expressive of rational structures of human life. But Honneth wants to detach the process of recognition from the ontological dimension that it is supposed to reveal. He wants to see recognition as a process that is at the same time an end. But Hegel sees that this is an error, and he realizes this early in his critique of Fichte's conception of recognition in the *Differenzschrift*, where Fichte is critiqued for being "unable to find a place in the objective world for an 'objective' Subject-Object."[37] More to the point, Hegel argues:

> In Fichte's system identity constitutes itself only as subjective Subject-Object. But this subjective Subject-Object needs an objective Subject-Object to complete it, so that the Absolute presents itself in each of the two Subject-Objects, and finds itself perfected only in both together as the highest synthesis that nullifies both insofar as they are opposed. As their point of absolute indifference, the Absolute encloses both, gives birth to both and is born of both.[38]

What Hegel has in view here is that the subject-object relation must be conceived as operating not simply within a phenomenological encounter with the "other," but as leading to a higher structure of consciousness that sees human social interdependence as the core essence of social being. If we take this line of thinking seriously, the theory of recognition must be embedded in a broader, rational grasp of social relatedness as an anchor for critique and judgment, not simply an end in itself. It is our social interdependence as social beings that is the real essence of the source of a more expanded, richer articulation of self and freedom. Recognition is therefore the phenomenological means by which the rational core of human social ontology can be revealed, allowing for it to be comprehended in thought and that leads us to think in a new space of reasons. But Honneth's thesis is that recognition stops at this phenomenological mechanism, whereas Hegel saw it as the beginning of a process of a higher form of reasoning ultimately allowing us to grasp the metaphysical essence of human sociality. For that reason, recognition is a crucial mechanism, but it can also be corrupted by defective social relations, institutions, and arrangements that are not detectable through recognition itself. In effect, this means that recognition is susceptible to the functional, centripetal pull of capitalist forms of social integration, and this is something the Idealism in Hegel (not to mention the neo-Idealism of Honneth) could not anticipate. Recognition on its own is no longer able to provide us with this critical cognition since it, too, can be colonized by defective social relations and defective forms of self. Pathologies of recognition therefore produce pathologies of reason, and recognition on its own cannot get us out of this dilemma. What Honneth is unwilling to recognize is that the powers of capitalism over socialization processes serves to negate the positive force of recognition as he reconstructs it.

Nevertheless, the thrust of Hegel's critique of Fichte was that recognition is a means of leaping out of the narrow forms of immediacy that plagued the "understanding." Recognition is a process, a kind of path that leads to an objective insight about the ontological features of the basis for human life.

Freedom lies in the insight into this conceptual structure of human life, and this is why Hegel and Marx lead us to the view that we cannot think of human consciousness outside of the objective structure (in Hegel's case Idealist and conceptual, in Marx's social and historical) that mediates all forms of consciousness. But Honneth's recognitive theory is limited by the same critique put forth by Hegel or Fichte—we are trapped within a hermeneutic circle that pens us into particularistic opinion structures and worldviews that are already present and dominant within the community rather than an objective standpoint from which we can form critical-rational judgments. Critique is the end process of a reconstruction of the social ontology that Hegel saw as the essence of our sociality. The key for critical theory, therefore, is to provide us with a theoretical vantage point that allows us to see the distortions of an "inverted world" and that can provide us with critical categories for social criticism and judgment. But the paradigm of mutual recognition on its own cannot secure for us the kinds of insights needed to call into question the forms of consciousness and cognition shaped by hierarchical social relations. Lacking an objective foundation, a ground in which to root critical cognition, it does not seem likely that the project of critical theory is a tenable one in any compelling sense of the term.

V. THE ROLE OF RECOGNITION IN CRITICAL THEORY

What, then, is the proper place for recognition within the context of critical social theory? As I see it, the act of recognition is not simply a phylogenetic process of ego development, since, as I have tried to show above, the social context—particularly that of contemporary administrative-capitalist societies—that the processes of intersubjective recognition operate within has too strong a distorting influence on the ways individuals relate to themselves as well as to others—that is, to the ontogenetic processes of socialization. What is lacking is an appreciation of the extent to which rational autonomy comes to be eroded, to be stunted, depleting the capacities for critical reflection. The processes of recognition embed individuals within a context of compliance, or at least one of relative acquiescence to the social order and the value-systems that legitimate it. Even though it can awaken consciousness to certain forms of disrespect, there is no sense that this is capable of penetrating the deeper structures of domination and injustice that characterize advanced capitalist societies. What is needed is a refashioned conception of critical subjectivity, of a strengthening of the cognitive capacities of individuals to call into question the value-patterns that produce system compliance and attitudinal congruence among groups.[39]

A reconstruction of critical theory can begin with the problem of reification as a critical entrée point. If we read Lukács's argument about reification as a thesis concerning the ways that the cognitive and epistemic powers of subjects are deformed (that is, how individuals fail to grasp the pathological nature of the social world they inhabit), then we can see that it is not from within the intersubjective lifeworld of recognitive relations that individuals grasp this social ontology. Rather, it is derived from the way that we choose to view the world, one that moves beyond immediacy and into the realm of a conceptually mediated consciousness. Since reification is essentially a category error on the part of our cognition, recognition must be a means of grasping an ontological, objective truth about the nature of human sociality. Modern capitalism and its crises and pathologies force us to see the social world not as an aggregate of individuals, or as static objects, but as an organic interdependence, as a series of processes, as dynamic and formative in nature. This is grasped not from a passive reflection of the social world but from active engagement with it, coupled with a critical-cognitive faculty.[40] We come to grasp an ontology of the social that can be used against the ideological forms and social-structural institutions that predominate capitalist societies.

In this sense, the argument is that the conceptual structure of unreified thought is able to comprehend the *actual* conceptual structure of a free, cooperative, shared social life in which the ends of individual actions are oriented toward shared purposes and needs.[41] This is why Hegel tied his conception of ethical life to his metaphysics: to a rational attempt to grasp the nature of the essence of objects (in this case, the human community itself and its essential structure). Honneth wants to detach recognition from these philosophical moorings and their implications for a critical cognition and instead make it into a phylogenetic process between subjects. But if we follow this path, we have no objective, ontological referent for critique, no way to secure critical thought against merely reflecting power relations that are already extant. Recognition is supposed to awaken in us an ethic of respect for others, but in truth any culture can calibrate its conception of respect in line with the forms of hierarchy and control. No, the radical implications of Hegel's theory of recognition must lie in its *capacity to reveal to us the essential, rational structure of social life*, that the deeper purposes of our life together is a common interest and not the exploitation and dominance of others for the benefit of the few. We cannot obtain this insight through the recognitive relations of everyday life alone; rather, we are forced to move in a more conceptually demanding space of reasons, one that is facilitated by the structural transformation of social relations made possible by capitalism.

Rather, a key seems to me to be found in a rereading of Hegel's understanding of recognition and the way it was absorbed into the structure of the

Philosophy of Right. According to this reading, the process of recognition is not simply a phenomenological one in which individual subjects encounter others. Rather, it is one in which the phenomenological process is meant to disclose an ontology of human sociality and interdependence; in other words, *the actual conceptual structure of what human social life essentially is.*[42] Recognition is therefore not only an intersubjective process but also a subjective, cognitive one in which the rational individual moves in the space of universal reasons, recognizes the ethical structure of the state, of a society shaped and oriented toward the common interest, toward what is needed by the essential nature of society itself.[43] The object of this consciousness is the essence of human sociality, the very fact that this is itself not simply a structure of relations but also an ontologically distinct way of being, one that can be either stunted or *actualized* based on the ways in which any society organizes itself and its purposes. There is, then, an *ontological claim* fused to the *phenomenological* one.[44] What individuals grasp, *recognize* in their movement from *Moralität* to and through that of *Sittlichkeit*, is the conceptual structure of what it means to be human, to be social, to be part of complex forms of relations and processes that have as their *telos* the realization of their potentialities as members of the community.[45] We are constituted by a system of processes, of relations; we have shared purposes; we ought to orient our subjective actions and purposes toward common ends.[46] Recognition is not only a matter of the intersubjective-phenomenological but also a recognition of the conceptual structure of the dynamics of human social life, of a social ontology.[47]

Recognition of the ethical state therefore becomes a crucial element to a critical form of cognition in that it is able to disclose the depth of the pathological nature of what exists at any given moment.[48] As Hegel remarks in his lectures on the *Philosophy of Right*, "The whole, the state, achieves inner stability only when what is universal, what is implicit (*an sich*), is recognized as universal."[49] The deepening of rationality through recognition is the ability to grasp rationally the objective structure of our interdependent sociality as a kind of essential determinate for individual human actuality.[50] This social ontology provides the foundation for further claims about the state, culture, freedom, and so on. We begin to see—through the family, the actions of the market society, and finally realized in the state—that we are components of a broader fabric of dependencies and that reveal to us an objective insight into the essence of what it means to be a free being. We move from recognizing others to recognizing the state as an embodiment of the universal, of the common interest of the political community itself. As Hegel notes in his lectures from 1817, "The right of the state is that its idea be recognized and realized."[51] And this idea is that the actual (*Wirklich*), rational, ethical state is one that embodies in its institutions and its basic principles the universal, or the common interest according to reason. Recognition is a higher form of cognition in which subjectively bound forms of self-consciousness come to take on a wider form of thinking. As such, self-reflection becomes reflection on the common forms of interdependencies that make up the essential structure of human social life. In this sense, recognition should lead us to a republican conception—not unlike Rousseau's *volonté général*—that will allow us to move in an enlarged space of reasons capable of cognizing the common welfare. But this requires, as Lukács points out, that the cognitive shackles of reification (caused by defective socialization under capitalism) be shattered and a new form of critical-cognition emerge in its place. Honneth does not have a path out of this dilemma. We are asked to rely only on the intersubjectivity of recognition to shoulder the burden of this task, but there is no way for him to show how reified forms of thought, reified forms of identity, or the kind of identity formation that occurs as a reflex to those forms of thought and identity can be overcome. Instead, it seems more likely that recognition places us in a cultural situation in which we are asked to recognize particularist identities rather than foster the consciousness necessary for social critique in any meaningful, rational sense.

Rather, what I have in mind here is that recognition be viewed as embedded in the cognitive process of coming to realize the centrality of the cooperative, interdependent essence of human sociality. In this sense, recognition would be the phenomenological layer of a more critical-cognitive process that grasps the social ontology of human social relations and that they should be arranged for the common ends of the community and the realization of individuality. In classical critical theory, this argument also emerges in Lukács's thesis concerning the notion of an "expressive totality," where, in the third part of his essay "Reification and the Consciousness of the Proletariat," he argues that the working class can shatter reification only once it sees itself as the subject-object of history—that is, they recognize their place within an objective set of historically produced conditions and their normative role within that structure. But on a deeper level, it is an argument about what an unreified form of cognition ought to see as the essence of human life: that it is a cooperative, shared form of being, that the current social order is worthy of rejection not because of a utilitarian calculus to increase its interests as a class, but rather that capitalist relations distort the potentiality that lies latent within human subjects.

It is the grasping of this social ontology that stems from the process of cognizing the essential determinants of our existence *as social beings* that leads to the conceptual framework of a social ontology that can serve as a means of bridging the gap between the implications of the theory of recognition and the need to resurrect a more radical sense of cognition as well as a more foundationalist approach to ground a critical theory that can still call the irrational nature of capitalist society into question. Even more, this means that the theory of recognition needs to find its place within a broader critical framework in that it should be seen as a capacity to recognize the ontological structure of rational, human sociality, the kind of interdependence that is at the essence of what it means to be human. And this means that rationality also demands that the institutions of a rational society—of the family, of economic life, of the state, of culture—must be accountable to the features of this basic sociality and its needs. Recognition, as Honneth conceives it, does not bring us here, since it seeks to weave a normative theory out of intersubjectivity alone, to distance itself from questions of social ontology and the material (or perhaps better, ontological) qualities of human social life, and to eschew the pervasive and insidious power of capitalist social relations on the capacities of critical cognition. In this sense, I do not mean to suggest that recognition is somehow an idea lacking value and salience in an age of dehumanized social relations and intolerance. I only mean to suggest that it cannot serve as the basis of a critical theory of society and that it must take into consideration the theoretical insights from which it seeks to distance itself if it is to achieve a more compelling account of the modern social order and its pathologies.

NOTES

1. Axel Honneth, *Disrespect: On the Normative Foundations of Critical Theory* (Cambridge: Polity Press, 2007), 66.
2. Ibid., 71.
3. Charles Taylor, *Philosophical Arguments* (Cambridge, MA: Harvard University Press, 1995), 225.
4. Honneth derives this from a parallel reading of Hegel and Mead. Interestingly enough, he does not point to the fact that Mead overlooks problems of alienation and pathological subject-formation in his theoretical model. For a discussion of this element in Mead, see Tom W. Goff, *Marx and Mead: Contributions to a Sociology of Knowledge* (London: Routledge and Kegan Paul, 1980), 92ff. For a critique of Mead's social interactionism on the theme of power and domination, see Lonnie Athens, "Mead's Analysis of Social Conflict: A Radical Interactionist's Critique," *American Sociologist* 43 (2012): 428–47.
5. Honneth, *Disrespect*, 71; see also Axel Honneth, *Das Ich im Wir. Studien zur Anerkennungstheorie* (Frankfurt: Suhrkamp, 2010), 78–102.
6. Axel Honneth, *The Struggle for Recognition: The Moral Grammar of Social Conflicts* (Cambridge, MA: MIT Press, 1996), 118.
7. Ibid.
8. A critique along broadly similar lines is outlined by Frédéric Guillaume Dufour and Éric Pineault, "Quelle théorie du capitalisme pour quelle théorie de la reconnaissance?" *Politique et Sociétés* 28, no. 3 (2009): 75–99. They point out, correctly I think, that "[l]a théorie sociale contemporaine qui s'inspire de la Théorie

critique pour comprendre le capitalisme avancé se trouve ainsi devant une sociologie du capitalisme avancé sans théorie de la subjectivation des salariés ou des élites. . . . C'est pourquoi nous croyons qu'une théorie critique du capitalisme avancé doit de nouveau s'approprier l'outil d'analyse qu'est la structure de la reconnaissance inégale pour comprendre les formes de polarisation propres au capitalisme avancé," 97.

9. Honneth, *Disrespect*, 72.

10. Honneth places great emphasis on the need to move away from structural-functional concerns and toward an autonomy of moral philosophy and a social theory of praxis. "Today, social theory based on Marx can regain its critical potential only if the functionalist prioritizing of the economic sphere is dropped and the weight of other domains of action is brought to bear: an analysis in which the achievements of all remaining spheres has been investigated as contributing to the one systemic aim of material production must give way to a research program that investigates the historically specific interrelationships of independent spheres of action." *The Fragmented World of the Social: Essays in Social and Political Philosophy* (Albany, NY: SUNY Press, 1995), 5 and *passim*. However, there have been attempts to work out a recognition-theoretic interpretation of the early manuscripts in order to show Marx's inclusion within the normative-critical framework of recognition. See Michael Quante, "Recognition as the Social Grammar of Species Being in Marx," in Heikki Ikäheimo and Arto Laitinen (eds.), *Recognition and Social Ontology* (Leiden: Brill, 2011), 239–70, and Daniel Brudney, "Producing for Others," in Hans-Christoph Schmidt am Busch and Christopher Zurn (eds.), *The Philosophy of Recognition: Historical and Contemporary Perspectives* (Lanham, MD: Lexington Books, 2010), 151–88.

11. Elsewhere, I have elaborated this insight of rationalization, routinization, and internalization as central mechanisms of domination relations. See my paper, "A Functionalist Theory of Social Domination," *Journal of Political Power* 6, no. 2 (2013): 179–99.

12. For a related but distinct critique of the effect of structural power relations on the process of recognition, see Lois McNay, *Against Recognition* (Cambridge: Polity Press, 2008).

13. Honneth, *The Struggle for Recognition*, 96.

14. Ibid., 97.

15. Herbert Marcuse, "The Obsolescence of the Freudian Concept of Man," in *Five Lectures* (Boston, MA: Beacon Press, 1970), 44–61, 46.

16. As Horkheimer notes on this point, "Even more than through actions deliberately aimed at forming men, this social function is exercised through the continuous influence of the prevailing situation itself, through the formative power of public and private life, through the example of persons who play a role in the individual's life; in short, through processes not consciously directed." Max Horkheimer, "Authority and the Family," in *Critical Theory: Selected Essays* (New York: Continuum, 1971): 47–128, 98. Horkheimer indeed operates within a thoroughly Freudian model of the family, one attached to the bourgeois stage of economic life. Honneth suggests that this constellation of the family has been eclipsed, at least since the 1960s, and that a new, more humane form of family life has emerged. See Axel Honneth, *Das Recht der Freiheit. Grundriß einer demokratischen Sittlichkeit* (Frankfurt: Suhrkamp, 2011),

281ff. But one can still quarrel with the idea that even if the family has become less domineering and hierarchical, as in Horkehimer's model, Marcuse's post-Freudian paradigm of familial socialization (which he sees as occurring in the late, or consumptive, mass-society stage of capitalist culture) can be observed.

17. Elsewhere, I have outlined a theory of alienation along the lines of an "atrophied moral cognition," which means a withering of the critical capacities of moral cognition as a result of efficient forms of socialization that are able to shape subjects' sense of legitimate authority. See my paper, "Alienation as Atrophied Moral Cognition and Its Implications for Political Behavior," *Journal for the Theory of Social Behaviour* 43, no. 3 (2013): 301–21.

18. Parsons notes that "the fact remains that all social action is normatively oriented, and that the value-orientations embodied in these norms must to a degree be common to the actors in an institutionally integrated interactive system." *The Social System* (Glencoe, IL: Free Press, 1951), 251.

19. Ibid., 213.

20. Honneth, *The Struggle for Recognition*, 104.

21. Horkheimer explains that "[t]he decisive thing here is not whether coercion or kindness marked the child's education, since the child's character is formed far more by the very structure of the family than by the conscious intentions and methods of the father." "Authority and the Family," 111. It should be added to Horkheimer's thesis, which is more in the shadow of the classical Freudian model of ego development, that it is also the *style of parenting* that affects the ways that individuals come to understand and to conceive of authority. See George Lakoff, *Moral Politics: How Liberals and Conservatives Think* (Chicago: University of Chicago Press, 2002), as well as Marc J. Hetherington and Jonathan D. Weiler, *Authoritarianism and Polarization in American Politics* (New York: Cambridge University Press, 2009). For an empirical test of the hypothesis that strict families tend to produce conservative authoritarians and liberals the reverse, see David C. Barker and James D. Tinnick, "Competing Visions of Parental Roles and Ideological Constraint," *American Political Science Review* 100, no. 2 (2006): 249–63.

22. Robin Celikates has argued on this point that "social and political institutions are primarily seen as the objects of recognition by the members of a society who credit the social order they live in with a seemingly inevitable authority in which recognition and misrecognition are not easy to disentangle." "Recognition, System Justification and Reconstructive Critique," in Christian Lazzeri and Soraya Nour (eds.), *Reconnaisance, identité et intégration sociale* (Paris: Presses Universitaires de Paris Ouest, 2009), 82–93, 86. Andreas Kalyvas argues on a similar point that "[i]f moral claims emerge out of cultural conflicts, they have to be the effect of contingent power relations among competing groups. In that case, the appeal to recognition loses its normative relevance. What has to be recognized amounts to the identities the strongest groups have succeeded in forming after surviving, and winning, an antecedent to the struggle for recognition, cultural conflict. Within this model, recognition is equivalent to the justification of internalized unequal power relations, and not their repudiation." "Critical Theory at the Crossroads: Comments on Axel Honneth's Theory of Recognition," *European Journal of Social Theory* 2, no. 1 (1999): 99–108, 102. Neither of

these critics, however, probe the actual recognition model itself upon which Honneth relies.

23. Parsons, *The Social System*, 211.

24. It is interesting to note Honneth's more recent discussion of Parsons and the function of "role obligations" in the formation of the family, particularly his view "daß der Haushalt aus einer ganzen Reihe von weiteren Mitgliedern bestand, sowie schließlich das räumliche Arrangement der Wohnanlagen verhinderten, da sich zwischen Vater, Mutter und Kind die Art von intensiver Gefühlsbindung entwickeln konnte, die uns heute für die Beziehungsform der Familie als charakteristisch erscheint." *Das Recht der Freiheit*, 278. He relies on Parsons and the theory of complementary role obligations to show how the structural transformation of the modern family can create an inchoate environment for recognitive relations. Ibid., 282ff. However, this seems to me to be largely peripheral to the concern over identification and the eclipse of the central role of the family and its ability to form the subject without the influence of extrafamilial institutional imperatives. See my treatment of Parsons on this theme of role obligations and its ability to coordinate isonomous value-systems of compliance and control in chapter 6.

25. Honneth addresses this critique, but in a deeply unconvincing way. He chooses to critique Althusser on this point rather than less mechanistic approaches. Nevertheless, Honneth claims that "Die Anerkennung sollte als Genus von verschiedenen Formen einer praktischen Einstellung begriffen werden, in der sich jeweils die primäre Absicht einer bestimmten Affirmierung des Gegenübers spiegelt. Im Unterschied zu dem, was Althusser vor Augen hatte, besitzen solche affirmierenden Haltungen einen eindeutig positiven Charakter, weil sie es den Adressaten erlauben, sich mit den eigenen Eigenschaften zu identifizieren und daher zu größerer Autonomie zu gelangen; weit davon entfernt, eine bloße Ideologie darzustellen, bildet Anerkennung die intersubjektive Voraussetzung für die Fähigkeit, autonom eigene Lebensziele zu verwicklichen." *Das Ich im Wir*, 111. But this gets us nowhere, since the point is that there is a naturalization of the social structures of power that are rendered legitimate. This is the real meaning of the theory of reification: the naturalization in the human mind of the social hierarchies that ensconce us. Therefore, recognitive relations need be not only positive but also *negative* since they can just as easily reproduce legitimation of hierarchies as to call them into question on the basis of a feeling of "disrespect."

26. See the interesting discussion by Éric Pineault, "Quelle théorie critique des structures sociales du capitalisme avancé?" *Cahiers de recherche sociologiques* 45 (2008): 113–30.

27. Marcuse, "The Obsolescence of the Freudian Concept of Man," 47.

28. Maurice R. Stein, *The Eclipse of Community: An Interpretation of American Studies* (New York: Harper Torchbooks, 1960), 213.

29. In many ways, this is a category mistake that is embedded within Mead's theoretical model of intersubjectivity. For a different perspective that sees social hierarchy and subordination as primarily deriving from the work of Robert Park, see Lonnie Athens, "Human Subordination from a Radical Interactionist's Perspective," *Journal for the Theory of Social Behaviour* 40, no. 3 (2010): 339–68.

30. Christopher Zurn has argued on a similar point that Honneth's theory of recognition "must retreat to a high level of abstraction in order to save the empirical phenomena under the recognition analysis, or it must descend to a sufficiently substantive level of social analysis in order to provide strategic guidance. However, in the former case it loses requisite socio-theoretic insight, while in the latter case it cedes empirical accuracy." "Recognition, Redistribution, and Democracy: Dilemmas of Honneth's Critical Social Theory," *European Journal of Philosophy* 13, no. 1 (2005): 89–126, 110. In my view, Zurn is too cautious in his critique, for it can be said that Honneth's model of recognition is so abstract that it becomes essentially Idealist in the sense that material factors of social life and structural concerns of the organization of concrete power forms are seen as wholly separate from the recognitive mode Honneth lays out.

31. For a discussion of this from a hermeneutic dimension that incorporates the problem of alienation on the capacities of individuals to interpret their world, see Hans Herbert Kögler, "Alienation as Epistemological Source: Reflexivity and Social Background after Mannheim and Bourdieu," *Social Epistemology* 11, no. 2 (1997): 141–64. Also see Bourdieu's discussion of this problem in Pierre Bourdieu, *Language and Symbolic Power* (Cambridge, MA: Harvard University Press, 1991), 163–70.

32. Stéphane Haber has argued on this point that since Honneth's theory of reification is a critique "dedicated to the critique of symptoms rather than to the pathological facts themselves, [it] will remain dependent on what Honneth refers to as the 'critique of civilization' (*Kulturkritik*). A style of critique which more appropriately reflects the work of Nietzsche than that of Marx, simultaneously divests itself from the field of economic and social reality and from the lived experience of work." "Recognition, Justice and Social Pathologies in Axel Honneth's Recent Writings," *Revista Ciencia Politica* 27, no. 2 (2007): 159–70, 167.

33. Jean-Philippe Deranty, "Marx, Honneth, and the Tasks of a Contemporary Critical Theory," *Ethical Theory and Moral Practice* 16, no. 2 (2013): 745–58, 749.

34. Specifically see Frances Fox Piven and Richard Cloward, *Regulating the Poor: The Functions of Public Welfare* (New York: Vintage, 1993).

35. Axel Honneth, *The Pathologies of Individual Freedom: Hegel's Social Theory* (Princeton, NJ: Princeton University Press, 2010), 5.

36. Cf. Allen Wood, *Hegel's Ethical Thought* (New York: Cambridge University Press, 1990), 256ff., as well as Andrew Buchwalter, *Dialectics, Politics, and the Contemporary Value of Hegel's Practical Philosophy* (New York: Routledge, 2012), 214ff.

37. Paul Redding, *Hegel's Hermeneutics* (Ithaca, NY: Cornell University Press, 1996), 104.

38. G. W. F. Hegel, *The Difference between Fichte's and Schelling's System of Philosophy* (Albany, NY: SUNY Press, 1977), 155.

39. Joel Whitebook has correctly written on this theme that the role of critique is to "picture a self that can stand outside the world—outside of any given traditional world—and evaluate it. And this capacity, in turn, has generally been viewed as a necessary anchoring point for critique." "Mutual Recognition and the Work of the Negative," in William Rehg and James Bohman (eds.), *Pluralism and the Pragmatic Turn: The Transformation of Critical Theory* (Cambridge, MA: MIT Press, 2001), 257–92,

272. Mark Sacks also reinforces this idea: "If the self, or at least the substantive self, is an intersubjective constant all the way down, the individual cannot transcend his or her socio-cultural reality. . . . The norms of critical judgement would themselves have been left behind." "The Conception of the Subject in Analytical Philosophy," quoted in Whitebook, "Mutual Recognition and the Work of the Negative," 272.

40. As Lukács puts the matter, "For every purely cognitive stance bears the stigma of immediacy. That is to say, it never ceases to be confronted by a whole series of ready-made objects that cannot be dissolved into processes." *History and Class Consciousness* (Cambridge, MA: MIT Press, 1971), 205.

41. The reading I privilege here places emphasis on the logical structure of Hegel's metaphysics and its relation to the critical forms of cognition that Lukács takes as crucial for exploding the deficient forms of social life under capitalism. The idea here is that thought and being, for Hegel, are unified in the Absolute Idea or, as Stephen Houlgate has argued, "[f]or the metaphysician Hegel, on the other hand, thought is not primarily the conceiving of possible objectivity but is above all the direct awareness of immediate being—the intuitive understanding that there is being and of what being is. The forms of being set out in the *Logic* are thus not just forms of possible becoming, but forms that actually inhere in being itself." *The Opening of Hegel's Logic* (West Lafeyette, IN: Purdue University Press, 2006), 128. Also see the important discussion by André Doz, *La logique de Hegel et les problèmes traditionelles de l'ontologie* (Paris: A. Vrin, 1987).

42. For an interesting discussion on this theme, see David A. Borman, "Labour, Exchange and Recognition: Marx Contra Honneth," *Philosophy and Social Criticism* 35, no. 8 (2009): 935–59. For an interesting discussion of the theme of human interdependence as an objective feature of human nature in Marx's early writings, see Michael Quante, "Das gegenständliche Gattungswesen. Bemerkungen zum intrinsischen Wert menschlicher Dependenz," in Rahel Jaeggi and Daniel Loick (eds.), *Nach Marx. Philosophie, Kritik, Praxis* (Frankfurt: Suhrkamp, 2013), 69–86.

43. Mutual recognition cannot serve as the central feature of the *Philosophy of Right* since Hegel sees that the universal, or the rational common interest, ought to be at the forefront of a rational, modern, ethical state and a politics that buttresses modern social freedom. For a critique of Honneth's reading of the *Philosophy of Right* from this perspective, see Karin de Boer, "Beyond Recognition? Critical Reflections on Honneth's Reading of Hegel's *Philosophy of Right*," *International Journal of Philosophical Studies* 21, no. 4 (2013): 534–58.

44. As Robert R. Williams argues, "Recognition is the phenomenological framework (*Zusammenhang*) for the concept of freedom, within which and through which the concept of freedom is realized. Recognition is the existential-intersubjective actualization of the concept (*Begriff*) of freedom, that is, its phenomenological dimension." *Hegel's Ethics of Recognition* (Berkeley, CA: University of California Press, 1997), 262.

45. In this sense, we should say that the institutions of modern capitalism effectively distort the capacity of subjects to perceive this universality of human sociality and interdependence. It does this by corrupting the social relations that ought to lead to the recognition of this concept, something *ontologically prior to consciousness*.

See my exploration of this thesis in "Capitalism as Deficient Modernity: Hegel against the Modern Economy," in Andrew Buchwalter (ed.), *Hegel and Capitalism* (Albany, NY: SUNY Press, 2015), 117–32.

46. For a non-Hegelian, but nevertheless important, account of the dimensions of social ontology, see David Weissman, *A Social Ontology* (New Haven, CT: Yale University Press, 2000), 147ff., as well as chapter 7.

47. Robert Williams makes mention of this interpretation, but he does not develop it to any significant degree. See *Hegel's Ethics of Recognition*, 262ff.

48. As Robert Williams correctly points out, "Hegel believes that just as individuals have a right to be recognized by others and by the state, so also they owe the state a duty of recognition in return. The ethical state has a right of recognition as well. Failure to recognize the state is a violation of and a refusal to participate in the universal *Anerkanntsein* constitutive of the state." *Hegel's Ethics of Recognition*, 271.

49. G. W. F. Hegel, *Lectures on Natural Right and Political Science* (Berkeley, CA: University of California Press, 1995), §121.

50. This view runs counter to that put forth by recent interpretations of Hegel, in particular by Robert Pippin's view of Hegel's ethical thought as providing the context for rational agency or autonomy. For Pippin, "[t]his state is defined as a rational self- and other-relation, and thereby, because rational of universal, counts as being free, the product of reason and not a matter of being pushed and pulled by contingent desires or external pressure, or of merely strategically responding to such pushes and pulls." *Hegel's Practical Philosophy: Rational Agency as Ethical Life* (New York: Cambridge University Press, 2008), 187. However, this interpretation robs Hegel of his deeper power since he is also putting forth an argument about the rational structure of human sociality and the kind of interdependence that sustains and supports a free individuality. What is needed for a true form of critical consciousness is the ability to grasp the social ontology that underlies the pathological forms of life that the subject may encounter and deploy this against it. Perhaps even more, the point I am making here is that this needs to be cognizant in the minds of rational agents.

51. Hegel, *Lectures on Natural Right and Political Science*, §124.

Part II

RECONSTRUCTING THE LOGIC OF CRITICAL SOCIAL THEORY

Chapter 4

Structure and Consciousness

Reconsidering the Base-Superstructure Hypothesis

I. INTRODUCTION

As I have been suggesting thus far, a central development of contemporary
critical theory has been the thesis that theories of social action—of communication, intersubjective recognition, forms of justification, and so on—are to
be given primacy over the influence of the structures and functions of social
institutions and their grounding in the economic structure of society. According to this view, the original project of critical theory was mistaken in that it
placed too much emphasis on the dynamics of social structure and its ability
to inhibit individual autonomy.

But these attempts to offer an emancipatory form of praxis fall into a
deep and dangerous form of abstraction in that they eschew the concrete
mechanisms of political power and the kinds of logics necessary to contest
the power of capital politically. My aim now is to try to address this problem
by showing the relevance of the base-superstructure hypothesis for critical
theory and to argue that it should be seen as residing at the core of a critical
theory of society. Although this may seem to conjure visions of orthodox
Marxism, my claim here is that Marx's critique of capital must be seen as
not only a means of organizing material, productive life but also the norms
and forms of thought that produce capital as a social fact. This thesis, therefore, will have implications on the ways that cognition and mental states are
shaped, something that was at the root of Marx's hypothesis.

My basic thesis is that critical theory must retain a base in Marxian
theory for it to sustain its essentially critical character and that the "base-
superstructure" hypothesis that Marx puts forth in his preface to the *Critique
of Political Economy* is a central model of understanding how material forms

of social power are able to shape the cognitive and symbolic domains of thought and action. Marx's basic premise was that the forces of economic power necessitate certain social, political, legal, cultural, and mental forms of life. The relation is rightly seen as *determinist*, but wrongly seen as *mechanistic*. As I will argue here, it should also be seen as the core of critical theory since the project of the critique of consciousness, of *Ideologiekritik*, was always the main concern of critical theory whose radical character has always consisted of its ability to explode false forms of consciousness, to identify the expansive ways that the imperatives of modern, capitalist economic systems can transform consciousness in order to reinforce the extractive imperatives of society through the expansion of the commodity form, the embedding of instrumental rationality, and the domestication of radical critique of these things as systems of power, domination, and control. However, traditional critical theory was unable to meet these challenges politically because, at least under the impulse of the later work of Adorno and Horkheimer, a move was made that placed renewed emphasis on subjectivity as a realm of contesting reification in terms of a "negative dialectic," the cynical indictment of Enlightenment rationality, a turn to aesthetics as a domain of resistance, not to mention its lack of any kind of political theory.

In my view, critical theory can be relevant once again only by regrounding its link with Marx by seeing the central ways in which capital—itself a specific mode of organizing the ensemble of social relations—is also able to determine consciousness in such a way that we can diagnose the irrational forms of social and political consciousness that in fact allow for the persistence of a hierarchically organized social order of extractive social relations. This conception of determination is not meant to invoke metaphors of mechanistic causality. Rather, my task here will be to show how Marx's basic idea of the causal model of social structure and consciousness can be grasped through modern theories of values and of forms of collective intentionality. In essence, since material forms of production and consumption in modern societies require the proliferation of specific institutional imperatives and values to allow for the legitimacy and internal efficiency of the system, the social epistemology of subjects will be shaped by these dominant constitutive rules and value-systems that come to make up the logic of these institutions. Marx's hypothesis about the relation between base and superstructure lies, for me at least, at the heart of the attempt to understand how economic forms of power can pervade and shape noneconomic forms of life and cognition.

I argue that a reconstruction of the base-superstructure hypothesis can be effected along the two basic lines of argument. According to the first, there is an essential *primacy of functional forces of social organization to those of consciousness* in the sense that social facts are able to impress and shape cognitive frames of thought. My idea about what "functional forces" actually entails, however, is meant to convey the ways that social institutions and their rule-governed nature are able to affect social cognition and the ways that the kinds of collective intentionality involved are able to create social reality. The key to this approach is to fuse aspects of a constructivist social ontology that theorizes the ways that social facts are articulated through collective forms of thinking and acting along with the value-orientations and systems of normative meaning that bind together institutional orders and how these spheres of social life are rooted in logics of capital and economic organization. The material organization of the social world operates according to certain logics of power in which institutions are hierarchically organized based on the capacity of economic life to force some degree of harmonization with its own logics. Second, the social-theoretic argument deals with the problem of the *constitution of subjectivity*. This "constitution problem" occurs along two lines as well: (1) through the constitution of certain forms of cognitive capacities that individuals possess and use in the operation of their consciousness, and (2) through the shaping of moral-evaluative forms of reasoning and value-orientations that affect the nature of how individuals act in the social context of norms and obligations. This constitution problem, as I see it, is distinct from many recent approaches that emphasize social practices but lack a theory or model of *how consciousness is shaped by social forces and how those forms of consciousness legitimate practices and institutions.* This will form the basis of the model I provide explaining the constitution of subjectivity by showing how value-orientations and intentional mental states are shaped by social-structural forces.

In this way, therefore, my reconstruction of the base-superstructure hypothesis shows how the imperatives and logics of capitalist institutions are able to shape institutions, culture, and the subjective lifeworld of individuals. But it does this in a way that dispenses with a merely phenomenological approach and instead embraces mechanisms of collective intentionality and social cognition. This process is not mechanistic, even though it is deterministic. It is deterministic in the sense that the power to shape consciousness comes from specific and identifiable institutional logics. It is also nonmechanistic in the sense that it is not structured in such a way that the causality of the model is total, but rather *functional*. More precisely, I advance the thesis that capitalist forms of rational-economic life shape and condition (i.e., determine) the *mental states* of individuals as well as the broader personality complex. It does so imperfectly, however, not totally. But my proposition is that it is effective enough to constrain the critical capacity of subjects and, to go further, corrupt significantly their capacity to cultivate and obtain an active critical consciousness through the means of communicative action, recognition, or other forms of intersubjective praxis. In this sense, the Marxian premise of an economic base that has functional primacy to forms of consciousness can be defended and the premises of communicative and discursive forms of social action can be seen to be defective in the face of capitalist forms of social organization and institutionalization. I submit that the base-superstructure model stands at the center of any genuine form of critical theory because of its ability to deal with the constitution of consciousness and subjectivity and hence with the central connection between the nature of sociohistorical formations and the shaping of subjectivity. This means opening up once again the problems of alienation, false consciousness, and reification as challenges to pragmatist-inspired theories of action and epistemology. I end by considering the ways in which current trends in critical theory can be reworked to reintegrate the constitution problem and its relevance for contemporary social and political philosophy.

II. THE CRITIQUE OF BASE-SUPERSTRUCTURE IN NEO-IDEALIST CRITICAL THEORY

The reconstruction of the base-superstructure model that I advance here is meant to further a reconstruction of critical theory along Marxian lines. This means reconnecting theories of mind and consciousness to forms of economic power and to mitigate against a domesticated form of critical theory that places emphasis on subjective and intersubjective forms of agency at the expense of structural and economic sources of social power and their respective capacities to shape, determine, and distort the consciousness of subjects. This domesticated critical theory has ushered in a kind of neo-Idealism, turning its back on the radical insight of Marx that "social being determines consciousness." In many ways, this begins with Jürgen Habermas's thesis that emphatic weight needs to be shifted *away from* the systemic and structural-functional institutional processes of modernity toward the intersubjective and discursive forms of action that comprise the essence of solidaristic forms of socialization and democratic ego and will formation. This intersubjective and linguistic turn in critical theory has culminated in a vision of critique that undervalues the persistent and consistently pathological ways that the economic organization of society (especially under capitalism) is able to pervert the powers of subjective and intersubjective reason and socialization from achieving critical power against oligarchically structured forms of social power.

Habermas made the first move against the Marxian foundation of critical theory when he attacked the base-superstructure model for its reliance on a conception of rationality that placed too much emphasis on the technical-rational mode of rationality at the expense of communicative rationality. Since Marxist theorists conceived of economic relations of production as characterized by forms of technical and strategic rationality, "The dialectic of productive forces and productive relations has often been understood in a *technicist* (*technizistischen*) sense. The theorem then argues that techniques of production necessitate not only certain forms of organizing and mobilizing labor power, but also, through the social organization of labor, the relations of production appropriate to it."[1] On this view, the relations of economic life are characterized by modes of rationality that do not exhaust the types of action and interaction characteristic of the species. He sees communicative action as distinct from the technical-rational modes of thought and action that Marxian theories took as basic: "However, we must separate the level of communicative action from the instrumental and strategic action combined in social cooperation."[2] This results in the thesis that "the species learns not only in the dimension of technically useful knowledge decisive for the development of productive forces, but also in the dimension of moral-practical consciousness decisive for structures of interaction. The rules of communicative action do develop in reaction to changes in the domain of instrumental and strategic action, but they follow *their own logic.*"[3]

My proposition here is that this move by Habermas was made without properly theorizing the power of the base-superstructure model. Rather than reducing the economic sphere to technical and strategic action alone, it is crucial to see that a connection exists between the ways that economic logics shapes those institutions that in turn socialize members of society. Capitalism therefore is concerned not only with the aims of production but also with the ability to harness as many institutions as possible to its logic in order to secure increased growth, consumption, legitimacy, and social stability. The communicative competence, the cognitive power of subjects, is dialectically related to these forms of socialization anchored in institutions that are increasingly aligned with economic logics. We cannot escape the materialist thesis through a model of intersubjectivity and socialization that is *external* to the processes of dominant economic forces, mainly because Marx's basic idea is that we continually reconstitute the social reality through our beliefs and practices without being aware that these beliefs and practices are the very cause, the very foundation constituting the social totality. My counterclaim to Habermas therefore concerns the mechanisms that facilitate the creation of value-orientations within subjects that are shaped by those economic logics as well as that shape their cognitive and mental powers.

The crucial weakness of neo-Idealist expressions of critical theory lies in their assumption that the logics of capitalism are somehow contained within an economic sphere separable both analytically and empirically from the other domains of society (something that perhaps could have been deduced given the state of capitalist development in the late 1960s and 1970s—that is, before the neoliberal transformation of capitalism), particularly the cognitive processes and powers that are developed through discursive or recognitive forms of intersubjectivity. However, I submit that this thesis is not tenable— that, despite its philosophical appeal, it fails to take into consideration the ways that capitalist forms of social integration shape consciousness in such a way that solidaristic forms of social action and social consciousness become increasingly scarce and, when it does in fact occur, it is decreasingly radical and threatening to the nature of the contemporary social order. More crucially, I think that it is more likely to argue that the very mental states, cognitive patterns, and attitudinal structures of modern subjects are deeply formed by institutional logics within everyday life that are harnessed to capital and the rhythms of economic rationality. My central aim in what follows is to resurrect the Marxian hypothesis of the base-superstructure model of society in order (*a*) to show how critical theory is rooted in its basic premises, and (*b*) to show that the intersubjective, discursive, and recognitive theories that dominate neo-Idealist critical theory fail in their attempt to formulate an immanent critique of domination in modern societies.

III. CRITICAL THEORY AND BASE-SUPERSTRUCTURE: A BASIC AXIOM

The limitations of the classical Marxist model of base-superstructure is plagued by an inability—despite its intrinsically dialectical character—to account for the mechanisms that shape subjectivity and the ways that this leads to the quiescence of political movements and the distortion of rational, critical consciousness more generally. Critical theory's basic project was, from the beginning, to explore the categories of the superstructure; to seek to tease out the ways by which capitalism creates subjects compliant to the interests and imperatives of capital—in short, to legitimate an oligarchically structured community that could sustain a highly technical, highly consumptive phase of capitalism. It was, from the beginning, a reaction to the mechanistic form of consciousness and praxis that characterized orthodox and classical Marxism. What unites Gramsci, Korsch, and Lukács in this sense is that all were seeking to theorize a new means by which to confront and explode the cultural and cognitive clenches that deflected critical consciousness and nullify critical activity and emancipatory forms of social praxis. This means explaining the pathologies of modern life in terms of the ways that the economic imperatives of the capitalist are able to distort the subjective (i.e., cognitive, moral, aesthetic, psychological, etc.) attributes of modern personalities. The dehumanization of modern man is seen as a symptom of the permeation of commodification, reification, exchange value, *et cetera*, into deeper domains of cultural and personal life. In what follows, I will therefore seek to outline the basis for a nonmechanistic understanding of the base-superstructure hypothesis, one that I will call an organic-functionalist model of base-superstructure. According to this model, social values and mental states are shaped by economic logics capable of shaping norms and institutional patterns of thinking that become the basis for social facts. Providing this alternative interpretation of the base-superstructure hypothesis, I will then show how it is relevant as a basis for any critical theory of society.

1. Axiom: Social Being and the Determinants of Mental Life

We should begin with an analysis of Marx's basic hypothesis. According to him, "The totality of [the] relations of production forms (*bildet*) the economic structure of society, the real basis (*reale Basis*), on which rises (*erhebt*) a legal and political superstructure (*Überbau*) and to which correspond (*entsprechen*) definite (*bestimmte*) forms of social consciousness. The mode of production of material life conditions (*bedingt*) the social, political, and cultural life process (*geistigen Lebensprozeß*) in general. It is not the consciousness of men that determines (*bestimmt*) their existence, but their social being that determines (*bestimmt*) their consciousness."[4] It is important to analyze this passage with some precision. First, Marx's use of the words *determine, constitute*, and *condition* are important since they are the words he uses to describe the causal nature of the mechanisms that constitute the base-superstructure model. First, the distinction between *bestimmen* and *bedingen* is an important one. The verb *bestimmen* indicates a more definitive, stronger sense of determination or causation, whereas *bedingen*, rendered here as "condition," is one that sets the necessary preconditions for an event to take place. Rather than one event causing another to occur unidirectionally and directly, *bedingen* implies that one structure will come to correspond with another, that the kind of causation is softer, more pliable, less acute than a billiard ball type of causality.

For Marx, saying that something "determines" something else does not imply a mechanistic form of causation. Rather, Marx means by "determine" (embedded in the use of both *bedingen* and *bestimmen*) the act of placing limits on something, by "blocking or selecting out all such phenomena that do not comply with it."[5] *Determinare*, in Latin, is the verb that means "to confine within limits," or "to set bounds to," or "to delimit boundaries." This semantic dimension to the term is important, since it means that the act of determining, for Marx, means controlling the fundamental, rule-governed structure of any process or structure. When applied to the life processes of individuals, the economic structure, the "real basis," for the community sets up the preconditions, the rules of the game, so to speak, that regulate, shape, and therefore determine those life processes. In this sense, the act of *determining* any thing

is the result of the kinds of patterned forms of life and action that any structure (in Marx's case, the economic structure) can impose on agents. But the
key here is that these structures and institutions are themselves constituted by
human beings and their respective beliefs and practices. The key aim of social
criticism, therefore, must seek to make conscious what the purposes and ends
of the social structures and institutions in which we participate actually are.[6]

The result is a dialectic between structure and agency in which subjects
come to take on the patterned forms of structured life into which they are
socialized and that pervade their lives. The determinative relationship of
base and superstructure is therefore the result not of the classical or orthodox
causal model, one influenced by positivist conceptions of scientific reasoning, but rather the result of a structural-functional adaptation of subjects to
social structures. This means that the base-superstructure model is *historical*
in nature in that it is a diachronic process of adapting institutional forms, as
well as forms of consciousness, practices, culture, and so on, to the imperatives of the valorization of capital. But this thesis relies on a prior one that
articulates the nature of the determinative relationship between different
kinds of structures. The first iteration of the axiom of base and superstructure
can be stated as follows:

A_I: *Structure A determines structure B if structure A is able to place limits on*
the functions (rules, norms, laws, etc.) that govern structure B.

These structures can be social in nature—as in formal institutions such as
schools, firms, and so on, or it can refer to informal institutions such as social
relations, or to "structures" of consciousness, or the personality. Nevertheless, what is necessary is that one structure or set of constitutive rules is able
to set limits on some other set of rules or norms. This means that, as a first
approximation, structures can be hierarchically related to each other to the
extent that one is able to limit the attributes of another or a plurality of others.
In Marx's basic formulation, the basic organizing institution or structure is
capital. Capital is, as Marx reminds us, not a thing, but a "social process," a
"relation among men," and, in the *Manifesto*, a concrete "social power" (*eine
Gesellschaftliche Macht*). But capital is also a conglomeration of practices,
attitudes, and patterns of thinking that are rule oriented, imposing constraints
and requiring the collective acceptance of others for its existence. Capital
achieves its actual reality in the world through the specific set of rules, norms,
practices, and attitudes that constitute it. One does not see, taste, or feel capital
as such: it is a social fact—objective with material needs and consequences
to be sure, on the environment, on people, on communities—but nevertheless
a social, not a natural, fact. As such, the assemblage of rules, practices, and
attitudes that is capital possesses the capacity to shape other, noneconomic

institutions and their respective rules, practices, attitudes, and so on. The basic form of the base-superstructure hypothesis therefore lay in *the ability of capital to order the dynamic processes of those institutions it requires for its maintenance and/or expansion even as it extinguishes others based on their vestigiality with respect to the imperatives of capital.* In terms of capitalist society, this axiom can be filled out to give us a more concrete one:

A_2: *The logic of capital determines the structure and function of social institutions that rely on sets of constitutive rules and values for their successful operation.*

These two formulations have much in common, but they also differ in certain senses. A_1 maintains that there exists a relation of structural dominance of a specific set of rules over another specific set of rules. This means that *determination* denotes a form of power in which one structure of rules is capable of rewriting or restructuring the rules or scripts of another structure or institution. Constitutive rules are those rules of thinking and acting that assign different forms of meaning to things, thereby producing social facts. A constitutive rule effectively creates the very meaning that I and others in a community share in common. Since all social structures constrain only to the extent that enough people internalize their respective schemas, we derive A_2, which begins to bring us into the sphere of the superstructure—that is, to the reality of the noneconomic forms of social life. According to this iteration of the thesis, one kind of economic structure begins to impose constraints on other structures (institutions), which are themselves defined as sets of cognitive rules, attitudes, practices, and values that need to be internalized by agents.[7] But in this sense, we are forced to move from an abstraction of a dominance of one set of rules over another, and into the realm of social being and consciousness, respectively. We should perhaps break this axiom down into its core constituent parts:

A_3: *Constitutive rules and values determine the basis of how subjects legitimate their social world and the institutions that constitute it.*

This postulates a distinct, causal relation between the structure of rules and norms that govern two spheres of social institutions: capital as a social relationship and those social institutions that are external to the sphere of economic relations. The key here is to note that in A_1 we defined the fundamental base-superstructure relation as residing in the capacity of one structure to place limits on the rules that govern another structure. But, in addition to this, we see that institutional norms possess a socializing function on agents, thereby granting them a determining character on the personality system of subjects. This process of subject-formation, of *subjectivation*, occurs as a result of the ability of institutions to place limits on the content of norms to which individuals come to assent as well as the cognitive and epistemic structures of thought (i.e., the thought categories, or *Denkformen*) that come to constitute their reflective and rational capacities. Hence, the last axiomatic claim in this series of arguments is:

A_4: *The structures and patterns of subjective norms, mental states, and cognitive capacities are determined by routinized logics of social institutions.*

This suggests that the link between capitalist imperatives, the logics of social institutions, and subjective mental states, powers, and capacities come to be linked through a determining chain of causation in which economic forces shape institutions that in turn socialize or "subjectivize" agents. Therefore, we see that both A_3 and A_4, when combined, give us the basic axiom of the base-superstructure hypothesis:

A_5: *Economic logic shapes social relations and institutional logics that in turn socialize individuals according to the norms necessary for those logics and economic goals to succeed and operate efficiently.*

It is clear that much remains to be filled in here. First, the important feature of this axiom is that it is functionalist in nature: it presupposes that the efficacy of the economic imperatives is premised on their ability to root themselves in noneconomic institutional logics (or the values of work, of consumption, of cultural taste, and so on). Second, there is also the assumption that we understand that what is meant specifically by the terms *logics*, *patterns*, and *structures* is essentially the norm- and rule-governed attributes of social life and the ways these are altered in accordance with the interests of the economic structure of the community. There is a reason why, for Marx, capitalism was a unique, total institution, since it was the first that was able to colonize almost every noneconomic institution in modern societies.

This seems to lead us to a unidirectional causal model where economic imperatives impress themselves on the other institutions of the community.[8] However, the expansion of the field of explanation beyond the sphere of politics is crucial since at its root, we are dealing with the problem of norms and values that come to organize the social and individual forms of consent and legitimation that is required for modern forms of authority to congeal.[9] As a first approximation for a general model of base and superstructure, we can begin by delineating it not as a dichotomous relation between economic forces and noneconomic institutions and structures, but rather as a *tripartite* one that shows a cascading chain of determinative causation between the various layers of economic relations and imperatives, institutional norms and logics, and the processes of individuation, self-formation, and cognition that occurs at the level of the individual.

Key to this model, as suggested by A_1, is that the determining character between each different level of social reality occurs within the realm of the normative structures of each sphere. In this sense, we are dealing with a functional form of causation in which each level of societal functioning is able to impress its imperatives onto subsequent normative orientations. But the problem with this becomes apparent when we think about the lack of subtlety that characterizes the model.[10] For one thing, it presupposes a form of causation that is too simplistic and mechanistic. The premise that economic logics of capital form and shape subsequent forms of consciousness through institutions is not in itself problematic, it is that the means by which this happens is simply lacking. But this model ends with the formed subject rather than seeing the proper logic of causation as being one in which subjects are shaped by interpenetration between the value-systems of their personality and the institutional logics that dominate their socialization processes. Since productive forces and productive relations are internally related, we should be able to show that the different elements of the model are related internally, not simply causally as external elements impinging on others.[11]

What exactly is the connective tissue between the layers or part of the model? As I have been suggesting, the key to a model of base-superstructure that can serve as the basis of a critical theory of society needs to recognize the ontological status of values and value-orientations that come to be the very substance of modern institutions and subjective adherence to administrative norms. This itself structures the symbolic realms of language and other forms of communication as well as forms of signification and meaning formation for agents.[12] But before I consider this, I must show why functional arguments are essential to this thesis. Briefly stated, functionalist arguments in critical theory are those that are able to show how economic imperatives are able to shape noneconomic institutions that then come to shape forms of consciousness and subjectivity necessary for those economic imperatives to achieve success.

2. A Functionalist Theory of the Dominance of Base over Superstructure

According to the understanding of functional argumentation, we need to focus on the *ontological status of values* as the means by which social institutions as well as cognitive functions are held together as complexes.

The reason for this is that values or value-orientations are, to take up a definition from Parsons, "the commitments of individual persons to pursue and support certain *directions* or types of action for the collectivity as a system and hence derivatively for their own roles in the collectivity."[13] To say this means that "they are directions of action rather than specific objectives,"[14] and that these directions are the very things that form the connective element between the objective world of institutions and the subjective domain of mental states. The functionalist element of explanation here is not, as G. A. Cohen proposes, reducible to an analytic statement regarding the nature of causation where "the occurrence of the *explanandum* event (possession of the *explanandum* property, etc.) is functional for something or other, whatever 'functional' turns out to mean. Thus consequence explanations which are functional explanations may be conveyed by statements like 'The function of x is to φ,' whatever may be the correct analysis of the latter."[15] But this seems too rigid when we look back to Marx's text, particularly because Marx seems unable to commit himself to the view that there are such discrete forms of meaning in explanation, that it is more dialectical in nature, and that the social processes of life are far more subtle and nonreducible to an analytic formulation. Rather, it seems to me that Marx's thesis can be better understood as suggesting that determination and causation be seen in the light of the dominance of certain functions over others. The purpose of this, of course, is that the imperative be efficiently carried out, that the goal set by subsystem A can be achieved (only or perhaps more efficiently) through the cooperation or manipulation of subsystems $B, C, D \ldots n$.[16] In this way, the base-superstructure model is able to provide us with a working model for a critique of modern society.

The premise that I am working with here is that functional statements in social criticism are those that are able to identify the ways that institutions are capable of (1) *patterning value systems* and (2) successfully *routinizing* those value systems, in order (3) to adapt forms of institutional action and *subjective agency* to those very value-patterns and orientations.[17] Therefore, we cannot simply state that economic imperative p obtains goal x. Rather, we need to show that for goal x to be obtained, p must adapt function φ (or any set or complex of functions, $\{\varphi_1, \varphi_2, \varphi_3 \ldots \varphi_n\}$) to secure goal x. Each of the functions in question are the properties of a social institution, I. So, in this sense, base acts upon superstructure in order to reorient the purposes of institutions toward economic goals; these institutions must change their internal logics in order to perform new functions to achieve that economic imperative (or to act under its limitations), and these logics must be accompanied by new value-patterns and value-orientations that individuals must come to adopt if they are to be successful within the new institutional environment structured by p.

In this sense, any intended economic imperative, p, that seeks goal x_1 will need to adapt institution, I, away from achieving its own goal, x_2, and toward the goal of p. Since t_1 is inefficient for the purposes of p, there exists a need to change the orientation of the goals and purposes of I. The proliferation of this process over time leads to a series of institutions, I_1, I_2, and so on, to be oriented toward the goals of the economic imperative. If we recall that each institution possesses a series of functions $\{\varphi_1, \varphi_2, \varphi_3 \ldots \varphi_n\}$, then we can also see that imperative p must also shape those functions if it is to be able to secure broader social goals. Hence, each sphere of society can be adapted to the goals of economic imperatives: schools away from education and toward training for the demands of the business community, artistic expression and taste toward the most profitable forms of entertainment, the ends of scientific research away from genuine human needs and toward marketable ends, and so on. Resistance to these imperatives therefore creates inefficiencies within the social system as a whole and, as the social system is increasingly colonized by the imperatives and goals of economic calculus and interests, the various social functions of social institutions—formal and informal—come under the dominance of that calculus as well.

Hence, for economic goals to be secured, the functions and logics of institutions must be reoriented toward the goal in question. In other words, for capital to be able to achieve any given goal requires that the functions of all necessary subsystems within society be adapted to the logic of capital.[18] But recall that the essence of the model for Marx is a relation between the economic, social-institutional, and mental/psychological states of subjects and that the character of the relation between economic structure and social institutions is one of "conditioning" or "shaping." In this sense, the real question is not simply the ways that any given event can come about or be explained, *it concerns the specific ways in which social systems are able to adapt its constituent parts according to different imperatives from within the system.* By an imperative I mean the force that a specific component of society is able to exert on other subsystems within the society as a whole in order to adapt them to its own functions and logics. Hence, different periods in history have seen the relative strength of religion, of the state, and so on. But modern capitalist societies are characterized by the dominance of economic rationality and the interests of production-consumption for the ends of profit (i.e., the circulation of capital). It is obvious that the coordination of individual actions to secure specific outcomes is a prerequisite for the success of the expansion of capitalism. The rationalization of the industrial order and political institutions of the state did in fact precede the colonization of cultural and personal spheres of life through the culture industry.[19] But the key to the story is the thesis that there exists a diachronic process of adaptation by the imperatives of capital absorbing the political, legal, institutional, cultural, and psychological subsystems of society.

The functional element in the argument is dependent on the question of whether a given social system is made to operate according to the imperatives of any single subsystem—that is, whether the functions of society as a whole become colonized by the functional logics and imperatives of capital. Indeed, as I have been suggesting, the base-superstructure model is one that gives us insight into the basic framework for a critical theory of society because the colonization of society by the logics of capital is dependent upon the capacity of rationalized social institutions to inculcate specific value-orientations within the subjective matrix of the personality system of individuals. Recall that, for Marx, the forms of social consciousness "correspond" (*entsprechen*) to the political and legal forms that arise out of the relations of production. Further recall that the means of production "shape" or set the conditions for (*bedingt*) the social, political, and cultural life-processes in general. This indicates that we are dealing with a kind of causation that is subtle, pliable, and complex. I propose that this thesis is best understood through a functionalist understanding of value-acquisition: the process whereby institutions are able to disseminate and inculcate specific value-patterns into the personality system of individuals. Lacking this, individuals would not grant legitimacy to social institutions, and the economic structure of the community would no longer be able to dominate the logics of noneconomic domains of life. The extent to which this kind of adaptation of subjectivity to economic relations is successful is the extent to which domination can be secured. It is from this basic thesis that much of the structure of critical theory is derived.

3. Functionalist Arguments and the Ontology of Values

Thus far I have suggested that the real essence of the model of base and superstructure is a functionalist logic in which the imperatives of one subsystem of society, the economy, come to dominate and to *determine* the functions, logics, imperatives, and goals of other noneconomic institutions within that society. The economic subsystem therefore comes to map its imperatives and goals on to those of society as a whole. Now, in order for this argument to defend against the charge that it is mechanistic, I will seek to show how this determinative dominance of the base over superstructure requires and includes the shaping of subjective mental states, forms of cognition, and other basic elements of the personality system. This is important because it has been left out of much of the discussion of how capitalist institutions constitute subjectivity. Overcoming the mechanistic nature of older Marxian theories of subject-constitution, Moishe Postone argues that Marx "seeks to establish the intrinsic connectedness of objectivity and subjectivity by means of a theory of their constitution though practice."[20] For Postone, the mediating element between objectivity and subjectivity—between base and superstructure—resides in the ways that practices are shaped: "Marx's theory of constitution through practice is social, but not in the sense that it is a theory of the constitution of a world of social objectivity by a human historical Subject. Rather, it is a theory of the ways in which humans constitute structures of social mediation which, in turn, constitute forms of social practice."[21] What this misses is that practices must also mediate consciousness, the very structures of thought and feeling that orient behavior. The legitimacy of social institutions and practices require a cognitive and evaluative layer for them to be stable and to be recreated. Postone stops at practice, but consciousness and the personality is the true seat of the source of legitimacy and the very essence of where the action is for the base-superstructure hypothesis. What is needed, therefore, is a theory of the mechanisms of consciousness and of cognition itself that can be susceptible to social forces and practices.

In order to expand the base-superstructure model into a theory about the nature of consciousness, it is important to consider how functional arguments and values play a central role. In order to make functional arguments more fitting to the actual working of social and psychological life, it is important to modify the *mechanistic* form of functional argumentation with a more *organic* mode of argument. To do this, I will insert the crucial concept of *value-orientations* as an element that fuses the structural and agentic attributes of the model. A *value-orientation* is a mental state that combines the cognitive, evaluative, and affective (or the rational, normative, and emotional) elements of the personality and that directs the beliefs and modes of evaluating and thinking about the world as well as one's place within it. Value-orientations collectively make up a *value-complex* or a system of beliefs that come to constitute a distinct belief system that is essentially a cognitive map of the world that the subject uses to orient his behavior within and conceptions about society.[22] Since individuals are socialized into society through the inculcation of value-orientations, it is important to show how individuals are dependent on these value-orientations to be able to participate in society without deviance, but also how institutions and coordinated social action also require that these value-orientations be subscribed to.[23] Both are derived from *values* that have ontological status as social facts since they are the products of social relations: the particular, legitimate mode in which any given social relation should be ordered and the ways that agents ought to behave within those roles. On this view, values possess an ontological status in a twofold sense: (1) to the extent that they are cultivated and rooted in the social relations that socialize the ego, and (2) that the values that ego comes to internalize are then used to endow social relations and roles with specific forms of authority and power.

In a certain sense, this is anticipated by Althusser and his account of ideology as the *interpellation of the subject*. For Althusser, the relation between base and superstructure is tied together by ideology: "It is not their real conditions of existence, their real world, that 'men' 'represent to themselves' in ideology, but above all it is their relation to those conditions of existence which is represented to them there."[24] This means that ideology functions to represent a false world to the individual, to mask the real conditions that pervade his world. But Althusser goes further to suggest that the essence of this process is one in which the individual is "transformed" into a subject (a process he calls "interpellation") and "which can be imagined along the lines of the most commonplace everyday police (or other) hailing: 'Hey, you there!'"[25] The thesis here is that the result of this hailing by the policeman would evoke within the subject the impetus to turn around, to respond to this hailing: "By this mere one-hundred-and-eighty-degree physical conversion, he becomes *subject*. Why? Because he has recognized that the hail was 'really' addressed to him, and that 'it was *really him* who was hailed' (and not someone else)."[26] Althusser is here proposing that ideology is something that totally subjectifies the individual to the extent that it becomes the total world of meaning that he inhabits.

However, his thesis lacks a precise mechanism.[27] Althusser proposes that ideology transforms the subject, but he also seems to suggest that it is in the very act of being formed into a subject that we are shaped by ideology. But what this actually means is not systematically worked out. I think Althusser is essentially correct in the sense that subject-formation is deeply shaped by the institutional imperatives of economic life, but that this process is not total. Rather, I will propose here that the process of subject-formation is one in which the mental states of individuals are routinized by rationalized institutions shaping forms of cognition that legitimate the social relations that pervade the world. I will therefore, in contrast to Althusser, look to the philosophy of mind to complement the base-superstructure thesis and to work out a more plausible, more precise theory of subject-formation.

What is needed, then, is an account of mental states and forms of consciousness that shows their relation to social-structural forms and functions. To do this, I will proceed by building a model of socialization that includes the ways that institutions serve as crucibles of socialization through the shaping of social relations and, more centrally, the mediation of values and value-orientations. As I pointed out above, value patterns are a central means for the determination of consciousness as well as social coordination since institutions are responsible for socializing subjects in accordance with them. If, as Parsons suggests, the "values of the society will define the main framework of attitudes toward the attainment of collective goals, the broad types of goals to which commitment is likely to be made, and the degree of 'activism' with reference to such goals,"[28] then we can see that the value-orientations of subjects can be a powerful mode of legitimation articulating stable forms of legitimate authority and domination. Values link the institutional domain and the subjective domain through socialization processes in which certain value-patterns and orientations are acquired through a process of internalization that requires an intricate reworking of the transformation of the norms and rules of institutional functions such as schools, the workplace, and so on.[29]

But in addition to Parsons's theory of value-acquisition, there is the second feature of values that I pointed to above, that once they are acquired by the subject, they can then be used to legitimate specific relations of social power. John Searle argues that an ontology of social power exists once we consider the existence of "status functions" and "constitutive rules." Both of these stem from the imposition of statuses and rules onto social relations and actors. A status function is when human agents "impose functions on objects, which, unlike sticks, levers, boxes and salt water, cannot perform the function solely in virtue of their physical structure, but only in virtue of a certain form of the collective acceptance of the objects as having a certain sort of status."[30] Hence, it is the result of *intentionality*, or the capacity to endow an object with specific meaning, functions, and statuses.[31] An intentional mental state is one that allows agents to give meaning and status to objects in the world, and we can extend Searle's basic account by fusing it to Parsons's thesis that the key to social life itself is the value-orientations that individuals possess as a result of socialization. In this sense, the intentional state of any subject is also the source of the forms of social power that exists in any society since such power relations are the product of subjects assigning value and power status to an object, person, role, or whatever. When this happens in a routinized way and is internalized, it becomes a *constitutive rule*: a rule that essentially creates the social reality one moves within. The socialization of norms and values shape not only our evaluative capacities but also the kinds of intentional expectations we have of others given that we are routinized into certain logics of behavior and action, certain forms of meaning that we come to attribute to the world and the way people in it should act, how we should act, and what kinds of behavior and beliefs we come to see as having authority in that world. The (intentional) mental state that I possess is dependent upon the institutional rule-set that governs the institutional context that I inhabit at any given moment. Now, each institution requires that the agent, and all agents who participate in that institution, be properly socialized into the values that govern that institution. Therefore, any mental state will be dependent on the subject *internalizing* the rules and norms of the institution, and also on the fact that others within the institution have internalized those rules and make them an element of their mental states, at least within that institution.

Searle's account of social ontology as *collective intentionality* and *constitutive rules* means that we possess the cognitive capacity to posit specific

functions and statuses to people, objects, and practices such that we collectively accept those statuses as "real" in an ontological sense. What this
means, for Searle, is that constitutive rules produce the very reality of social
facts. Hence, playing a game of poker requires that all those involved follow
certain rules of the game, assign different values to the physical cards played
with, and so on. The game of poker is this set of rules and the behavior of
rule-following that poker entails. Similarly, a rock is simply a physical object
unless we collectively assign it some other function in a given context, such
as when it is used to decorate a garden, or cement a series of them together to
create a wall, and so on. The social field is essentially, for Searle, the result
of collective forms of intentionality that *produce social facts*:

> Collective intentionality exists both in the form of cooperative behavior and
> in consciously shared attitudes such as shared desires, beliefs, and intentions.
> Whenever two or more agents share a belief, desire, intention or other inten-
> tional state, and wherever they are aware of so sharing, the agents in question
> have collective intentionality.[32]

Searle next proposes that this collective process of being able to share
thoughts and intentions means that we can collectively assign functions to
objects. Assignment of function means that we have the ability to "count
certain things as having a status that they do not have intrinsically, and then
to grant, with that status, a set of functions, which can only be performed in
virtue of the collective acceptance of the status and the corresponding function, that creates the very possibility of institutional facts."[33] It is when the
assignment of function becomes routinized and regularized by a group of
people that they become "constitutive rules," which "not only regulate, they
also create the very possibility of, or define, new forms of behavior."[34]

This implies that the capacity to shape and to arrange the various constitutive rules of any social group would entail a certain degree of power over that
group as a whole.[35] But even more, it can also be extended to show how social
relations themselves constitute particular social facts. The relation between
capitalist and worker, for instance, is one that not only has a material dimension of reality but also, more basically, requires that certain normative statuses
and intentional states be embedded in the community as a whole for those
distinctions to have any real social meaning in any realist sense.[36] Indeed, it
would not be a direct form of power—as, say, coercion or force—but it would
nevertheless constitute a distinct form of power over others. Here is where the
constructivist view on its own becomes problematic. Whereas Marx saw that
social power was rooted in the uneven control over resources and the kinds of
social logics to which that gives rise (i.e., the competitive search for surplus
value), he also saw—in instantiating his base-superstructure hypothesis—that
there was a basic relation between the economic forms of life or a society and

its mental, cultural, legal, and political forms of life. Although Marx gives us no concrete mechanism for this relation, I think that the *uneven control over natural and social resources (i.e., the material-economic base) entails an uneven power over the institutions of the community that in turn opens up the capacity to control and to shape the constitutive rules of that community.* Searle's account of constitutive rules suggests that they create forms of social reality; lacking this power, there is no way to maintain social power outside of coercion and force. It is therefore essential that we see domination as possessing both the material problem of uneven resource control and its link to shape institutional forms of life and constitutive rules. Social power, when successful, creates its own social reality in accordance with itself.[37] Social power now has an ontological character in that it consists in the capacity to not only control and deploy social and natural resources but also, and more important, *shape and constitute the nature of social reality itself.* This is the superstructural expression of material-economic power.

But even economic power cannot be seen as something nonsocial. The issue here is that power is the expression of specific kinds of norms and collectively accepted rules of thinking and acting that constitutes the social world. My relation to others is not simply a script, in this sense, but it is embedded in the very mental capacities, the very *intentional system* that any institutional or social context provides for me and in which I participate.[38] What this means is that an *ontology of values* can be derived from the ways that they provide an intentional system for social agents and the ways that these values are independent of my own subjective choice. A value obtains an ontological significance once it is a norm or rule that multiple individuals share and that also directs social action and behavior. Such a rule or norm is a value, however, only once it achieves a social significance for directing the consciousness of individuals as well. Values orient subjective behavior not according to the spontaneous desires and goals of the agent, but from norms and goals that shape their personality system and structures of cognition through the inculcation of value-orientations. In this sense, we can see that the cognitive and cathectic elements of the subject must come to be mapped on to the functional logics of the institutions in which any individual participates. To the extent that this is successful, then the subject has been successfully socialized. The success of institutions, as I argued above, therefore requires that such socialization is secured for large segments of the population, and, to this extent, if we see social institutions as increasingly determined by the logic of economic calculation and capital, we can see a relation between the logic of economic life, on the one hand, and the formation and shaping of institutional and subjective value-systems, on the other. Hence, we can begin to glimpse a functionalist model of the base-superstructure hypothesis that is still consistent with the basic axiom defined above.

Constitutive rules and collective intentionality—the very things that make up the mental production of social facts—are therefore shaped by specific institutional logics and also permeate the social field more generally. What results is a deeper, more pernicious kind of reification than the classical critical theorists had even imagined. The extent to which social institutions—which are themselves simply a series of rules that become embedded in the processes of cognition and intentionality—are able to routinize these constitutive rules and successfully imbue subjects with them is also the extent to which they become the very social reality for those agents. Marx's base-superstructure hypothesis therefore takes on a more powerful edge when reconstructed in these terms, and its capacity to shape the very subjects that recreate their own domination is describable in very real terms. Capital itself is a congealed grouping of such norms and collectively accepted values and rules of thinking and acting, for it grants certain individuals to establish private property laws, to create financial and banking systems, and to organize the community as a whole according to the ends of accumulation. Capital, in this sense, is a social fact, not a materially existing object; it is fundamentally social, even though it has material consequences.

The shaping of personalities that will accept the social order and the goals of that order is one that is produced by economic imperatives of the social system and that also comes to secure the goals of those imperatives. This seemingly circular logic is best seen as the product of how mental states are the product of value-systems that are themselves shaped and structured by the determinative forces of economic logics. This is the essence of the critical-functionalist proposition: social power congeals through the colonization of social-institutional functions and logics that then come to shape subjective and agentic mental states and forms of cognition and other features of the personality of individuals. As I have suggested above, this is itself achieved through the shaping of value-orientations as well as the kinds of learning and socialization processes that institutions provide. As the theory of intentionality demonstrates, social facts can be seen, at least in one basic sense, as the result of the constitutive rules that individuals project on to the world and in which they participate.[39]

Now, if we consider the base-superstructure model I have been proposing, it is crucial that it possess the feature of a nonunidirectional type of causation. In other words, the key characteristic of a functionalist understanding of the base-superstructure model is that it is reciprocal or *self-reinforcing*: the success of any system is the result of its capacity to colonize and harmonize the institutional and agentic structures that pervade the society. What I term here a *critical-functionalist* model of base and superstructure, summarized below in figure 4.1, is therefore meant to show how the values and constitutive rules that produce social reality for subjects are altered and modified by the logics

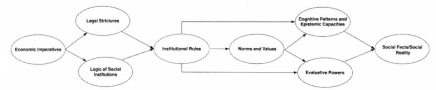

Figure 4.1   Functionalist Model of Base and Superstructure

of institutions influenced by the needs and pressures of the logic of capital. Hence we produce what Marx knew as a "social formation": a complex of economic imperatives and purposes that come to construct new norms, legal structures, forms of political authority, and cultural and personal values and ways of life and thought that come to characterize any given society. Lacking this, there is no way for it to be able to secure and to reproduce itself with any degree of efficiency.

IV. THREE FUNDAMENTAL THEOREMS OF BASE AND SUPERSTRUCTURE

I can now restate my central thesis: The logics of capitalist economic forms and imperatives, and their search for increasingly efficient forms of accumulation, map their logics onto noneconomic social institutions that, in turn, shape the value-patterns and intentional systems of meaning of subjects. Hence, the above discussion can be broken down into three separate theorems that cover the general model of base and superstructure in the sense that I am reconstructing it here. Central to this approach is the existence of value-orientations as the very social and psychological variable that glues together the structural realm of economic rules and imperatives, on the one hand, and the forms of consciousness and social action, on the other. I will elaborate each of them below so that we can see the overall structure of the mechanisms of the model, after which I will consider its relevance for renewing the tasks of a critical theory of society.

1. Theorem A: Structural Determinism and Institutional Isomorphism

The first, and necessary, theorem that derives from the base-superstructure model described above is that there exists a significant degree of *institutional isomorphism* that comes to proliferate over time in order for the capitalist imperatives to expand and to be secure from threats to its aims. As I showed above, isomorphic tendencies among social institutions occur because of the power that economic logics can exert on them over time or, in another sense, to the extent that certain social forms and institutional logics simply can no longer operate within a changed social-institutional environment. What is meant here is the ways in which different sectors and subsectors of society become increasingly adapted to the needs and logic of capital. Put more clearly, the functions of different institutions come to "correspond" to the functional imperatives of the economic system as it becomes the dominant mode of logic for other spheres of society.[40] This was what was meant by the basic axiom of the base-superstructure hypothesis formulated above—that the determination of one institution by another means that one has the ability to place limits on the logics and rules of the other. In this sense, the nature of technology, of the legal system, of the educational and cultural spheres, as well as aesthetic and religious domains, all come under the determining pressure of economic growth and the valorization of capital on pain of extinction. The isomorphic character of these institutions means that an increasingly unified system of rationalization comes to predominate late capitalist societies.[41]

This should not be taken to mean that there is no critique of these imperatives, no room for dissent. What it does mean is that such forces and counterpressures become less frequent, and less politically viable the more such a universalization of expansion-rationality takes hold. The force of the determinative logic of capital on other social institutions produces an isomorphism in which the logics of capital come to be mapped on to the logics of other institutional forms and, in the end, onto the personality system of the individual. As a result, capitalism as a system becomes not only more firmly rooted into the social system as a whole over time but also more reified in the consciousness of its subjects and is seen less and less as the source of social pathologies.

2. Theorem B: Routinization of Authority and the Persistence of Social Domination

The acceptance of the social order means that individuals—or at least a significant number of them—have come to see the collective goals of the society as a whole as valid and not in need of questioning or justification. Institutions are not simply congealed forms of practice and rules, they are processes whereby the subjectivity of subjects comes to be shaped by a particular set of values and goals that individuals come to not only recognize but also, at least in some nominal sense, adopt themselves. As I have suggested above, the connective tissue between the institutional forms and the subjective complex of the individual is the ontology of values and value-orientations that come to shape the intentionality of subjects. This means that if we take the theory of intentionality seriously, the very cognitive powers and mental states of individuals come to be redirected by the institutional patterns that socialize them. Since, as I argued above, there exists an ontology of values, the only way for a social action to exist in a social sense and as a social fact requires that the individuals involved in the act assign a legitimacy to that act and that they follow rules that are shared among them. These values of legitimacy and rules mean that they have internalized, to some basic degree, the norms of the institutions they inhabit. This can only occur, however, not by mere rational choice, but through a process of socialization that inculcates value-systems into the personality of the subject.

If any institution that sustains and/or is an expression of a hierarchically organized society is to maintain itself, it cannot efficiently do so with the threat of violence as its primary mode of power. Even though such institutions may at first be subject to the "double-movement" described by Karl Polanyi over time if such institutions are to last, it is only because they are able to *routinize* and *rationalize* their logics of the organization of power. And this routinization of power can only succeed to the extent that it can be internalized by the agents that make up and that will themselves sustain the institution.[42] This internalization takes place as a result of the routinization of the shared value-system that dominates the institution, setting its rules and norms, and rooting its logics into the psyche of individuals. The logic of any institution is essentially made up of the complex of norms that govern the forms of legitimate action and behavior that channel individual actions to coordinate group behavior. The subject's relation to institutions and their socialization by them is essentially the mapping of institutional logics on to the basic personality drives and values that comprises the subject.

As a result, *domination becomes a reality once an elite subgroup within the community is able to organize the logics of institutions to benefit them rather than the general interest of the community as a whole.* Domination becomes a secure form of power within any hierarchical social formation once the subjects socialized into that hierarchy *accept the logic and values of that social formation in some basic sense.* It is easy to see, then, that the early growth of industrial capitalism was able to spark more resistance to its imperatives since these were not yet internalized and legitimated by social actors. If the institutional isomorphism that I have described above can take place more quickly than the counterpressures and movements against it, then the base becomes unable to affect, or to determine, the superstructure; if, however, this is not the case, then the routinization, rationalization, and internalization of institutional logics and values come to predominate more and more of the socialization processes of society and culture. Recall that Weber's theory of modern, legal-rational forms of domination (*Herrschaft* or *Autorität*) maintains that domination is "the chance of commands being obeyed by a specifiable group of people." He also adds that the ruled makes "the content of the command the maxim of their conduct for its very own sake."[43] Taking both of these, the forms of hierarchical and extractive power that constitutes the essence of the capitalist system can be secured only by the internalization of domination into the consciousness of subjects. They come to see the authority relations that constitute their world as intrinsically valid.

3. Theorem C: The Reification of Consciousness and Defective Cognition

We can now see how the structure of consciousness is affected and shaped by the previous two theorems. If we see the causal path from the thesis of institutional isomorphism to that of the routinization of value-patterns, then this provides a strong socialization context for the structure of consciousness and the personality giving the phenomenon of reification a new and more deeply relevant role. Traditionally conceived as the infiltration of the commodity form into the realm of thought resulting in the translation of human phenomena into the rationalized categories of exchange value, reification should also be expanded to cover the problem of defective forms of cognition that arise from the processes associated with the universalization of capitalist logics described above. Indeed, for Lukács, the problem of reification was a problem of being confined to the realm of the "understanding" or of the kind of mental relation to the world that was unable to discern the actual, essential kinds of social relations and the ways they were perverted by capitalism forms of rationalization and exchange relations. Reification was the inability for the subject to grasp rationally and correctly the object of consciousness. The reification of consciousness is therefore a *cognitive and epistemic pathology*, not a pathology of recognition or whatever.[44] It refers centrally to the defective forms of rationality that constrains the critical capacity of the subject, thereby limiting, misdirecting, or even extinguishing any sense of practical activity or ethical reflection.

Reification of consciousness therefore needs to be seen as a cognitive pathology wherein the subject's power of cognition (of forming reasons about the world) and epistemic capacities (of the ability to receive information about the world) become aligned and see as valid the dominant value-patterns of the social world. The extent to which this occurs is a metric for the extent to which a social system is becoming rooted in the everyday life and consciousness of its members. But from the standpoint of reification, the key element is that these value-systems serve to distort the cognitive processes of the individual, rendering him unable to think through the world rationally or to simply apply the internalized value-patterns and value-orientations uncritically to the world. Reification, therefore, becomes a phenomenon in which the object of consciousness actually disappears from cognitive view.[45]

What results is a kind of defective form of cognition *characterized by an inability to grasp the totality within which different moments or aspects of reality relate*. This means, in our case, the inability to grasp the nature of capital as a social relation—but a social relation that shapes consciousness in such a way as to misperceive the ontological category of what it means to be human—that the true nature of human life is social, associational, and, as a result, capitalism constitutes a system of social life that is deficient, unjust, and not attuned to the true nature of human life. The determinate negation— as opposed to the negative dialectic, in this sense—would require the transformation of society based on the reorientation of the organization of social labor; a reorientation grounded in the social essence of human activity and the premise that all social production ought to be for common, not particular or private, ends. This is something that can only be learned and understood socially, not generated from within by the subject.

But the effects of reification go deeper than the inability cognitively to grasp the totality of social relations and the logic that dominates that system; it also is rooted in the contradictory nature of the base itself. Even though the routinization of domination and authority is generally effective for the majority of society's members, those that deviate from those legitimate authority relations can also be affected by an irrationalism of political consciousness. In an important sense, this results in forms of reaction to the system that ultimately results in an ineffectual form of extroversion that seeks to expiate the tensions that derive from the unsatisfied desires created by the system itself.[46] Since the economic system is riddled by contradictions and crisis, the irrationalist reacts to it through seeking to transcend it, rather than through immanent critique. Reification and defective cognition become the *telos* of the model, the place that enables the maintenance of the system as a whole to reproduce itself. Hence, these three theorems constitute what I am calling a functionalist model of base and superstructure. It remains now to see how this is relevant for critical theory and how contemporary forms of critical theory have strayed, to their detriment, from this basic theoretical doctrine.

V. THE LIMITS OF INTERSUBJECTIVE RATIONALITY

The problem of base and superstructure is therefore a problem of the particular sociological mechanisms by which the present oligarchic and hierarchical social order of modern capitalism is able to secure itself and to reproduce itself. The nullification of critical consciousness is real, and it should be taken seriously as a threat to the practical realization of discourse ethics and theories of "recognition" that are in vogue in critical theory. But at a deeper level, it is also a problem not only of subjective but also of intersubjective forms of consciousness. In this sense, we should turn our attention to the ways in which the current forms of critical theory that rest upon the linguistic, communicative, and recognitive theories of socialization and of moral consciousness are affected by what I am calling here the "perversion" of subjectivity.

Consider the foundational argument laid out by Habermas on the autonomy of communicative forms of action from other forms of social action: "The grammar of language games links symbols, actions, and expressions. It establishes schemata of world interpretation and interaction. Grammatical rules establish the ground of an open intersubjectivity among socialized individuals. And we can only tread this ground to the extent that we internalize these rules—as socialized participants and not as impartial observers. Reality is constituted in a framework that is the form of life of communicating groups and is organized through ordinary language."[47] But there are problems with this basic idea that Habermas lays out. For one thing, as I have suggested above, the power of language to constitute the world for any subject *is not prior to the powers of institutional forms to organize the context of meaning that shapes the intentional states that serve as the very content of thought and meaning.* Intentional states, in this sense, need to be seen as wired into the social-institutional contexts that socialize us and that come to shape subjective senses of meaning and action. Put another way, *linguistic meaning (as social practice and as a system of syntactic and semantic meaning) is not prior to the existence and force of social formations and the kinds of constitutive rules and value-systems that make them cohere.* Communication itself cannot be separated out from the kinds of moral-cognition and the normative categories that, in many instances, are embedded in the personality system of individuals. And this process of embedding normative categories is itself a strong product of institutions that, as I suggested above, are increasingly shaped by the determining power of capital. The thesis that language is some kind of separate sphere that can be used autonomously against the conformist effects that accompany the forms of socialization under capitalism is not tenable. The very powers of judgment that are required to demand justifications, articulate reasons, and so on, that can call into question the broader structure of injustice under capitalism are themselves shaped by the value-systems that secure the legitimacy of the system.

Base-superstructure is therefore a model that suggests that the mental states of individuals—which comprises the linguistic, conceptual, emotive, moral-cognitive, epistemic, intentional, and so on—are deeply affected by the socialization that occurs within a capitalist system. The isomorphism of institutional functions and logics come to permeate the collective intentionality of individual subjects and their consciousness. Hence, Habermas's theory about the nature of discourse ethics seems to fall into a neo-Idealist trap in which the structure and content of consciousness as well as the capacities of subjects is premised on a detached conception of the social from its economic foundations. Now, as I have been trying to demonstrate, this is not tenable given the thesis that the functional argument of the base-superstructure puts forth—namely, its ability to shape, to condition the consciousness of its members. This basic premise is something that grounds critical theory in alternate conceptions of human rationality, socialization, and of social practices as well. It means that we should view the problem of *perverted subjectivity*—or the condition that results from the inculcation of heteronomous value-patterns and systems—as a central critical concern in the analysis of political, social, and cultural phenomena.

NOTES

1. Jürgen Habermas, *Zur Rekonstruktion des Historischen Materialismus* (Frankfurt: Suhrkamp, 1976), 159.

2. Ibid., 160.

3. Ibid., 163.

4. Karl Marx, *Zur Kritik der Politischen Ökonomie*, in *Marx-Engels Werke*, vol. 13 (Berlin: Dietz Verlag, 1971), 8–9.

5. John McMurtry, *The Structure of Marx's World-View* (Princeton, NJ: Princeton University Press, 1978), 161.

6. Robert Meister insightfully argues on this aspect of Marx's thought that "when he speaks of a material reality that is transforming itself he generally recognizes that it is doing so through our actions and as a consequence of our beliefs, but not necessarily in accordance with them. To a significant extent the objective world of which he speaks is the one we objectify in the theories by which we interpret ourselves—a social world that includes the behavior of individuals who are actively and consciously interpreting that behavior in the process of engaging in it. Essentially, *The German Ideology* is about the relationship between one's beliefs and one's participation in the objective processes by which the world is transforming itself, whether one is aware of it or not." *Political Identity: Thinking through Marx* (Oxford: Basil Blackwell, 1990), 87.

7. Cf. the useful discussion by Sally Haslanger, "What Is (Social) Structural Explanation?" *Philosophical Studies* (forthcoming).

8. This was the idea initiated by Plekhanov and his five-part model of base and superstructure that was more concerned with the explanation of law and state and the ways that rights were articulated by economic forces. See his *Fundamental Problems of Marxism* (New York: International Publishers, 1992), as well as Steven B. Smith, "Considerations on Marx's Base and Superstructure," *Social Science Quarterly* 65, no. 4 (1984): 940–54.

9. Cf. Loic Wacquant, "Heuristic Models in Marxism," *Social Forces* 64, no. 1 (1985): 17–45.

10. Cf. Franz Jakubowski, *Ideology and Superstructure in Historical Materialism* (London: Allison and Busby, 1976).

11. See the discussion by Melvin Rader, *Marx's Interpretation of History* (New York: Oxford University Press, 1979).

12. See A. Bergesen, "The Rise of Semiotic Marxism," *Sociological Perspectives* 36, no. 1 (1993): 1–22.

13. Talcott Parsons, *Structure and Process in Modern Societies* (Glencoe, IL: Free Press, 1960), 172.

14. Ibid.

15. G. A. Cohen, *Karl Marx's Theory of History: A Defence* (Oxford: Oxford University Press, 1978), 263.

16. On this view, if there exists an imperative p of the economic subsystem for goal X, and Y the goal of another institutional subsystem I, and φ the function of that institution, the logic of this kind of process would be $p \to I \to \varphi \to X$, where the success of Y is necessary for the success of p. Hence, the expansion of consumption requires the reengineering of subjective desires and tastes; the maximization of relative surplus value is dependent upon the alteration of previous ideas about time, leisure, work, and so on. The imperatives of capital will constantly need to reformulate the functions of institutions in order for them to secure the promotion of its ends. Put another way, *it produces and cultivates those kinds of social functions and accompanying value-orientations that it requires for its own agglomeration.*

17. This thesis differs from those based on a game-theoretic model advocated by Daniel Little: "Economic structure rests on the notion of a social relation of production. A social relation is an objective relation among men and women that is embodied in the structure of society through some set of incentives and penalties." Daniel Little, *The Scientific Marx* (Minneapolis: University of Minnesota Press, 1986), 44–45. But this misses the way that value-orientations play a central role in human action and thought, particularly in the way that individuals come to grant legitimation to rational forms of authority and domination. Little's account seems too mechanistic, and lacks the kind of subtlety that critical theory requires to be an adequate theory of modern society.

18. Marx and Parsons seem to disagree on this point. For Parsons, the economy "is a functional subsystem of the society—not, as such, a 'structure,' which primarily articulates the institutional and collectivity levels of the organization of social action in this field." Parsons, *Structure and Process in Modern Societies*, 181. However, it seems to me that this can still be altered to show that the economy, as a functional subsystem of society, can come to dominate the other subsystems within society, thereby organizing them around its needs and interests.

19. For important historical and sociological accounts, see Martin J. Sklar, *The Corporate Reconstruction of American Capitalism, 1890–1916: The Market, the Law, and Politics* (Cambridge: Cambridge University Press, 1988); Stephen Skowronek, *Building a New American State: The Expansion of National Administrative Capacities, 1877–1920* (Cambridge: Cambridge University Press, 1982); and D. Carpenter, *The Forging of Bureaucratic Autonomy: Reputations, Networks, and Policy Innovation in Executive Agencies, 1862–1928* (Princeton, NJ: Princeton University Press, 2001).

20. Moishe Postone, *Time, Labor, and Social Domination: A Reinterpretation of Marx's Critical Theory* (New York: Cambridge University Press, 1993), 217.

21. Ibid., 218.

22. Maurice Godelier argues correctly, I think, on this point that "the mental part of a social relation consists, first of all, in the set of representations, principles and rules which must be 'acted upon' to engender that relation between the individuals and groups which constitute a society needed to make it into a concrete mode of organization of their social life." *The Mental and the Material: Thought, Economy and Society* (London: Verso, 1986), 169. The mental is therefore to be seen as the foundation for the various social formations in that it is the specific mental states that orient the behavior and action of individuals but also, as I will show, grant validity and legitimacy to the values and goals that underwrite those social formations themselves.

23. Lucien Sève argues that we should see the individual in what he terms a "juxta-structural" relation to the base and superstructure: "It is vital not to confuse the purely external connection of two structures which are independent in themselves, a connection which therefore tends towards an *equalizing reciprocity*, with what I call here a juxtastructural relation in which, although its support has an independent existence and source one of the structures is entirely subordinated to the other, their necessarily reciprocal functional determination then having the form of an *oriented circularity*: one of the structures is always the determinant structure in the last instance." *Man in Marxist Theory and the Psychology of Personality* (Sussex: Harvester Press, 1978), 144–45. In this sense, the personality system of the subject is "meshed into" the structural logics of social institutions, thereby becoming persistently subordinate to social roles, rules, functions, and so on.

24. Louis Althusser, *Lenin and Philosophy and Other Essays* (New York: Monthly Review Press, 1971), 164.

25. Ibid., 174.

26. Ibid.

27. Althusser proposes (correctly, I think) that the educational system has taken the function in modern times of conditioning the subject: "I believe that the ideological State apparatus which has been installed in the dominant position in mature capitalist social formations as a result of violent political and ideological class struggle against the old dominant ideological State apparatus, is the *educational ideological apparatus.*" Ibid., 152.

28. Parsons, *Structure and Process in Modern Societies*, 187.

29. Cf. Talcott Parsons, *The Social System* (Glencoe, IL: Free Press, 1951), 211ff. Also see the discussion in the next chapter of this volume.

30. John Searle, *Freedom and Neurobiology: Reflections on Free Will, Language, and Political Power* (New York: Columbia University Press, 2007), 87.

31. Elsewhere, Searle defines intentionality as "that property of many mental states and events by which they are directed at or about or of objects and states of affairs in the world." John Searle, *Intentionality: An Essay in the Philosophy of Mind* (New York: Cambridge University Press, 1983), 1. In this sense, intentionality covers a large field of subjective mental states. Theorists of intentionality have not explored the ways in which the social processes of institutional life come to shape the content of those intentional states, and it is this that I will sketch in brief here.

32. Searle, *Freedom and Neurobiology*, 85. Also cf. John Searle, *The Construction of Social Reality* (New York: Free Press, 1995), 15ff.

33. Searle, *Freedom and Neurobiology*, 89.

34. Ibid., 88. Cf. John Searle, *Making Sense of the Social World: The Structure of Human Civilization* (New York: Oxford University Press, 2010), 42ff.

35. See Raimo Tuomela, *Social Ontology: Collective Intentionality and Group Agents* (New York: Oxford University Press, 2013), 160ff. Tuomela's treatment of authority within group action lacks a critical edge, but he lays a basic foundation for authority's relation to collective intentionality.

36. Cf. the discussion by Sally Haslanger, *Resisting Reality: Social Construction and Social Critique* (New York: Oxford University Press, 2012), 183–218.

37. For a somewhat different, but interesting, view of social ontology from a critical perspective, see Titus Stahl, "Praxis und Totalität: Lukács' *Ontologie des gesellschaftlichen Seins* im Lichte aktueller sozialontologischer Debatten," *Jahrbuch der Internationalen Georg-Lukács-Gesellschaft* 14/15 (2015): 123–50.

38. Daniel Dennett argues on this point that "we approach each other as *intentional systems*, that is, as entities whose behavior can be predicated by the method of attributing beliefs, desires, and rational acumen." Daniel Dennett, *The Intentional Stance* (Cambridge, MA: MIT Press, 1987), 49. If we see the relations between individuals in this way, then it means that they are shaped and structured by the kinds of beliefs, desires, and so on that each attributes to the other within any social relation. Another way of saying this is that each individual predicates his relation with another by attributing certain beliefs about them that they also expect, in some basic sense, to be reciprocated back to them. Lacking this, there would be no stable means of sustaining social relations.

39. See John Searle, *The Construction of Social Reality* (New York: Free Press, 1995), 27ff.

40. I think this goes against the thesis put forth by Althusser and his followers that "overdetermination" is at work in the social and cultural sphere. According this thesis, "a social process *does not express* or *represent* any or all of its constituent aspects; rather, it is the *product of a complex process of transformation*, where the determinations emanating from each social process are acted upon and altered as they interact. Overdetermination is a concept that stresses a 'decentering' of discourse and history in its rejection of all forms of essentialism." Jack Amariglio, Stephen Resnick, and Richard Wolff, "Class, Power, and Culture," in C. Nelson and L. Grossberg (eds.), *Marxism and the Interpretation of Culture* (Urbana: University of Illinois Press, 1988), 488.

41. Paul DiMaggio and Woody Powell contend that institutional isomorphism occurs "as the result of processes that make organizations more similar without necessarily making them more efficient. Bureaucratization and other forms of homogenization emerge, we argue, out of the structuration of organizational fields. This process, in turn, is affected largely by the state and the professions, which have become the great rationalizers of the second half of the twentieth century." "The Iron Cage Revisited: Institutional Isomorphism and Collective Rationality in Organizational Fields," *American Sociological Review* 48, no. 2 (1983): 147–60. The emergence of

these "highly structured organizational fields" is the result not only of aggregations of individuals and their rational attempts to deal with uncertainty but also, it must be added, the need to secure compliance with the broader social and institutional goals of economic growth. Lacking this latter condition, there would be no sense of interest at stake in the structuring of institutional fields, and we would be left with a kind of Luhmannian "autopoietic" logic of institutional development.

42. Cf. Anthony Giddens, *The Constitution of Society: Outline of the Theory of Structuration* (Berkeley: University of California Press, 1986).

43. Max Weber, *Wirtschaft und Gesellschaft* (Tübingen: J. C. B. Mohr/Paul Siebeck, 1972 [1922]), 544.

44. This conception of reification has become popular since Axel Honneth's reconstruction of the concept along the lines of recognition. See his *Reification: A New Look at an Old Idea* (New York: Oxford University Press, 2008). Also see the discussion by Titus Stahl, "Verdinglichung als pathologie zweiter ordnung," *Deutsche Zeitschrift für Philosophie* 59, no. 5 (2011): 731–46, for this view with respect to false consciousness.

45. According to this interpretation, *Verdinglichung* is interpreted according to the terms of subjective Idealism, as literally "becoming-*Ding*-like." According to Kant, a *Ding* is some thing that is hidden from the subject's power of reasoning. Only by becoming a *Gegenstand* does it first become an object of awareness for the subject before finally becoming an *Objekt*, or a thing that can be an object of rational investigation and knowledge. The *Dingheit* of any thing refers therefore to the extent to which the thing is obscured from cognitive awareness.

46. Cf. Göran Therborn, *What Does the Ruling Class Do When It Rules?* (London: Verso, 1978), 224ff.

47. Jürgen Habermas, *Knowledge and Human Interests* (Boston: Beacon Press, 1971), 192.

Chapter 5

System and Function

The Normative Basis of Social Power

I. INTRODUCTION

The legitimacy of the social order—of any social order—is the primary area of research for any critical theory of society. The mechanics of domination work in such a way in modern societies such that it is necessary to shape the value systems of culture as well as the value-orientations of individuals. The deep structures of socialization and of the personality system of individuals are therefore the place where the tendrils of power reach and shape a cohesive system of legitimacy for any system of power and hierarchy. Seen from this point of view, it can be said that critical theory is centrally concerned with the issue of norms. Norms are the mechanism by which social power is concretized. They are social facts while also being cognitive concepts, and they organize not only cognitive forms of knowledge but also the evaluative and judgmental capacities of subjects as well. They are the very sociological means that allow for the shaping of the subjective states of individuals, affecting their cognitive, affective, and evaluative capacities. The shaping of a normative order is also the way that social power is effectively created and constructed. Any kind of material form of power—say, the ownership of property, of the ability to control political or other forms of economic power, and so on—are only really possible through the shaping of a normative order that unifies and in some basic sense stabilizes the power relations within the community. Structure and function are therefore essential aspects to understanding the actual mechanisms of social power and to understand the ways that individuals as well as whole societies come to accept and acquiesce to the prevailing forms of social power that pervade their world.

Perhaps one of the most significant turns in critical social theory has been the collapse of the structural and functionalist understanding of the institutions

123

that make up modern social life. The general thesis that guided social theory and much of the social sciences—"critical" and otherwise—held that there existed a background logic for the systems of action and behavior that social actors performed. There was a systemic logic to the patterns of behavior that bound individuals at the most internal, personal level to the system of norms and expectations that existed outside of them. The vision of society that it promulgated was one that was in contrast to conflict theories that emphasized differential interests, asymmetrical relations of power, and the real possibility of concrete social change and transformation.[1] By contrast, an emphasis on the equilibrium of systems glossed over these differentials and struggles over power, influence, and resources. But jettisoning the systemic, structural-functionalist understanding of social life—particularly as brought forth by Talcott Parsons—prevents us from seeing the deep mechanisms of personality adaptation, subject-formation, diagnosis of social and personal pathologies, and a critical appreciation for the strong, centripetal power of modern—particularly capitalist—institutional arrangements that predominate in modern society. In this chapter, I would like to reconsider the contributions of Parsons with respect to this complex of problems, and show his deep relevance for reviving a more robust critical social theory.

At the heart of much of classical critical theory and Western Marxism was the thesis that saw modern industrial civilization as promoting a consensus of value-orientations that allowed for a passive acceptance of capitalist economic institutions and patterns of culture that legitimated them.[2] Basic to this idea in critical social theory was that modern society rested on a certain passivity of ethical agency that allowed the interests of capitalist social relations and production to embed themselves in their subjective drives and interests. As Marcuse was brought to remark, "The political needs of society become individual needs and aspirations, their satisfaction promotes business and the commonweal, and the whole appears to be the very embodiment of reason."[3] At the heart of this theory was a structural-functional reasoning that gave critical theory coherence and organized it as a way of approaching all aspects of modern society. Parsons, when seen in this light, despite his anti-politics and the conservatism that surrounded his theory at the time, can be reconstructed to provide a return to a structural-functional analysis that can return critical theory to its central purpose in understanding the cognitive and cathectic fusing of individual thought and action to the structural imperatives of capitalist society.

The move toward subjectivity in the late Frankfurt School critical theory is partially to blame for this move away from structural-functionalism. Implicit in Marx was a theory of capitalist society that relied on the integrative power of social, political, and cultural institutions. For Marx, this was seen largely as a theory of false consciousness, something that was removable through the penetration of an alternative ideology informed by a critical, structural analysis of the motion of capital and its effect on social power. Central to the merging of theory and practice was a labor movement informed by the scientific analysis of capitalism and its dynamics. This emphasis on the base-superstructure thesis was at the heart of critical theory from the inception. By incorporating Weber and Freud, Fromm, Adorno, Horkheimer, and Marcuse were able to move toward a theory of modernity that laid bare the ways that modern society was able to shape pathological forms of subjectivity. But they were unable to lay out the precise mechanisms of this approach; they relied, oftentimes, too heavily on Freudian concepts that tied them to themes of psychoanalysis and, in the later work of Adorno and Horkheimer in particular, to a move toward a radical subjectivity as a means of resisting the all-encompassing forces of reification.[4] Even Fromm, whose social-psychological analyses of capitalist society did not make such a move, only offers a sketch of the precise ways the social order is able to pervert the personality system of the individual. But in Parsons, in my view, we see a systemic approach to the ways social structures are able to secure compliance to its imperatives and produce new forms of social stability. His approach shows that this is not a matter of ideology nor a manipulation of some "libidinal economy." Quite to the contrary, the personality system of the individual is shaped and formed at an early age toward cognitive and emotive forms of obedience, foreshadowing—in a more satisfying way—the later approaches of thinkers such as Bourdieu on the same question.[5] Parsons shows us how a structural-functionalist approach is able to flesh out the precise ways personality systems are adapted to the functional norms of modern institutions and create what we can call a "culture of passive compliance" to the imperatives of capital and its pathological effects, or what Weber referred to as "the domestication of the dominated."

Contemporary social and political theory has decidedly moved away from this paradigm of thought, and the collapse of structural-functional thinking has had deleterious effects on progressive thought in general and critical theory in particular. I want to argue for a modified return to some of the central theoretical insights of Parsons's work to help us think in a deeper, more incisive way about the modern social systems that ensconce individuals and their agency. I want to urge critical theorists to take up once again the concern of confronting the connection between capital as a specific institution that patterns power relations and systems of domination, subordination, and control and the ways that this affects and shapes modern forms of subjectivity—especially with reference to the systems of power in everyday life. Parsons in particular is a powerful thinker because of the extent to which he was able to lay the foundations for a comprehensive understanding of the most elementary ways that individuals are socialized to orient themselves—in thought, feeling, and action—within the context of certain normative constraints and to attain a value-consensus around the goals of the prevailing social order. Taking this analysis further, we can say that capital as a system of organizing society can be seen as increasingly able to secure such a value-consensus.

Parsons's ideas about social integration and normative mechanisms of social control are also more advanced and, I contend, more far reaching in terms of their consequences than ideas such as Foucault's "governmentality" that are in fashion today.[6] The main reason for this is that these theories abstract us from the specific nodal points of power: that the capitalist system itself is able to shape and construct social relations in ways that, over time, have become able to secure it from the kind of threats posed from mass mobilizations and cohesive social movements. If I am right and Parsons's theories can be used to breathe life into the functionalist powers of modern institutions, then the kind of resistance needed to dislodge them must be rethought. Despite Parsons's own distance from so-called materialist explanations in social science of his own time (particularly Marxist analysis), I believe we can see in his work a powerful corrective to the excesses of subjectivity and the cult of praxis in leftist social and political thought as well as the illusory emphasis on discourse theory and deliberation as a means of outflanking the traditional impulse of critical theory.

If critical social and political theory are once again to grasp the most central mechanisms of social control, domination, and subordination, then it requires a turn away from the current of thought that has been prevalent on the left that has placed excessive emphasis on agency and praxis at the expense of structure and function. It must also confront the mainstream understanding of the nature of domination in the modern context that employs the language of a sterile liberalism or a revived neorepublicanism[7]—the radical vision must be reworked through a more accurate understanding of the deeply rooted forms of social power that shape our lives. Focus needs to be placed on the ways that value-orientations of individuals are shaped and patterned by the structural domain of society, specifically by the economic organization of the social order. This is crucial because the sphere of values—defined here as the ways the personality relates to the objective world epistemologically as well as affectively—is decisive in the ways that individuals and groups grasp and make sense of their world. The problem of reification is therefore, on this view, a problem of value-orientation.

The current intellectual fetish around issues such as identity politics, neo-anarchism, and so on all need to be seen in this context. These are expressions of a distorted, false way of thinking about the world; they are ways of conceptualizing social relations, the nature of human subjectivity, and the nature of society itself that take us away from the objective realities that shape our lives and impede broader forms of resistance from taking shape. In Parsons's work, I believe we find an entrée back into a more concrete, more objective, more powerful way of critically engaging not only the sclerotic effects modern capitalism has on political resistance, consciousness, and social solidarity but also a critical bulwark against the irrationalist tendencies in contemporary critical theory. If we return to the interdisciplinary orientation of Frankfurt School theorists, we see that this was the central conviction that ran through the best of their work: that modern (capitalist) social systems have the effect of adapting the personality of agents to the systemic patterns of society itself. I think the insights of Parsons can help us rethink a more general paradigm for understanding the deep consequences of the ways that forms of authority and domination permeate and serve as the central mechanism of modern societies.

Primary among these is the ways that we are able to conceive of one of the more pervasive problems of modern political and cultural life: the increased stabilization of modern liberal-capitalist societies. Perhaps the most important problem critical theory faces in contemporary society is to explain the ways in which mass democracies are able to tolerate the pressures of capitalist crises as well as the deleterious effects of contemporary hypercapitalism. The extremes of economic inequality, the degradation of social solidarity, and the flattening of cultural and personal life, are all accepted and legitimated by modern society. Although social and personal pathologies persist and deepen in modern culture, correct knowledge of the mechanisms of social control as well as psychological and cultural processes of authority-legitimation remains abstract. What Parsons is able to open up for us in a crucial way are the mechanisms that have led to a decline in the frictive, conflict-oriented nature of civil society and democratic politics. The erosion of the effectiveness of large-scale social movements, the solidity of capitalist economic systems of material reproduction, the ideological firmness of the legitimacy of this system, and the general integration and cohesiveness of these various social systems—polity, economy, culture/society—speak to real problems for critical theorists. I will seek to outline a basic logic for critical social theory: a logic that allows us to see the tendency of modern societies to become more stable in the face of increasingly extractive economic and administrative social structures as well as the norms that govern them.

II. HABERMAS'S CRITIQUE OF PARSONS

The decisive attack on Parsons did not come from conservatives, but from critical theory itself. Habermas elaborated his critique of Parsons in the second volume of his *Theory of Communicative Action* in the early 1980s, arguing that Parsons's theory of society collapsed because of the particular way he fused the action-theoretic and systems-theoretic aspects of his theory of society.[8] More to the point, Habermas saw that Parsons did not leave adequate space for a theory of action to be independent of the theory of systems. "In my view," writes Habermas, "Parsons underestimated the capacity and degree of self-sufficiency of action-theoretical concepts and strategies; as a consequence, in constructing his theory of society he joined the system and action models too soon."[9] Of course, from the point of view of the state of critical theory in the 1970s, this was an accurate and well-timed criticism. What Habermas correctly pointed to was the lack of space for the processes that unleash rational forms of political critique and resistance as well as a more satisfying conception of democratic validity for ethical postulates. A rational, democratic transformation of society would need to come about through the communicative activities of individuals oriented toward mutual consensus. From this point of view, Parsons was seen as imprisoning the subject and its ability to act (action-theoretic frame) within the systems of social norms and institutional logics (systems-theoretic frame). In place of the supposed rigid theorization of social action elaborated by Parsons in which individuals were oriented toward egocentric motivations for success, Habermas puts forth a theory of social interaction and socialization based on the paradigm of reaching mutual understanding.[10] From this point of view, Habermas consigns Parsons—as well as Hegel, Marx, and Lukács—to an outdated paradigm that he wants to upend through a theory of consensus built on the theory of communication. In place of a theory of society that sees relations between the structural differentiation of complex social systems, on the one hand, and cultural forms of meaning, on the other, as reflected in each other, Habermas contends that there is a communicative mechanism that lends the notion of public reason a decisive importance. As a result, the paradigm of structural-functionalist modes of socialization and social integration are seen as essentially vestigial.[11]

We should examine this critique by Habermas with scrutiny. To be sure, the move from subject-centered reason to that of an intersubjective paradigm oriented toward mutual understanding was a crucial move toward revealing and deepening the discursive processes that could lead toward a more flexible, more enlightened conception of civil society. For Habermas, the crucial insight was that modern societies were distinguished from traditional (or "conventional") ones by their decoupling of a system of reified norms from forms of action oriented toward mutual understanding. The more societies freed themselves from institutions that impeded communication, the more they would force themselves to call into question the validity of the social practices and values that gave traditional societies their cohesion. On this view, the paradigm of communicative action made the structural-functional argument essentially obsolete: now we would be able to conceive of social integration as separate from forms of system integration—social actors were now free to invent, through a rational form of consensus based on the paradigm of communicative action, new forms of politics and culture; they would be freed from the problem of being fused to the structural imperatives of institutional logics. What was prior, according to Habermas, was the communicative paradigm rather than the background conditions that shaped subjectivity and consciousness itself since individuals were mainly constituted through linguistically mediated forms of interaction.

Habermas effected a shift in social theory from a paradigm that emphasized objective forms of life that "preform the encounters of individuals with objective nature, normative reality, and their own subjective nature"[12] to one that emphasizes discursive practices as a means toward enlightened political action and critique. In a simultaneous critique of Lukács and Parsons, Habermas argued that the assumption that there exist "background conditions" that shape the subjectivity of subjects misses the crucial insight of the linguisitification of consciousness and the pragmatist insight of the fluid construction of worldviews through communication.[13] This has led to a wholesale rejection of the kind of structural-functionalism that was necessary to understand the macrostructure of modernity. Habermas's critique led to a fuller turn—one begun in the late work of Adorno and Horkheimer—away from a concern with the organizational structures and imperatives of the social order and its effects on subjectivity and consciousness. At the heart of critical theory is the teasing out of those mechanisms in modern society that erode critical reflection and encourage the democratization of social institutions. I think that Parsons can help revive this concern by showing the mechanisms of socialization that are fused to structural imperatives of social systems—mechanisms of socialization that in fact refute the thesis of Habermas and others that insist upon the pragmatist understanding of democratic will formation. In contrast to this view, I want to suggest that we take seriously once again the ways that social systems are able to distort critical consciousness and serve to adapt the personality structure of modern man to the structural imperatives of the social order. Understanding the durability of authority relations, the erosion of critical thought, and the movement toward an increasingly integrated, conservative social and political culture (in the sense of forms of thought and action that bolster or reinforce the status quo) can be more effectively achieved, in my view, by considering the ways that individuals are socialized (i.e., adapted) into modern social systems.

III. PARSONS AND THE FUNCTIONALIST THEORY OF VALUE-ORIENTATIONS

At the core of Parsons's understanding of modernity are several mechanisms that allow for the peculiar way modern societies are organized and maintain their cohesion. Parsons did not orient his research toward a critical stance on modern social institutions. He was interested in developing a grand theory of social action. But I think that Parsons is able to bring together certain strands of non-Marxian social theory that can serve as a sophisticated and deeply explanatory theory to complement a critical political economy. Parsons points to the ways in which modern social systems are capable of further fusing individual agents to social systems by forcing certain elements of the individual personality to conform to the norms of different institutional and systemic contexts. The central problematic of disclosing the systemic nature of social relations was to show how social actors are absorbed into the systemic processes of the domain of social institutions. Parsons argues that individuals choose to perform certain actions, orient themselves to certain goals, and cathectically shape their personal emphasis and emotional orientation toward certain social objects and values, but that these choices, although entered into willingly, nevertheless are constituted by the integrating power of the various social systems that we inhabit. Authority and social power is about the inculcation of certain values and symbols that individuals absorb in order for the systemic operations of modern institutions to operate. Overcoming the highly individualistic, atomistic conception of man—one that was being developed by the epistemological turn in neoclassical economics with thinkers such as Frank Knight, Carl Menger, and others—was central for Parsons to defend a sociological conception of man as opposed to the growing hegemony of *homo oeconomicus*.[14] In strong contradistinction to the epistemological trend that was forming neoclassical economics in the early half of the twentieth century, Parsons sought to reconcile the problem of human voluntarism with the reality of a highly institutionalized modern society. This means that he is able to give us insight into the ways in which individuals participate and legitimate institutions and social practices that can be seen as running against their interests, even that are pathological in nature.

To achieve this, Parsons takes Weber's conception of subjective value-orientation to a new level. He argues that social values are the means by which we form our roles and pattern our actions, expectations, and emotional investment in certain types of action.[15] Values are *socially grounded* in three distinct but interrelated spheres of direction: existential beliefs about the world, motivational needs, and relations to others. These three spheres build off the other; they are concentrically organized in that the motivational needs become a function of existential beliefs just as our relations to others is a function of our motivational needs. Individual agents are therefore brought into the fundamental problem of justifying, at the deepest subjective level, the values that orient their social action: "The existential propositions which men invoke to answer what Max Weber called the 'problems of meaning,' the more or less ultimate answers to questions on *why* they should live the way they do and influence others to do so, may thus be called the field of the *justification* of values."[16] Individual agents therefore absorb certain values that then form certain needs within the individual. It is not that we possess pregiven social needs; rather, we intake a set of values that themselves form needs. This Parsons discusses in terms of a "gratification-deprivation balance" within a given personality.[17] We orient our cognition, cathexis, and evaluative capacities toward the gratification of approval, of recognition, of respect, and so on and away from the lack of these things or the disapproval of others, their rejection of us. This means that the personality structure of the individual is shaped and formed by a need to comply with the basic rules and expectations of the value-system shared by others.[18]

This plays a crucial role for Parsons because it is here we begin to see the ways in which social systems are able to adapt individuals to their functional logics. For Parsons, institutions are "generalized patterns of norms which define categories of prescribed, permitted and prohibited behavior in social relationships, for people in interaction with each other as members of their society and its various subsystems and groups."[19] Institutions therefore constitute the patterns of behavior of individuals in the sense that they articulate "legitimated directionality of behavior."[20] Institutions that have a power to differentiate roles and individuals are expected, for the institution to be successful, to inculcate the required value-orientations requisite for those roles. This leads Parsons to consider the various mechanisms that exist for the formation of the internal value-system of individuals. What is crucial for a theoretical understanding of modern institutions is to bring Weber's insight about the nature of modern authority into the domain of the constitution of the personality, of subjectivity itself. The functionalist insight here is different from its previous incarnations, such as Evans-Pritchard and Herbert Spencer. In contrast to these older views of functionalism, Parsons sees modernity as a series of subsystems, the complexity of which cannot function without properly inculcating individuals with the appropriate orientations of action needed for those subsystems to function, something Parsons refers to as "functional prerequisites."[21] The functionalism is defined by the structuralism—the binding force of modern societies consists in the adaptation of the personality structure of individuals to the functional imperatives of its institutions.

It should be remembered that Weber's theory of modern authority or domination (*Herrschaft*) was premised on the idea that individuals were constituent agents in a relationship of domination (*Herrschaftsverhältnis*). This was achieved by orienting the value-systems of individuals toward the imperatives of institutional logics. Weber pointed to the category of "routinization" (*Veralltäglichung*) as the means by which the individual entered into a relation of obedience (*Gehorsam*) to the systems of power in modern bureaucratic societies.[22] But Weber was unable to flesh out the mechanisms

of routinization that shaped the personality structure of individuals, instead
relying on the hermeneutical device of *verstehen* to show how different
subjective worldviews and actions translated into broader patterns of social
coordination. Missing from this analysis were the actual processes were
responsible for this adaptation of individuals to systemic imperatives. For
Parsons, the answer was to be found in the mechanisms of social control, or
the ways in which social systems—the economy, the polity, and so on—are
able to fuse the personality structure of individuals to systemic imperatives.
This is achieved through "socialization," of the ways in which the personality is shaped to think (cognition), feel (cathexis), and value (evaluation) are
ordered according to the needs of the particular institutional goals that one
inhabits or functions within. We are formed within a culture that mediates our
subjective elements, that shapes our personalities:

> The keynote of the conceptualization we have chosen is that cultural elements
> of patterned order which mediate and regulate communication and other aspects
> of the mutuality of orientations in interaction processes. There is, we have
> insisted, always a normative aspect in the relation of culture to the motivational
> components of action; the culture provides standards of selective orientation
> and ordering.[23]

We are therefore concerned with the ways in which culture—which I will
argue later needs to be seen as framed by the economic logic of capitalism—
is able to mediate subjective value-orientations through the process of socialization. In many ways, the mechanisms of socialization are an elaboration and
deepening of this insight of Weber, but he also adds the dimension of social
psychology to give his account of the personality structure of individuals
more depth and complexity. Like Weber, Parsons sees that the mechanisms
of socialization constitute the means by which any system is able to function since it requires individuals to subordinate themselves to the logic of
the different institutions we inhabit. From Durkheim, he takes the notion of
a commonly shared set of values that a plurality of participants share to a
level in which the mechanism of legitimation and consciousness formation
can be opened up. In this sense, we leave the domain of traditional forms
of "coercion" (*Macht*, for Weber) and enter into a more pernicious form of
social control: one based upon the inculcation of value-orientations within the
personality structure of the individual himself.

Now, the issue of values and value-orientations is essential. Although Parsons seeks to use the concept of the personality structure of the individual as
a crucial layer of the process of societal legitimation, he does not wholly take
over the concept in a purely Freudian sense.[24] Rather, he sees the personality
as constructed, in a sense, by a series of social practices and social relations

that have the effect of orienting individuals toward certain goals. The relation between ego and alter(s) is a crucial one because it takes Weber's concept of "routinization" to a next level. The relation between them is important because it is the means by which value-orientations are absorbed by ego. "It implies that ego and alter have established a reciprocal role relationship in which value-patterns are shared. Alter is a *model* and this is a *learning process*, because ego did not at the beginning of it possess the values in question."[25] The realm of learning solves a series of moral problems for the individual in the sense that they no longer pose a problem for legitimate action. The process of learning through routinization therefore creates a constellation of value-orientations in which "moral problems are treated by the actor as solved."[26] In this sense, the individual no longer sees certain actions as morally problematic and accepts them as legitimate forms of action, cognition, feeling, and evaluation. Values therefore become central because they are able to harmonize our conceptual frames with the institutional and societal context of our world. These subjective value-orientations find their objective referents not only in the operations of institutions but also in the symbolic sphere of culture itself. This symbolic system is not enough, however, to hold all legitimacy in check. After all, the systems and subsystems within which we live and work must be able, in some way, to function and deliver on the goals toward which we have been socialized.[27] Beyond this, the individual is willing to tolerate other pathologies that may result from that systemic context.

Although in traditional societies authority worked by inculcating norms to which all members were expected to conform, Parsons is aware that modern societies must deal with the problem of subjective action and value-orientation. Weber was also aware of this, as was Durkheim. But Parsons is able to give this theory a new depth by isolating elements of sociation that shape and form subjective value-orientations. This leads him to a theory of action that is deeply socialized, but one that is also able to show us the ways that domination and authority require complex symbolic, cultural, and psychological forms of social control. By seeing social subsystems and institutions as tending toward either integration or disintegration, the stability of social systems depends on the extent to which individuals possess value-orientation that directs them toward role expectations that keep individual agents in check—in effect shaping them in accordance with the norms of other social actors within the given institution. For Parsons, this was the act of *identification*, which is a situation wherein the ego takes over, or internalizes, the values of the given model of action required of the institution or subsystem.[28] We do not merely imitate what we see around us, we come to *identify* with the values and norms we see others valuing and performing. This constitutes the essence of socialization or a "socializing effect" that is "conceived as the integration of ego into a role complementary to that of alter(s) in such a way that the common values are internalized in the ego's personality, and their respective behaviors come to constitute a complementary role-expectation-sanction system."[29] For Parsons, alter is a crucial variable in this process since ego is shaped by the role expectation-sanction system that the alter exhibits—teachers, family members, co-workers, and so on, all constitute alters responsible for the ego's formation of role expectations in different subsystem contexts. The expectation-sanction system is crucial because it is the base of the process of socialization: "The socialization effect will be conceived as the integration of ego into a role complementary to that of alter(s) in such a way that the common values are internalized in ego's personality."[30]

The act of identification is strong because it has the effect of anchoring the subjective orientations of the individual by molding both *cognitive* and *cathectic* layers of the personality structure, in turn forming the basis for the *evaluative* structure of the individual. For Parsons, this means that each agent is formed by the structural constraints placed on intersubjective ego formation. Mechanisms of social control work by implanting within the individual a counteracting force against tendencies to deviate from the role expectations that he occupies in any given subsystem. These role expectations are properly internalized by the ego through what Parsons terms a "relational possession," in which ego forms a reciprocal attachment to alter. The ego then "acquires a 'stake' in the security of his possession, in the maintenance of alter's favorable attitudes, his receptiveness-responsiveness, his love, his approval or his esteem, and a need to avoid their withdrawal and above all their conversion into hostile or derogatory attitudes."[31] In this sense, the individual is turned into his own self-regulating actor, one who helps to reequilibrate the subsystem itself, but based on the intersubjective relations of norm-governed behavior. As opposed to traditional societies, modern societies need to invest these "mechanisms of value-acquisition" with remarkable power (i.e., reinforcement-extinction processes) because the norms are defined by the functional imperatives of the system rather than oriented toward mechanical forms of solidarity or based upon metaphysical worldviews. These "mechanisms of the personality" are distinct from mechanisms of the social system itself. Although distinct, they are complementary since without the required self-regulation on the part of the individual, the systemic imperatives of modern institutions cannot succeed. Parsons sees the systemic imperatives of social institutions as possible only through its capacity to successfully moderate forms of social control—that is, by managing forms of deviance. This becomes a crucial element in his theory of modern social systems since the imperatives of social systems require mechanisms that adapt members of society to its imperatives.

It seems clear that this shows us the extent to which systems of power require not only legitimation but also a deep-seated mechanism of ego formation based on systemic *and* intersubjective grounds. Parsons's insight into the nature of the ego's value-acquisition and internalization is that it operates within the domain of intersubjective conformity so that we learn to identify ourselves with certain roles and functions based on the ways others act and expect us to act. But also, and perhaps more important, his theory is that this process molds the emotional investment of the ego to seek to ingratiate alter(s); it is a process that can lead to the justification of systemic logics not based on a critical-rational faculty, but on the socialized cathexis of the personality toward goals shared by others within the specific subsystem. Indeed, one's very existential self is, to a great extent, functionally dependent on following norm-governed roles and maintaining the systemic nexus within which that personality has been formed.[32] The stability, or "equilibrium," of any system is dependent on such a process. This thesis implies that the system itself becomes a background condition for processes of ego formation. The durability of power systems are therefore structured by these processes of formation, not only at the level of cognition but also of the value-orientations and emotional investment of individuals. If we are to escape the dual positions of radical subjectivity as well as see through the limitations of discourse-based theories of democratic will formation, then we must see how Parsons's understanding of such a socialization process permeates and in some ways corrupts the prerequisites for those two positions. Here is where, as I see it, critical theory's enduring legacy lies: in the ways that capitalist institutions and imperatives have the power to reform and neutralize the background conditions necessary for forms of political resistance, in particular, for the higher-order forms of communicative action that would allow Habermas's pragmatic critique to be effective.[33]

This can be more firmly grasped when we see how Parsons theorizes the forms of deviance that accompany the various mechanisms of socialization since he conceives the domain of conformity-deviance as "inherent in and central to the whole conception of social action and hence of social systems."[34] Since social systems seek equilibrium, or a condition wherein they are able to function so as to maximize their goals, forms of deviance emerge not from a problem of the system itself but from a lack of motivation on the part of actors within the system to uphold the roles necessary for systemic equilibrium.[35] Now, since roles are constituted intersubjectively, deviance means a withdrawal of cognitive and emotional resources from the goals of the system or the role(s) the individual is required to perform, what Parsons refers to as "pattern responsibility." This equilibrium condition can only hold within institutional logics when the intersubjective relations of different individuals possess a "complementarity of expectations" among the different roles individuals fulfill. But when any given ego or personality structure has not properly absorbed the "expectations of the interaction system," there is a deviance in his social actions: one gives either too much of his personal resources to the role demanded (compulsive-conformity) or too little (alienative-withdrawal or rebellion).

What is insightful in this analysis is that we can begin to see the ways in which modernity is capable of disabling effective critical attitudes and, as a result, robust forms of political engagement with the system. Parsons points to the idea that power in modern societies is largely symbolic in the sense that the obedience of individuals to others within a hierarchy can only be secured once their personality has been adapted to systemic needs through a process of value-acquisition and internalization. Now, this means that deviance—in the sense of withdrawal or rebellion—is distinct from critical reflection since the latter requires a systemic understanding of the objective conditions of the system as well as a moral-evaluative perspective to open it up to critique. Mere deviance alone is little more than a pathology of the common value-system. The power of social systems, therefore, lies in their respective abilities to adapt individuals to the roles necessary for the functioning of institutions. Deviance under such systemic contexts becomes less politically or socially disruptive the more that these systems are able to secure actions and motivations toward compliance.[36] When deviance does occur, in other words, it becomes less effective in terms of its ability to disrupt the functional imperatives of the different subsystems. The main reason for this is that the cognitive ability to grasp the mechanisms of domination that cause the feelings of alienation and existential anxiety are disabled—not only does it become difficult to grasp conceptually the nature of the modern social order, but it also becomes difficult to accept its pathological nature.[37] In this sense, we can begin to see an explanation for the decreasing effectiveness and lessening attraction for countermovements against major systemic imperatives such as the economy, the state, and the culture of obedience to, or at least compliance with, authority.

The problem of deviance in modern societies, then, is quite different from what it had been before the permeation of modern forms of ego formation that accompanied and made complex industrial society possible. Whereas in previous historical periods, social systems—the economy, religion, the polity, and so on—would collapse as the values that underpinned them eroded, modernity creates pockets of deviance that do not threaten the systemic imperatives of the various subsystems; rather, these pockets of deviance become pathologies of society and the personality. A cult begins to grow around certain forms of popular culture, certain deviant forms of sexuality, and identity politics begins to take on an increasingly cultural, rather than really political, stance, and an emphasis emerges on symbolic ways of withdrawing from the nexus of values that stress conformity, what Paul Piccone once termed "artificial negativity."[38] Concerns with identity and postmodern ideas about emancipation become saturated with a "physical and erotic spontaneity against the ascetic routines of the modern working world."[39] Parsons's emphasis on value-consensus should be read in a more critical light: it means that for systems of such complexity—such as the modern economy, of the legal system, of the modern state, and so on—to be able to function with efficiency, a set of common values must be secured among social actors that reduce the friction of institutional logics. These values that underpin the legitimate domination of modern social systems means, from a political vantage point, that the notion of a "double-movement" of the type theorized by Karl Polanyi becomes ever more difficult to emerge. Instead, those periods in the past—say the tumultuous nineteenth century and early twentieth century as well—that saw upheaval, social unrest, dissent, and revolutionary activity were possible in a period before such forms of value-consensus were able to thoroughly permeate the culture, cognition, personality structure, and practices of social actors. Today, we witness the erosion of rational-radical politics as it competes with a left increasingly defined by passive, alienative withdrawal, on the one hand, and a mainstream of society that is saturated by conformity-dominance, on the other.

But all of this leads us back to the very criticisms that led critical social theory away from this paradigm—namely, the lack of insight into ways in which we can counter the systemic imperatives of capitalist society. Surely, it is argued, we are not that oversocialized; we possess some degree of agency, institutions are not that inflexible, and there are moments of crisis and opportunities for social change and transformation. Indeed, the latter phase of Parsons's work after 1970, with his turn toward a theory of social cybernetics, became more vulnerable to these criticisms.[40] But on the whole, the period of his work from 1950 through the late 1960s shows us a theory of modernity that we must consider in order for a more robust critical theory of society to be sustained. Parsons is emphatic that the connection between social systems and the personality is one of strong conformism, and this has led many to reject—prematurely, I believe—his ideas as inflexible, unable to formulate a theory of resistance. What Parsons is able to formulate is an interesting theory of the nature of deviance and the ways that our rejection of norm-governed patterns of action and belief leave us in a curious position of irrelevance.

By isolating this mechanism of socialization and the processes of social control, Parsons is able to point in a very distinct way to the mechanisms of authority relations, in a more concrete way than Weber was able to in his writings on authority and domination. In this sense, what we can call the "constitution problem" emerges as the central domain of Parsons's contribution to critical social theory. This can be understood as the ways in which personality structure is shaped and formed by objective, social conditions and institutions. In the more advanced ideas of critical theory, such as Lukács's idea of reification or Adorno's concept of the subject-object relation, we see a concern with the ways the objective world is perceived and framed by social subjects. They emphasized a Hegelian conception of consciousness and categories of cognition rather than the internal value-orientations of individual actors and their relation to the whole personality structure of the individual.[41] But Parsons, taking a view derived from Weber and Durkheim, adds to this way of thinking by emphasizing the internalized value-orientations of individuals as the self-regulating mechanism of the social order; he is able to point to the ways that these value-orientations are tied to broader, objective, institutional logics. For this reason, it seems to me Parsons's particular brand of structural-functional analysis ought to be revived, but in a more critical way. Integrating this way of thinking into the broader fabric of critical theory is therefore what I would like to consider next.

IV. STRUCTURAL-FUNCTIONALISM, LEGITIMATE AUTHORITY, AND SOCIAL DOMINATION

In spite of himself, Parsons shows us a way back to a series of crucial categories needed for the coherence of critical social theory. I would like to point to three different but interrelated concepts that we can see as crucial for anchoring a critical social theory/social science. First, there is an overcoming of the thin, utilitarian conception of social actors and their deep embedding within social systems. This does not mean, as with Luhmann, that agency is eclipsed by social context; it means that modernity places a particularly strong weight on the formation of individual agency. Second, there is the importance of seeing the personality as in tension with his social environment. What was missing in critical theory from the beginning was a cohesive theoretical paradigm that could explain the symmetry between the institutional power dynamics of capitalist institutional logics and the internalized obedience to these systems on the part of the subject. By blending Marx, Freud, and Weber, critical theory attempted to weld together these different theoretical paradigms in order to explain the crucial problem of the erosion of critical thought and its ability to confront the colonization of society, culture, and consciousness by the capitalist logic of valorization. Although Parsons cannot be seen as attempting this from his own theoretical vantage point, there is little question that he was able to achieve a highly integrated and cohesive theoretical understanding of this precise problem. In this sense, the relevance of Parsons needs to be seen in the extent to which the mechanisms he points to are able to help us come to grips with the further expansion and deepening of these forms of thought that persist in modern society.

The reaction in recent decades against all forms of structural analysis has taken social and political theory far from a position of conceptualizing and confronting forms of power relations that are deeply held as legitimate in modern society. To this extent, I think that Parsons can be read in such a way as to make him the opposite of how he was seen and interpreted for the past fifty years—namely, as a theorist of legitimate domination, of the ways that power relations can be embedded not only within the general culture of everyday life but also within the personality structure of individuals. More specifically, I think that this reading of Parsons can be fused to the theories of Marx in such a way as to make more compelling and satisfying the theory of base and superstructure, or the hypothesis so central to critical theory that the structural and systemic imperatives of capitalism is absorption of authority necessary for the continued accumulation process.[42] If Parsons was concerned with forming a theory of society around the norm-governed dynamics of systems equilibria, he was unable to locate a general source, a hegemonic point of origin for these normative systems. Parsons himself saw his reading of social theory as anti-Marxist in the sense that it focused on the problems of values and social integration. His anti-Marxism was reinforced by his reliance on Weber and Durkheim as the central pillars of classical sociological theory.[43] A straight reading of Parsons—one that has, wrongly I think, forced critical theorists to throw out the baby with the bathwater—leads us to the conclusion that he simply sees norm-governed systems as through a positivist lens, as ahistorical and part of the nature of man and society. But we can easily take his general apparatus and dislocate it from such assumptions and methodological dilemmas and provide a theory that can bring back the structural-functionalist understanding of modernity and its deep consequences on the nature of the personality structure. Although Parsons took an acritical attitude toward the strength of value-consensus in modern societies, there is no reason for us to take a similar view. Instead, I maintain that we need to blend his analysis with Marxian understanding of capitalist production process in order to provide critical theory with a firmer theoretical ground.

We can begin by seeing that whereas classical Marxism was content with an unsophisticated mechanistic understanding of the relationship between individual and group psychology, on the one hand, and the economic structure of society, on the other, the view adopted here is that the mechanisms of socialization, in particular of value-acquisition, is one of the central mechanisms of base-superstructure analysis. It constitutes the means by which individual consciousness and personality structure is constituted by the socioeconomic environment under the conditions of capitalist modernity. This was addressed, albeit abstractly at times, by the main thinkers of the tradition of Western Marxism—such as Lukács, Korsch, and Gramsci—but was then lost as Frankfurt School critical theory succumbed to subjectivist notions of resistance, especially in Adorno's *Negative Dialectics* and *Aesthetic Theory* as well as the cynical indictment of modern rationalism.[44] Before this turn, when considering the problem of the prevalence of domination in modern society, Horkheimer prefigures many of the ideas more fully elaborated by Parsons, although from a very different political and evaluative position: "Here it is in order to discuss briefly some of the aspects of this mechanism, e.g., the situation of man in a culture of self-preservation for its own sake; the internalization of domination by the development of the abstract subject, the ego; the dialectical reversal of the principle of domination by which man makes himself a tool of that same nature which he subjugates; the repressed mimetic impulse, as a destructive force exploited by the most radical systems of social domination."[45] For Horkheimer, these processes were based in the expansion of instrumental rationality and a preponderance of human domination over nature that was then extended to a domination of man by man.[46] Instead of following Horkheimer's path, we should see that the forms of domination in society have a structural basis and that its roots lie not in a particular epistemological trajectory but in the structural imperatives of capitalism itself, and these *structural* imperatives—that is, the accumulation of capital—require a *functionalist* form of social integration wherein modern forms of legitimate authority are grounded not only in the norms of formal institutions but also in the symbolic elements of the broader culture. This is Parsons's understanding of culture in modern societies as "patterned or ordered systems of symbols which are objects of the orientation of action, internalized components of the personalities of individual actors and institutionalized patterns of social systems."[47] We are therefore brought back to the Marxian thesis of base and superstructure: the creation of background conditions within culture, law, the state, consciousness, the very personality of the subject that have as their root the structural needs of capitalist accumulation. The adaptation of social actors to this system constitutes the very essence of modern forms of authority.

Taking this view shows us that Parsons's notion of a normative functionalism grounded in an intersubjective system of ego formation need not be attached to the values that he himself saw in modern society—that forms of socialization and integration were based in a consensus of common values shared by the majority. Rather, we can see that blending his ideas with Marx shows a fit between his ideas about value-orientation and internalization, on the one hand, and the Marxian understanding of political economy, on the other. Indeed, it shows us that the binding force of legitimate authority has become so deeply rooted within modern (specifically American) culture and society that resistance to its imperatives become increasingly weak in their effectiveness to dislodge its imperatives. What Parsons refused to see was that the structural elements of modern society are themselves governed by the necessities of capitalist accumulation; that patterns of economic growth, the agglomeration of capital, and so on require an increasingly tighter layer of legitimate authority as a means of securing the structural demands of the system as well as to stave off forms of deviance that stem from the social, economic, and cultural costs that it produces. The functionalist element refers to the extent to which this process of system integration is able to succeed, to the extent to which ego formation and personality structures are shaped to accept the values required for the continuation of the systemic imperatives of capitalist institutions.[48] This can be seen in Parsons's understanding of social power where he argues, contra C. Wright Mills, that power needs to be seen as a medium for the securing and obtaining compliance with "collectively acknowledged obligations."[49] Parsons argues that "[t]he capacity to secure compliance must, if it is to be called power in my sense, be generalized and not solely a function of one particular sanctioning act which the user is in a position to impose, and the medium used must be 'symbolic.'"[50] Power in the modern sense, therefore, must be able to absorb as many of the symbolic-creating institutions and mechanisms in society in order to secure functional imperatives.[51] Hence, stronger motivation is created for the adaptation of schools, cultural institutions, and so on in order to create a significant hegemony of norms that individuals feel compelled to follow and see as legitimate, and it also erodes the collective cache of values that could serve as a basis for legitimate deviance from the growing network of norms that congeal around a strong inducement-coercion mentality among individuals.

V. THE NATURALIZATION OF THE SOCIAL ORDER

The relevance of these insights for the revival of critical social theory ought to be seen as obvious. First, the onslaught of postmodernism and other forms of irrationalism that began to permeate critical theory have had the effect of thoroughly disabling any genuine sense of political resistance. What concerns these trends in political thought are the ways in which subjectivity is capable of being a resource for political resistance. On this view, the structuralist and the functionalist are conservative in the sense that they somehow deny subjectivity its rightful place in being able to shape its own sense and vision of what is politically possible and desirable. But where this goes wrong is in lacking a mechanism for the production and re-production of a specific kind of authority and power: one that is organized around the imperatives of an increasingly integrated social system that requires the production of forms of consent based on intersubjective means. More to the point, what Parsons provides us with is a mechanism for understanding the way that modern forms of power are rooted in personality formation, and the Marxist rereading

I privilege here shows that Parsons's normative functionalism can and must be read alongside the structural understanding of capitalist institutions illuminated by Marxist political economy to rejuvenate critical theory. We are able to deal with the problem of "false consciousness" in a more satisfying way by providing a mechanism that can account for its generation and content.[52]

But where this way of thinking goes terribly wrong is in its inability actually to grasp the correct object of critical thought. There simply is no subjectivity that can be unmasked, no reservoir of pent-up libidinal energy to be released, that can serve as the source for political resistance. The deep ways that individuals are socialized to accept the patterns of modern institutions as legitimate is underrated by such approaches. From a political point of view, the kind of resistance that we have witnessed has been unable to pose a serious threat to the system for precisely this reason.

Indeed, the crucial issue is to be able to point to, tease out, the mechanisms of social and cultural life that have the ability to weaken forms of resistance within the society as a whole. Whereas the current vogue of exaggerated subjectivity sees resistance as simply defining oneself against the system and its imperatives, what is really needed is the transformation of those systems of socialization, not their eradication *tout court*. Defined by what they oppose, these theorists escape into subjectivity, into a crude neoanarchism, situational ethics, and so on, and thereby cripple our ability to organize politically around the real institutional problems of the capitalist social order. What is needed is a translation of the current systems of socialization—to find ways in which the powers of modernity can be shifted toward common ends, not the creation of a utopian alternative culture that poses no threat to the system but is simply seen as deviant and, quite simply, irrelevant. Subjectivity does not *precede* the objective context within which it finds itself; rather, it is dialectically shaped by it. In this sense, the current manifestation of radical politics has become increasingly ineffective in terms of its ability to dislodge the institutional forms that constitute and reproduce capitalist modernity. As Parsons was able to show in his discussion of deviance, modern forms of legitimate authority are able to integrate the personality structure of the individual to such an extent that detaching from the system of norms that have become so hegemonic means that our withdrawal from the systemic nature of role orientation becomes nullified as a mode of resistance. The system reequilibrates itself by coding such behavior as deviant, and, as long as the system remains generally legitimate, deviance is unable to become true dissent. In this sense, I think that these insights emphasize even more the Marxian thesis of base-superstructure relations and the reasons why radical thought and praxis needs to be focused on the functional imperatives that integrate the social order.

On this view, the core problem remains to confront the mistaken idea that human agency is independent of the strong forces of systemic logics and their ability to constitute the value-orientations of individuals. If Lukács had seen this problem in neo-Kantian and Hegelian terms with his concept of "reification," Parsons sees the problem in a more elaborate way: in terms of the actual process of the personality development of the ego itself.[53] This means inquiring into the ways that our thickly constructed subsystems of modernity have the ability to pre-form the cognitive and emotive structures of individuals, orienting them toward obedience and conformity in very specific ways. This means approaching questions of subjectivity with great care since it cannot be taken for granted that subjectivity is something that can be used as a starting point for theoretical analysis. Instead, we are forced back onto the Hegelian notion that our own subjectivity is an immanent property of the system of mediations that any individual acquires. Critical thought can only gain real ground again once we see that the system logics of capitalist society necessitate a cohesion of legitimate domination that can only be countered by direct intervention into the systems of accumulation that serve as the point of origin for the outer shells of legitimate domination. Radical politics needs to embrace once again a radical stance with respect to the economy and privilege the state's power to encourage new directions for institutional activity. An economy oriented toward public concerns, a state that privileges public interests over private interests, and social movements that seek to enlarge the sphere of public accountability of social institutions such as capital—all are means of countering this trend, and they are ends to which radical politics needs to orient itself. In many ways, this was the reason Marx moved toward a social scientific paradigm of critique: the mechanisms of capitalist institutions serve as the organizing principle for other social, cultural, and political institutions.

I think this resonates with the deeper, more radical insights of Marx and the classical phase of critical theory. It lies in the insight that the objective, material, economic imperatives of modern society have deep, rhythmic effects on subject formation.[54] The Marxian thesis of "base-superstructure" takes on a more nuanced, more compelling form once we see that the capacities for critical, democratic will formation are severely hampered by the substance and logics of modern institutions, especially once we see that the integration of subsystems have become increasingly subordinated to economic imperatives. It is questionable to what extent the communicative paradigm of discourse ethics is capable of serving as a compelling mode of resistance and critique to this tendency. Quite to the contrary, reconsidering Parsons's powerful understanding of the nature of social systems and ego formation, we are forced to confront that reality that subjective orientations are increasingly fused to such systems. The lingering notion that modern forms of global capitalism will begin to create their own gravediggers, that spontaneous movements will begin to emerge to challenge the system, that capitalism's latest crisis foreshadows its own demise, are all absurd if we take Parsons seriously even in the slightest. A critical social theory with true political aims must focus on the ways that large-scale mass movements cannot be created without the erosion of ideology and false consciousness that we can reframe in this analysis as an absorption into a value-system that prevents individuals from engaging critically with the systems that govern their lives. On this view, Parsons can lend to Marxism and to critical theory a powerful force in understanding the reproduction of authority and a "culture of compliance" that prevents the accumulation of critical capacities within modern culture. We are thrown back to the Lukácsian dilemma of creating class consciousness within a society that is constituted by ever increasing, ever more tightly bound forms of socialization and legitimation and to a system ever more organized toward capitalistic growth at the expense of human development. This means an impoverishment not only of the symbolic culture of political resistance but also, and more important, the erosion of the cognitive structures and patterns of thought needed to counter the systemic imperatives of modern capitalism.

NOTES

1. This argument was most forcefully made by Rolf Dahrendorf in the late 1950s. See his "Out of Utopia: Towards a Re-Orientation of Sociological Analysis," *American Journal of Sociology* 64 (1958): 115–27. For a more extended discussion, see his *Class and Class Conflict in Industrial Society* (Stanford, CA: Stanford University Press, 1959), 157ff.

2. See T. W. Adorno and Max Horkheimer, *Dialectic of Enlightenment* (New York: Continuum, 1995), 120–67; and Herbert Marcuse, *One-Dimensional Man: Studies in the Ideology of Advanced Industrial Society* (Boston: Beacon Press, 1964).

3. Marcuse, *One Dimensional Man*, ix.

4. This is particularly pronounced in Adorno's *Negative Dialectics* (New York: Continuum, 1973) as well as his parallel argument in *Aesthetic Theory* (Minneapolis, MN: University of Minnesota Press, 1998).

5. Bourdieu's theory of *habitus* also relies, in my view, on a problematic thesis of the ways individuals orient themselves to contexts of social power. His idea of the "practical sense" (*le sens pratique*) one possesses is seen as inscribed in the body itself, as "bodily hexis." As such, it moves from being a feature of the *personality* of the individual to a *corporeal* predisposition: "Bodily hexis is political mythology realized, *em-bodied*, turned into a permanent disposition, a durable way of standing, speaking, walking, and thereby of feeling and thinking." *The Logic of Practice* (Cambridge: Polity Press, 1990), 69–70. Bourdieu approaches a more convincing theory of power and domination in his analysis of "symbolic power" and its relation to language. Here, however, there is a move toward a theory of ideology detached from concrete institutional logics even as it lacks an analysis of the process of ego formation in social agents. See *Language and Symbolic Power* (Cambridge, MA: Harvard

University Press, 1991), 163–70. As I will show, Parsons's basic theoretical schema offers a more detailed analysis of the social and personality variables that secure obedience and forms of modern domination.

6. See Michel Foucault, *Naissance de la biopolitique: Cours au Collège de France (1978–1979)* (Paris: Gallimard & Seuil, 2004). For the neo-Foucauldian reworking of this idea, see Mitchell Dean, *Governmentality: Power and Rule in Modern Society* (London: Sage, 1999), as well as Barbara Cruikshank, "Revolutions Within: Self-Government and Self-Esteem," in Andrew Barry, Thomas Osborne, and Nikolas Rose (eds.), *Foucault and Political Reason: Liberalism, Neo-Liberalism, and Rationalities of Government* (Chicago: University of Chicago Press, 1996). For an application of this to critical theory, see Eric Boehme, "Embodiment as Resistance: Evaluating Stephen Bronner's Contributions to Critical Theory," in Michael J. Thompson (ed.), *Rational Radicalism and Political Theory: Essays in Honor of Stephen Eric Bronner* (Lanham, MD: Lexington Books, 2011).

7. The neorepublican theory of "freedom as nondomination" has become an influential new thread in political theory. See Philip Pettit, *Republicanism: A Theory of Freedom and Government* (New York: Oxford University Press, 1997); Quentin Skinner, "Freedom as the Absence of Domination," in C. Laborde and J. Maynor (eds.), *Republicanism and Political Theory* (Oxford: Blackwell, 2008), 83–101; John Maynor, *Republicanism in the Modern World* (Cambridge: Polity, 2003), 108–40; and Frank Lovett, *A General Theory of Domination and Justice* (New York: Oxford University Press, 2010). I critique this theory in "Reconstructing Republican Freedom: A Critique of the Neo-Republican Concept of Freedom as Non-Domination," *Philosophy and Social Criticism* 39, no. 3 (2013): 277–98.

8. Habermas outlines a preliminary criticism of Parsons in *On the Logic of the Social Sciences*, trans. Shierry Weber Nicholsen and Jerry A. Stark (Cambridge, MA: MIT Press, 1988), 78–88.

9. Jürgen Habermas, *The Theory of Communicative Action*, vol. 2, trans. Thomas McCarthy (Boston: Beacon Press, 1987), 204.

10. Jürgen Habermas, *The Theory of Communicative Action*, vol. 1, trans. Thomas McCarthy (Boston: Beacon Press, 1984), 271–86.

11. This is also a position adopted by Axel Honneth in his reworking of the tradition of critical theory. See his essay "Critical Theory" in *The Fragmented World of the Social: Essays in Social and Political Philosophy* (Albany, NY: SUNY Press, 1995), 61–91.

12. Habermas, *Theory of Communicative Action*, vol. 2, 187. Also see the discussion by David Ingram, *Habermas and the Dialectic of Reason* (New Haven, CT: Yale University Press, 1987), 148–71.

13. For an important critique of Habermas on this point, see Byron Rienstra and Derek Hook, "Weakening Habermas: The Undoing of Communicative Rationality," *Politikon* 33, no. 3 (2006): 313–39.

14. See Parsons's early essay of 1935, "The Place of Ultimate Values in Sociological Theory," in Charles Camic (ed.), *Talcott Parsons: The Early Essays* (Chicago: University of Chicago Press, 1991), 231–58.

15. See the discussion of the relation of values and value-orientations and their relation to social action in Talcott Parsons and Edward Shils (eds.), *Toward a General Theory of Action* (Cambridge, MA: Harvard University Press, 1951), 159–89.

16. Talcott Parsons, *Structure and Process in Modern Societies* (Glencoe, IL: Free Press, 1960), 174–75.

17. Talcott Parsons, *The Social System* (Glencoe, IL: Free Press, 1951), 7.

18. André Gorz points to this insight as a critical move against Habermas in the sense that economic firms create patterns of rationality that are external to as well as prior to the choices and socialization of individuals. This raises the functionalist critique that individuals are fitted into the processes of social institutions, eroding crucial forms of spontaneous agency. Gorz refers to this as the "sphere of heteronomy," where the division of labor begins to have a regulatory effect upon social actors in that they begin to follow certain preprogrammed scripts of action and behavior: "Economic rationality has conferred increasing importance upon sub-systems functioning by programmed hetero-regulation: that is to say, upon administrative and industrial machineries in which individuals are induced to *function* in a complementary manner, like the parts of a machine, towards ends that are often unknown to them and *different from those offered to them as personal goals." Critique of Economic Reason* (London: Verso, 1989), 35.

19. Parsons, *Structure and Process in Modern Societies*, 177.

20. Ibid.

21. See Parsons, *The Social System*, 26–36.

22. See Max Weber, *Wirtschaft und Gesellschaft* (Tübingen: J. C. B. Mohr/Paul Siebeck, 1972 [1922]), 122–48. This is also developed by Herbert Marcuse; see his "A Study on Authority," in *Studies in Critical Philosophy* (Boston: Beacon Press, 1972). Marcuse points out that "the recognition of authority as a basic force of social praxis attacks the very roots of human freedom: it means (in a different sense in each case) the surrender of autonomy (of thought, will, action), the tying of the subject's reason and will to pre-establish contents, in such a way that these contents do not form the 'material' to be changed by the will of the individual but are taken over as they stand as the obligatory norms for his reason and will" (51).

23. Parsons, *The Social System*, 327; also see Clyde Kluckhohn, "Values and Value-Orientations in the Theory of Action: An Exploration in Definition and Classification," in Parsons and Shils, *Toward a General Theory of Action*, 388–433.

24. In this sense, I see Parsons's use of psychology and theories of the personality as distinct from Frankfurt School critical theory, particularly those of Marcuse and Adorno, and certain aspects of Fromm's work, as well as that of Wilhelm Reich.

25. Parsons, *The Social System*, 211.

26. Parsons and Shils, *Toward a General Theory of Action*, 166.

27. The early Habermas is more Parsonian on this point: "[O]nly when members of a society experience structural alterations as critical for continued existence and feel their social identity threatened can we speak of crises. Disturbances of system integration endanger continued existence only to the extent that social integration is at stake, that is, when the consensual foundations of normative structures are so much impaired that the society becomes anomic. Crisis states assume the form of a disintegration of social systems." *Legitimation Crisis*, trans. Thomas McCarthy (Boston: Beacon Press, 1975), 3. Hence, like Parsons, we can see that crisis is not associated with the conditions of social systems, but the threats they pose for the ego upon their disintegration.

28. Parsons takes, but deepens, the concept of "identification" from Freud, who defines it as "the earliest expression of an emotional tie with another person." But it is further elaborated in tripartite form: "First, identification is the original form of emotional tie with an object; secondly, in a regressive way it becomes a substitute for a libidinal object-tie, as it were by means of introjection of the object into the ego; and thirdly, it may arise with any new perception of a common quality shared with some other person who is not an object of the sexual instinct." *Group Psychology and the Analysis of the Ego* (New York: Norton, [1921] 1959), 46, 50. Parsons takes this as a basic mechanism of the way a personality is shaped, but he adds to this the layer of values: the individual comes to value in a conscious way the feelings of attachment he experiences in following certain roles, the rules of which are shared by others. His participation in that norm-governed network of rules requires some degree of attachment in terms of cognition, cathexis, and evaluation for them to become legitimate. Without this conscious legitimation through value-orientation, the operation and existence of complex social systems would be impossible.

29. Parsons, *The Social System*, 211.

30. Ibid.

31. Ibid., 213.

32. This phenomenon has been elaborated by a different and unrelated body of theoretical literature in political psychology known as "systems justification theory." See John T. Jost, Mahzarin R. Banaji, and Brian Nosek, "A Decade of System Justification Theory: Accumulated Evidence of Conscious and Unconscious Bolstering of the Status Quo," *Political Psychology* 25, no. 6 (2004): 881–919. Also see Tom R. Tyler's interesting paper, "The Psychology of Legitimacy: A Relational Perspective on Voluntary Deference to Authorities," *Personality and Social Psychology Review* 1, no. 4 (1997): 323–45; as well as Tom R. Tyler and E. Allen Lind, "A Relational Model of Authority in Groups," *Advances in Experimental Social Psychology* 25 (1992): 115–91. For a different theoretical approach to the phenomenon of hierarchy justification, see Jim Sidanius, Felicia Pratto, Colette van Laar, and Shana Levin, "Social Dominance Theory: Its Agenda and Method," *Political Psychology* 25, no. 6 (2004): 845–80. Also see Jim Sidanius and Felicia Pratto, *Social Dominance: An Intergroup Theory of Social Hierarchy and Oppression* (New York: Cambridge University Press, 1999), 61–126.

33. To a certain degree, Habermas admits this by pointing to the possibility of "systematically distorted communication," which prevents social actors from reaching mutual understanding in social contexts. "Such communication pathologies can be conceived as the result of a confusion betweens actions oriented to reaching understanding and actions oriented to success. In situations of concealed strategic action, at least one of the parties behaves with an orientation to success, but leaves the others to believe that all the presuppositions of communicative action are satisfied." *Theory of Communicative Action*, vol. 1, 332.

34. Parsons, *The Social System*, 249.

35. It should be pointed out that this is considered one of the more vulnerable areas of critique for functionalist theory. As Wolfgang Streeck has recently argued, "Research shows that functionalist constructions that view capitalist systems as seeking and remaining in static equilibrium are wishful thinking at best. In an institutional

perspective, capitalist actors are most realistically stylized as endowed with an ethos of unruliness that makes them routinely subvert extant social order in rational-egoistic pursuit of economic gain." *Re-Forming Capitalism: Institutional Change in the German Political Economy* (New York: Oxford University Press, 2009), 4–5. But this misses the point that I am developing here. It may be true that firms and their directories seek constant movement and disequilibrium in order to make gains in the broader market. But this says nothing about the actual conditions *interior to firms and everyday working life*. The reality speaks against Streeck's criticism, in this regard: in order to guarantee certain kinds of productivity and maximize certain kinds of extractive power over workers, an equilibrium of social control is not only necessary but also a broader cultural imperative.

36. In this sense, we see the rise of the culture industry and its ability to absorb certain cultural elements of deviance and transplant them back into the symbolic culture of the system as nondeviant objects of mediation. One can think of the commodification of certain kinds of music, film, and other forms of expression that have become integrated into the broader culture of compliance.

37. This thesis is developed by Erich Fromm in *The Anatomy of Human Destructiveness* (New York: Henry Holt, 1973). Fromm argues in this regard, "If others threaten him with ideas that question his own frame of orientation, he will react to these ideas as to a vital threat. He will say that the new ideas are inherently 'immoral,' 'uncivilized,' 'crazy,' or whatever else he can think of to express his repugnance, but this antagonism is in fact aroused because 'he' feels threatened." Ibid., 223.

38. Paul Piccone, "Artificial Negativity as a Bureaucratic Tool?" in Gary Ulmen (ed.), *Confronting the Crisis: Writings of Paul Piccone* (New York: Telos Press, 2008). This problem of the conflation of radical culture with radical politics is usefully probed by Stephen Eric Bronner, *Moments of Decision* (New York: Routledge, 1992).

39. Peter Dews, *Logics of Disintegration: Post-Structuralist Thought and the Claims of Critical Theory* (London: Verso, 1987), 176. Relevant to this discussion is his analysis of Lyotard and Foucault, 134–207.

40. Of course, this move in Parsons was echoed in Germany by the evolution of Niklas Luhmann's more comprehensive systems theory. See his *Social Systems*, trans. John Bednarz Jr. (Stanford, CA: Stanford University Press, 1995). For a more critical exploration of Luhmann's ideas in the face of modern trends in critical theory, see the debate between Luhmann and Habermas, *Theorie der Gesellschaft oder Sozialtechnologie. Was leistet die Systemforschung?* (Frankfurt: Suhrkamp, 1971).

41. Lukács saw this in terms of "reification" (*Verdinglichung*), in which certain objective attributes of the social world are rendered invisible to consciousness. This is the etymological implication of the word *Ding*, which in Kantian and neo-Kantian language was meant to denote the subject's inability to perceive any object as an object of knowledge, or *Objekt*. See his *History and Class Consciousness* (Cambridge, MA: MIT Press, 1971). Adorno, by contrast, emphasizes the need to hold on to a critical space between subject and object so that a genuine agency can be protected from the reifying tendencies of modern social systems. See his "Subject and Object," in Andrew Arato and Eike Gebhardt (eds.), *The Essential Frankfurt School Reader* (New York: Continuum Press, 1994), 497–512.

42. Note David Harvey's interesting, but theoretically thin, analysis of the phenomenon of the "culture of consent" in *A Brief History of Neoliberalism* (New York:
Oxford University Press, 2005). "[T]he neoliberal revolution usually attributed to
Thatcher and Reagan after 1979 had to be accomplished by democratic means. For
a shift of this magnitude to occur required the prior construction of political consent
across a sufficiently large spectrum of the population to win elections. What Gramsci
calls 'common sense' (defined as 'the sense held in common') typically grounds consent. Common sense is constructed out of long-standing practices of cultural socialization often rooted deep in regional or national traditions. It is not the same as the
'good sense' that can be constructed out of critical engagement with the issues of the
day" (39). The question remains what mechanism exists at the social-psychological
level to create this kind of consent building. I think the turn to Gramsci remains a
seductive but theoretically weak move and suggests that we consider an analysis
derived from Parsons instead.

43. Parsons put forward this view in his first major work, *The Structure of Social
Action* (New York: Free Press, [1937] 1968). In his preface to the 1968 edition of the
work, Parsons legitimated his exclusion of Marx from his reconstruction of modern
social theory. "Durkheim and Weber seem to me to be the *main* founders of *modern*
sociological theory. Both were in explicit revolt against the traditions of both economic individualism and socialism—Weber in the latter context perhaps above all,
because of the spectre of total bureaucratic 'rationalization.' In a sense, Tocqueville
and Marx provided the wing positions relative to this central core. Marx was the apos-
tle of transcending the limitations of the partial 'capitalistic' version of rationalization
through its completion in socialism. . . . Tocqueville, on the other hand, represented
the anxious nostalgia of the *Ancien Regime* and the fear that the losses entailed in its
passing could never be replaced. Indeed, to a preeminent degree, Tocqueville was the
apologist of a fully aristocratic society." *The Structure of Social Action*, vol. 1, xiii.
Parsons was unable to appreciate the sociological contributions of Marx, specifically
for a theory of social systems, instead choosing to see him in simplistic political
terms. But it is clear, in my view, that the concerns of more sophisticated Marxist
theorists such as Lukács as well as the Frankfurt School took seriously the need to
theorize the problem of ways that individuals were shaped by the logics of capitalist
social systems, something Parsons was simply unwilling to recognize or accept.

44. Adherents of structural analysis in Frankfurt School critical theory were Fried-
rich Pollock, the early work of Max Horkheimer, as well as Franz Neumann and Otto
Kirchheimer. All saw, from their respective points of view and areas of expertise, that
the structural nature of modern capitalism was the point of origin for other institutions of society, culture, and the psychology of the individual. For a discussion, see
Moishe Postone, "Critique, State, and Economy," in Fred Rush (ed.), *The Cambridge
Companion to Critical Theory* (New York: Cambridge University Press, 2004),
165–93. Postone correctly points to an understanding of "structuralism" that was
shared by these theorists: "'Structure' here refers to historically specific congealed
forms of practice, forms that are constituted by and constitutive of practice" (192).
In this sense, I believe we can perceive a fruitful point of intersection for Parsons's
understanding of practice as the process of value-internalization and ego formation,

on the one hand, and the substantive analysis of the structural nature of institutional action under capitalism provided by Marxist theory, on the other.

45. Max Horkheimer, *Eclipse of Reason* (New York: Continuum Books, [1947] 1974), 94.

46. Of course, this was also the argument of Horkheimer and Adorno's *Dialectic of Enlightenment*. See the important corrective to this move in critical theory by Stephen Eric Bronner, *Reclaiming the Enlightenment* (New York: Columbia University Press, 2004), 17–40.

47. Parsons, *The Social System*, 327. In this sense, Parsons's notion of ideology bears a striking affinity with later Marxian interpretations.

48. The separation of structure and function is deeply problematic, leaving us with a formalistic social theory. As Lucien Goldmann has argued, "The indissoluble link between structure and function, resulting from the relatively durable nature of functions and the relatively provisional nature of structures, constitutes the motive power of history or, to put it another way, the historical character of human behavior. Thus, if one separates structure and function, he has already committed himself to the creation of *either* an ahistorical and formalistic structuralism or a functionalism with the same orientation." *The Human Sciences and Philosophy* (London: Jonathan Cape, 1973), 14.

49. For an excellent discussion of the Mills-Parsons debate on the theory of power in modern society, see Dennis Wrong, *Power: Its Forms, Bases, and Uses* (New Brunswick, NJ: Transaction, 2002), 237–48.

50. Talcott Parsons, *Politics and Social Structure* (New York: Free Press, 1969), 362.

51. In many ways, this was also the thesis of the "culture industry" argument put forth by Adorno. See T. W. Adorno, "The Culture Industry Reconsidered," and "Culture and Administration," both in *Adorno: The Culture Industry: Selected Essays on Mass Culture* (New York: Routledge Press, 1991).

52. G. A. Cohen was perhaps closest to this position in his advocacy of seeing a Marxian theory of ideology in terms of a functionalist method, particularly in seeing Marx's theory of ideology as a functional development of a social system governed by capitalist laws of accumulation and reproduction. See his *Karl Marx's Theory of History: A Defence* (Oxford: Oxford University Press, 1978), 278–96. Also see the discussion by Michael Rosen, *On Voluntary Servitude: False Consciousness and the Theory of Ideology* (Cambridge, MA: Harvard University Press, 1996), 168–222.

53. See the discussion by Tom Rockmore, *Irrationalism: Lukács and the Marxist View of Reason* (Philadelphia: Temple University Press, 1992).

54. See the more recent discussion of this theme by István Mészáros, *Social Structure and Forms of Consciousness*, vol. 1 (New York: Monthly Review, 2010).

Chapter 6

Fact and Value

The Epistemological Framework of Critical Theory

I. INTRODUCTION

In his project of transforming the philosophy of ethics, Karl-Otto Apel has argued that a turn to hermeneutics and the concept of a "communication community" is an essential step for any approach to a philosophy of norms capable of achieving universalizability. One of his primary interlocutors was Marxism and its supposed inability to provide any rationally consistent foundation for ethics. According to Apel, this results from the way that Marxist philosophy attempted to solve the fact-value dichotomy. "Marxism does not accept," Apel writes, "Hume's distinction between what is and what ought to be as an insurmountable separation of scientifically knowable facts and subjectively established norms."[1] Rather, Apel suggests that the Marxian project is stricken with a crucial weakness that stems from its reductionism of normative statements to empirical statements: "In its orthodox version, at least, it adheres more or less avowedly to the classical Aristotelian-Thomist postulate of a teleological ontology, according to which what exists, if understood correctly, is identical with what is good. Stated more precisely: Marxism, following Hegel, interprets the historically real as what is rational and the rational as what is real."[2]

In what follows, I will argue that this view is deeply mistaken when applied to the classical ideas and epistemological strategy of classical critical theory. The logic of this kind of critical epistemology, one also maintained by Hegel and Marx, holds that the distinction between "facts" and "values" is a false dichotomy. Rather, any true knowledge of the world and its objects is simultaneously a descriptive and prescriptive knowledge. In other words, critical knowledge was that kind of rational grasp of an object such that we could distinguish its potential properties from its merely empirical and existent

151

properties. To show this, I will examine the methodological substrates of Erich Fromm's social theory to distill from it a critical epistemology that dialectically sublates the fact-value split into a coherent critical theory of society that can also be used to provide a critical-cognitive foundation for an alternative conception of ethics, an *objective ethics*, based on ontological principles rather than the hermeneutic move made by Apel and Habermas. In so doing, I will also suggest that a reconstruction of Fromm's social theory should lead us to refocus the energies of critical theory as a discipline, to rethink the current trends that have come to dominate not only critical theory but also the noncritical social sciences. Even further, the dynamics of Fromm's social theory allows for a more robust understanding of what it means to articulate an emancipatory interest within the context of the empirical social sciences. He elaborates a form of thinking that establishes a crucial dialectical connection between the descriptive, factual statements of modern subjectivity and culture, on the one hand, and the evaluative, ethical judgment of those forms of life, on the other. It is this, I will seek to show, that remains Fromm's most enduring, most salient contribution to critical social theory.

Critical theory had always contested the view, promulgated by the empirical, analytic, and positivistic trends in the social sciences, that a purity of knowledge was possible only under the conditions of the separation of facts from values, a problem that plagues all of modern ethics and social sciences.[3] Grounded in the Kantian distinction between theories of knowledge, on the one hand, and ideas about values and norms, on the other, the idea that normative judgments must be separated from empirical facts has become the cornerstone of mainstream contemporary social science. The idea that there is a form of knowledge that is able to move beyond this dichotomy was a crucial theme of the methodological writings of Adorno and Horkheimer, and a theme that I propose can lead us to a radical form of ethical reasoning. The reason for this is clear: there can be no critical social science that does not possess, in some sense, a normative foundation, a foundation in the questions of practical philosophy. But practical philosophy as an autonomous enterprise was seen as a defunct exercise since Hegel's critique of Kantian morality and, even further, Marx's analysis of the dynamics of social development and subject formation. The central aim of this kind of critical social science is therefore not only to make knowledge claims but also to make such claims that are grounded in normative understandings of social life—in short, to provide an antidote to the strong pull of reification.

To this end, I will seek to defend the thesis that Erich Fromm's concept of critical theory, as evinced in his various studies of the pathologies of capitalist society, is underwritten by a methodological perspective counter to the trends in mainstream social science. Even more, I want to suggest that this methodological perspective relates directly to a conception of critical thought that goes beyond method and into the sphere of a normative philosophical anthropology, one that is in direct contrast to current trends in critical theory. Fromm's basic, underlying methodological and epistemological insight is that facts and values cannot be separated but have to be sublated into a more comprehensive, more holistic understanding of the nature of human beings and their sociality than noncritical theories of society allow. From this, it follows that knowledge and judgment are dialectically related in such a way that any critical social science cannot ignore its import. For Fromm, knowledge and judgment serve as the means of knowing what is properly human and what is pathological; it serves as a method that can delineate not only a judgment of value but also an empirical hypothesis about descriptive and causal claims. I will focus on Fromm's idea of "normative humanism" that I believe serves as a model and exemplar of the kind of dialectical thinking that has been lost in contemporary critical theory and to which critical thought must return if it will be able to remain a means of making critical value judgments in the face of the pathological effects of modern capitalism on human individuality and freedom.

II. THE CRISIS OF CRITIQUE AND JUDGMENT

Judgment is the crucial activity by which we are able to make claims about the normative rightness or wrongness of things. It pertains to the moral, evaluative questions and concerns that individuals have about the nature of their personal and social worlds. Critique is the ability to articulate reasons behind things and about things, to explain and to understand. It is the activity of underwriting our worldviews with reasons, with explaining the world around us rationally, and with seeking explanations about the causes and rational structure of phenomena, natural, social, or otherwise. It is my contention that traditional critical theorists, working within the structure of thought initiated by Hegel and continued by Marx, saw these two functions as dialectically related, that the very idea of "critical theory" meant, and still must mean, that the rational, "critical" explanation of the social world contained within itself the normative guidelines for its own evaluation. In this sense, there are no *a priori* categories we can use to explain the world, nor are there are any *a priori* value-claims that can be used to orient judgment and evaluative thought. Rather, the very criterion for understanding the empirical nature of the social world can only be conceived through its effects on human beings and their developmental capacities.[4] *Judgment* asks: How do we know what is right and wrong? What is healthy and what is pathological? What is desirable as opposed to what should be opposed? On the other hand, *critique* asks: What causes this phenomenon? What mechanisms are responsible for generating this event? How is a particular state related to and determined by another cause or force? *Critical judgment* can therefore be seen as those kinds of judgment that take into account the causal structures of things rather than the nonfoundationalist view of pluralist, intersubjective consensus as the basis for judging. The basic idea that undergirds modern social scientific thinking and epistemology is that these two categories of question are to be seen as fundamentally separate. It was necessary not only to keep them apart for the sake of a kind of purity of knowledge—that is, to prevent the values of the researcher from biasing rational inquiry—but also (and, to a certain extent, more important) to prevent specific political values from gaining hegemony within the academic and political establishment. Historically, this was directed against Marxism and "scientific socialism." By setting a domain of value-neutral inquiry, it became easier to delegitimize these intellectual forces as "biased" and "non-neutral," and hence as an invalid form of science.[5]

It was Max Weber who most clearly outlined and forcefully imprinted this separation of fact and value on modern social science and theory, highlighting its importance for grounding a modern social scientific method. For Weber, the fusing of values and facts was problematic because he wanted to protect the sphere of values from the hard facts of social reality as well as the "purity" of science from the biasing influence of the worldviews of the researcher. At the backbone of neo-Kantian philosophy was the project of keeping the two spheres at bay in order to preserve an element of human reflection and judgment away from the influences of facts. The protection of the value-field from the realm of empirical reality was therefore not meant to instill a sterility to social scientific enterprise, but rather to protect ethical postulates from being limited by factual considerations. As Weber notes, "It can never be the task of an empirical science to provide binding norms and ideals from which directives for immediate practical activity can be derived."[6]

Even more, Weber's argument holds that values are something that are not objectively valid in the sense that facts can be. Rather, the key feature of normative values is that they are nonobjective, relative, held by individuals subjectively. Premodern cultures and religion (what Weber termed "positive religions" or "dogmatically bound sects") have been able to articulate value-systems that are objectively valid for the members of those societies in which such religions operate. But for all others, "cultural ideals which the individual wishes to realize and ethical obligations which he should fulfill do not, in principle, share the same status."[7] This means that values become unhinged from anything positive, anything that can be seen in objective terms. This is because values are seen to be anchored in the subjective orientations of individuals and their relations to the world; they cannot, therefore, obtain any degree of objectivity since they are constantly being revised and changed. There is an inherent incommensurability to all forms of value-ideas and normative standards that render them unable to be comprehensively binding on others.[8] Values, norms, cultural ideals (or *Wertideen* for Weber) all constitute a field in which individuals are able to create their own values, their own normative principles, and, hence, their own authentic sense of guiding their own lives. "The fate of an epoch which has eaten of the tree of knowledge," writes Weber, "is that it must know that we cannot learn the meaning of the world from the results of its analysis, be it ever so perfect; it must rather be in a position to create this meaning itself."[9] Such a paradigm shift in social-scientific epistemology meant that the spheres of critique and judgment were to be seen as estranged from one another, something that has persistently evoked reaction from critical theorists.[10]

The split between a critical scientific investigation into the forces of capitalist societies, on the one hand, and the moral judgment of the institutions and systems that comprise them, on the other hand, have grown ever farther apart to the extent that it is seen as illegitimate to make judgment claims in social scientific analysis. But at the same time, the sphere of judgment has been cleaved from the empirical facts and functional forces that continue to shape modern subjectivity and culture. For this reason, more contemporary thinkers have sought to ground a concept of judgment not in any kind of objective, generally valid set of values and interests, but have instead sought to pursue Weber's basic thesis that values must be worked out through discursive means external to the realm of social facts. Hannah Arendt's social philosophy is an example of this tendency, something that has taken a strong hold on contemporary political theory and that has had a decisive influence on the direction of critical theory. Arendt suggests that the concept of "action" be construed as an inherently political activity in which different individuals come to debate, share opinions, and seek to persuade one another of their positions. Since politics needs to be conceived as an "essential and nonreducible plurality and variability of opinions,"[11] judgment comes to be detached entirely from the context of social structures and forces. Rather, judgment comes to mean the ways in which we shape and form opinions through deliberative action: "I form an opinion by considering a given issue from different viewpoints, by making present to my mind the standpoints of those who are absent. . . . The more people's standpoints I have present in my mind while I am pondering a given issue, and the better I can imagine how they would feel and think if I were in their place, the stronger will be my capacity for representative thinking and the more valid my final conclusions, my opinion."[12]

Arendt then goes on to define judgment as the mental activity that occurs when individuals are engaged in this kind of action, of politics itself in her terms: "The capacity to judge is a specifically political ability in exactly the sense denoted by Kant, namely, the ability to see things not only from one's own point of view but in the perspective of all those who happen to be present."[13] Judgment is not about "facts," nor is it about truth, which she sees as essentially "coercive."[14] Rather, judgment is a kind of intersubjective-phenomenological process, a "sharing-the-world-with-others" that enables us to orient ourselves in the world and to live together. Politics ceases to be a question of domination and of the problems of obtaining freedom and instead becomes embedded in culture, in that realm that is (somehow) devoid of coercion and domination: "Culture and politics, then, belong together because it is not knowledge or truth which is at stake, but rather judgment and decision, the judicious exchange of opinion about the sphere of public life and the common world, and the decision what manner of action is to be taken in it."[15] Here we see the move toward a new paradigm of political judgment: one conceived as external to the structural relations of social power that give society its very substance, that indeed gives politics its very meaning. It is giving primacy to politics over society. Arendt's redefinition of judgment therefore moves us further away from the quest for some kind of objectively valid values that can ground the capacity for judgment in the sense that we do not consider the ways in which the opinions of individuals have been irrationally formed by forms of social power. For her, the concern of judgment is ungrounded; it becomes dependent upon the intersubjective exchange of reasons, feelings, intuitions, or whatever else that a plurality of individuals come to embrace.

Habermas would come to make this turn in critical theory, arguing that there is a "cognitive content" to a morality that can be established through discursive forms of interaction.[16] Since normative claims are articulated through language, Habermas maintains that the discursive procedures that individuals use to justify their claims with others can serve as the foundation and the criterion for justified norms. Judgment, morality in general, therefore comes to possess a cognitive content since individuals are forced to justify their normative claims to others. Ultimately, only those norms are valid that (1) meet with the acceptance of all concerned within the discourse, and (2) when the consequences of that norm are "*jointly* accepted by *all* concerned without coercion."[17] The idea that judgment is an activity of rational discourse about the moral norms holds with Weber's thesis that values are a matter of dispute, that they have no objective validity. Even though Habermas claims that the cognitive content of morality makes it plain that there is a certain objectivity of values, only when others come to see them as valid as well, there is no ontological grounding for validity claims outside of the structure of language. Judgment, in this sense, is more epistemically demanding than on Arendt's account, but there is still a separation between the values and social facts; moral and political judgment is still seen as separate from any objective features of human life and social processes.[18]

For classical critical theory, by contrast, there could be no separation between critique and judgment. Both needed to be seen as dialectically related *and* sublated. There can be no separation of "facts" from "values," and there can be no kind of praxis that is not tied to, embedded within an inquiry into the objective, social-structural conditions that shape subjectivity and our cognitive and evaluative capacities. Max Horkheimer, in his seminal essay on the method and purpose of "critical theory," argues this explicitly:

> The scholarly specialist "as" scientist regards social reality and its products as extrinsic to him, and "as" citizen exercises his interest in them through political articles, membership in political parties or social service organizations, and participation in elections. But he does not unify these two activities, and his other activities as well, except, at best, by psychological interpretation. Critical thinking, on the contrary, is motivated today by the effort really to transcend the tension and to abolish the opposition between the individual's purposefulness, spontaneity, and rationality, and those work-process relationships on which society is built.[19]

For Horkheimer, the foundation of critical theory is the move toward understanding critique not as a separate faculty of knowledge but rather as a deeper, thicker type of thought that seeks to render some idea of the capacities of human beings with the irrationality of the social systems in which they are ensconced: "Critical thought has a concept of man as in conflict with himself until this opposition is removed. If activity governed by reason is proper to man, then existent social practice, which forms the individual's life down to its least details, is inhuman, and this inhumanity affects everything that goes on in the society."[20]

Horkheimer's basic contention is that any theory of society that does not consider and account for the social conditions that shape human life is insufficient. The idea that the social facts that we consider are to be looked upon with an evaluative consideration goes against the very logic of the modern social sciences and its insistence on the separation between "facts" and "values." The basic problem that frames this discussion is the question of the possibility of values than can be described as "objectively valid" as well as causal knowledge of social phenomena and social facts that have the same status of objective validity. In this sense, the primary problem is how to articulate knowledge claims that in some sense escape the problem of relativism, or in some other sense, and the Critical Theorists railed against this tendency, seeing it as a path to abstraction, taking us away from the critical opposition to the social mechanisms and structures that shape individuality and the context of cultural life. As I have been arguing, contemporary social theory and the social sciences more broadly tend to see these two activities or practices as separate, leaving questions of judgment outside of questions of explanation. But at an even more serious level, the general texture of late capitalist societies can be described as having repressed the faculty of judgment almost entirely, leaving questions of explanation and fact to experts, on the one hand, and a bankrupt capacity for rational reflection for mass society, on the other. This problem is no less a concern in the area of contemporary critical theory in which we are asked to replace the critical inquiry into the structure of the social order and its pathological effects on subject-formation and instead adopt the view that discursive or recognitive relations can serve an emancipatory interest in contemporary societies.

I see these three trends—that of mainstream social science, the contours of everyday life and culture, and the communicative turn in contemporary critical theory—as evincing a crisis of the faculties of both critique and judgment in the sense that the dialectical relation between them has been driven asunder. What is powerful in Fromm's analysis of modern, capitalist society is his ability to continue the critique of capitalism as a social order that is capable of distorting, mutilating, shaping man in defective ways. This brings attention back to the problem of distinguishing between a materialist understanding of human subjects as shaped by the socioeconomic structures of any given historical formation, as well as that of the charge of *a priori* values as opposed to the social facts that constitute human forms of freedom and action. In this sense, the judgment paradigm pushed by contemporary theorists is unable to ground claims in anything objectively valid outside of the intersubjective context of discourse. In contrast to this conception of judgment, I want to juxtapose Fromm's theoretical insights to chart a path toward a more radical, more morally compelling conception of radical ethics: an *objective ethics* that is grounded in the rational, ontological, and material realities and dynamics of individual and social life. This is achieved, I will argue, by overcoming dialectically the split between facts and values and the abstract character of individual or intersubjective lifeworlds separated from the socio-relational contexts that shape them, instead moving toward an understanding of ethical postulates that can be considered valid only when they appeal to the structures of socialization and socio-relational contexts that constitute a genuinely free individuality. I submit that it is only through this path of analysis that we can arrive at a truly emancipatory ethics that can inform a rational-radical politics.

III. FROMM'S NORMATIVE HUMANISM
AND CRITICAL THEORY

Fromm's entire concept of critical theory, of ethics, and of social and cultural critique is premised on the thesis that there exist, in some sense, normative statements about the nature of human beings that are objectively valid and that must serve as an anchor to any theory of society if it is to be understood as critical in any sense. Given the discussion above, this will be a heavy burden to justify. The allure of deliberative and communicative approaches to political theory and political praxis seem to have eclipsed this older paradigm of critique and judgment. But my central contention here is that this is a mistake, that the collapse of social critique, the continued atrophy of moral revulsion and the paucity of social action against the contemporary social order, is due to the collapse of the very paradigm that Fromm's social theory epitomizes. For Fromm, there exist universal criteria from which we can make judgments, construct critique, establish a ground from which to grasp the pathological, destructive features of the modern social order. And this is itself related to a specific conception of the needs of human beings, of relatedness and of creativity, and of specific forms of relatedness and creativity.

Fromm orients his social theory against what he sees as "sociological relativism," which postulates that "each society is normal inasmuch as it functions, and that pathology can be defined only in terms of the individual's lack of adjustment to the ways of life in his society."[21] At the heart of Fromm's approach, by contrast, is an emphasis on what he sees to be specific laws of development that human beings all share, laws that are to be understood in psychic, no less than in social, terms:

> The species "man," can be defined not only in anatomical and physiological terms; its members share basic psychic qualities, the laws which govern their mental and emotional functioning, and the aims for a satisfactory solution of the problem of human existence. . . . The real problem is to infer the core common to the whole human race from the innumerable manifestations of human nature, the normal as well as the pathological ones, as we can observe them in different individuals and cultures. The task is furthermore to recognize the laws inherent in human nature and the inherent goals for its development and unfolding.[22]

The dichotomy between what "social" and what is "biological" is the chief error that mitigates against the fuller, more comprehensive and critical account of modern human pathologies: "The main passions and drives in man result from the total existence of man, that they are definite and ascertainable, some of them conducive to health and happiness, others to sickness and unhappiness. Any given social order does not create these fundamental strivings but it determines which of the limited number of potential passions are to become manifest or dominant."[23] Human subjectivity is not, in direct contrast to the postmodern social-constructivist view, created by individuals but is the result of the processual nature of the social order. There is no ready-made and fixed essence to man, but there is a universal set of *fundamental capacities* and drives that come into contact with the various relational matrices of any given social order. It is the dialectic of these two spheres that generates or produces the content of individual life.

The emphasis on "normative humanism" therefore comes more sharply into focus once we grasp that there exists a specific set of characteristics that can qualify as healthy or unhealthy, that can be seen, in some objective sense, to be correct and right. The distortion of human subjectivity by the social forces of capitalism is, for Fromm, only glimpsed from the standpoint of an objective set of social-psychological processes that allow for the capacities that lie inherent in human beings to be made manifest, to become realized in any real sense. Fromm's critique is partly grounded in the view shared by Aristotle, Hegel, and Marx that human development is grounded in the social conditions that form human beings, largely through the nature of social relations.[24] But it is also an attack on any kind of speculative understanding of human beings, based in the social scientific analysis of the traits and characteristics of man: "If we want to know what it means to be human, we must be prepared to find answers not in terms of different human possibilities, but in terms of the very conditions of human existence from which all these possibilities spring as possible alternatives. These conditions can be recognized as a result not of metaphysical speculation but of the examination of the data of anthropology, history, child psychology, individual and social psychology."[25] As Fromm sees it, this basic starting point shows that there is a particular social-psychological way of understanding the health of the individual. "There are many ways in which man can find a solution to the task of staying alive and of remaining sane. Some are better than others and some are worse. By 'better' is meant a way conducive to greater strength, clarity, joy, independence; and by 'worse' the very opposite."[26]

Returning to the concept and approach of "normative humanism," Fromm notes:

> If a person fails to attain freedom, spontaneity, a genuine expression of self, he may be considered to have a severe defect, provided we assume that freedom and spontaneity are the objective goals to be attained by every human being. If such a goal is not attained by the majority of members of any given society, we deal with the phenomenon of *socially patterned* defect.[27]

The problematic issue of "fact" and "value" can now be seen to be overcome in a particular argument rooted not in the *empirical* features of human life, but rather in the dialectical nature of human conditions of life. For Fromm, this is achieved by conceptualizing the essence of human life as socio-relational as well as developmental and processual. In this sense, Fromm reworks Marx's philosophical anthropology to expand its field of reference beyond labor as the nucleus of human action, absorbing this into other types of action. Central is the understanding of how these different relations contribute to the overall process of ego formation within the individual. For Fromm, the central question of critical theory must be to determine the mechanisms that prevent the critical attitude from arising within members of mass society. The phenomenon to be explained is why resistance to capitalist forms of life have not increased with their increased penetration into everyday life, but instead give way to the acceptance of domination and authority. For Fromm, the explanation lies in the ways that economic forces are able to rearrange social relations—starting with the family (or primary relations) and moving upward to other forms of socialization, such as school, work, and so on (the secondary bonds or relations). The distortion of family relations—primarily the weakening of the father figure in the nuclear family—constitutes the weakening of the ego in the child, leading to a lapse of critical consciousness and a tendency toward the herd mentality, to conformity, and to timidity to and acceptance of authority. In effect, the instrumentalized and authority-based forms of economic life of advanced capitalist society come to shape the very kinds of egos necessary for their own sustenance and reproduction.

This would seem to smack of a kind of functionalist form of reasoning, but I am not sure that should be seen as problematic, especially for advocates of critical social theory. The attack on functionalist forms of reasoning in the social sciences was motivated, within the confines of critical theory at least, by a desire to revive the agency of individuals within an instrumentalized and seemingly technologically determined understanding of modernity. Habermas and others sought to reinvigorate the Kantian paradigm of rational agency and democratic forms of activity through intersubjective and participatory forms of rational solidarity and consensus. But this came at the price of viewing the pathological effects of capitalist social relations and their ability to warp the rational and epistemic capacities of subjects socialized under such relations. As Fromm was able to point to again and again, however, it is precisely these kinds of pathological social relations that must be rooted out and transformed prior to communicative forms of relations to be of any political use. Fromm does not work within what thinkers such as Habermas and Honneth refer to as an exhausted paradigm of monological reason nor to a productionist paradigm in which an individual is merely constituted by his labor on things.[28] Rather, for Fromm, man's "nature," if we can call it such, is essentially *relational* in nature: his health is dependent on social relations, on the nature of those relations, and cannot be hinged upon communicative or recognitive relations alone.[29]

Indeed, communication and recognition are important features of social relations, but for Fromm, these are insufficient on their own to characterize the ways that social relations can shape and form subjectivity. What concerns

Fromm the most is the ways that the universal and "fundamental" drives of the human being become filtered and directed by social relations. "*The active and passive adaptation of the biological apparatus, the instincts, to social reality* is the key conception of psychoanalysis, and every exploration into personal psychology proceeds from this conception."[30] To know what it means to be human means knowing that human essence is *relational* and that this relational essence of human beings is something that has a *dynamic* effect on the formation of the character of any given person by structuring and shaping the directionality of the instinctual drives of the subject in specific ways. Of course, these relations are not under the control of direction of any one person, they are shaped and structured by the social and economic forces that come to predominate any given society. Fromm's theory of social and psychological pathologies is therefore rooted in a methodological viewpoint that synthesizes and grounds *knowledge claims* and *evaluative claims* in a broader critical theory of society.[31] Put another way, there is no way empirically to be able to know the fact of a social or personal pathology without understanding that such a pathology is the very inverse of the healthy social or personal characteristic. Just as a physician would know how damaged or sick, say, a human liver might be in a given patient only by knowing what a healthy, fully functional liver's characteristics and functionings actually are, so with human beings and with society: the need for critical theory is the need for the correction of those pathological tendencies that exist within individuals and within our culture more broadly that are rooted in the irrational nature of our social order and its various socio-relational structures.[32]

Fromm sees this as Marx's contribution to a particular form of consciousness, to a particular way of gaining knowledge about the world that is unalienated. For Marx, just as for Fromm, critical knowledge about the world can only be really formed once we have a concept of human essence: "Only on the basis of a specific concept of man's nature can Marx make the difference between true and false needs of man. Purely subjectively, the false needs are experienced as being as urgent and real as the true needs, and from a purely subjective viewpoint, there could not be a criterion for the distinction."[33] This passage is significant because it shows the connection between delineating the ontological conception of human beings (i.e., the concept of man's essence rather than his mere empirical existence), on the one hand, and the ability to make judgments about the social world, on the other. These two kinds of claims or kinds of knowledge cannot be neatly divided between "is" and "ought," since each requires the other to be made properly, in Marx's sense. When I come to conceive of human beings as social, as the essence of his being as social, then we see that the determining character of human consciousness, conscience, as well as cognitive powers, are the product of socialization. As Marx says in the *Theses on Feuerbach*, "The human essence is no abstraction inherent in each single individual. In its reality it is the ensemble of social relations."[34]

Even further, Fromm takes the Marxian hypothesis of the relation between "base and superstructure" as fundamental to his approach to critical theory. Whereas Marx argued that the human consciousness was determined by its social conditions, Fromm elaborates this model of explanation by incorporating Freud's theory of the character structure of individuals. But character is not, Fromm tells us, the property of an individual alone since it is functionally dependent upon its interactions with others, on social relations: "Character can be defined as the (relatively permanent) form in which human energy is canalized in the process of assimilation and socialization."[35] Now, this idea of "canalization" is central since it refers to the ways in which the impulses, forms of cognition, the epistemic capacities of the individual, as well as the affective and cathectic dimensions of the personality are formed. The canalization is functionally dependent upon forms of "assimilation and socialization," which means that the logic of our institutions—from informal ones such as the family to more formal ones such as school and work—have a powerful force in the formation of our character and upon our capacities to think and judge as well. Here Fromm is able to link the Marxian thesis of social relations as the essence of man with the dynamics of the personality as outlined by Freud.

If we begin from the premise, as Fromm does (and as I think we should as well), that the way to have critical knowledge of when there exists a pathological character is to know what a developed, healthy character is like, then we can ask what properties a healthy character should possess. Fromm's answer to this is drawn first off from Freud and then from Marx: "The healthy person, for Freud, is the one who has reached the genital level (as opposed to the oral or anal levels of development) and who has become his own master, independent of father and mother, relying on his own reason and on his own strength."[36] From Marx's *German Ideology*, we see a different dimension of human freedom, one that Fromm will incorporate into his theory of the free, healthy subject: "As long as a cleavage exists between the particular and the common interest man's own deed becomes an alien power opposed to him, which enslaves him instead of being controlled by him."[37] Social relations can mutilate the individual, preventing his capacities and functionings from being realized: "If the circumstances under which this individual lives permit him only the one-sided development of one quality at the expense of all others . . . the result is that this individual achieves only a one-sided, crippled development."[38] Fromm sees Marx's thesis as transcending Freud because at its core is the notion that "independence and freedom are rooted in the act of self-creation."[39] Unlike Freud, who saw the fate of man as tied to the repressive force of society, of "civilization," Fromm's social psychology places emphasis on processes of socialization that mutilate the implicit capacities and functions that human beings possess, albeit *in nuce*.[40] It is not only an independence from the commands of others and the dependence on their commands that makes the individual alienated and unfree but also that freedom contains the power of creation, of being part of a social order that has human ends as its ends, the common goal of the development of human powers as their particular, individual goals as well. A defective society, however, will reproduce pathological personalities, rendering this kind of freedom and personal health impossible.

This leads us to one of the central concerns of Fromm's social theory: that of domination and authority. It is important to note that Fromm's emphasis on this theme was central because of its importance for understanding the political shift away from democratic forms of resistance and dissent and more contemporary forms of conformity and attitudinal adjustment to authority-relations. This is what Fromm calls the "authoritarian conscience," which he defines as "the voice of an internalized external authority."[41] Starting from the basic Kantian distinction between autonomy and heteronomy, we can see that this violates the more basic understanding in moral philosophy of what it means to be free: you are not the author of your own acts. But at a deeper level, it employs Max Weber's thesis about the nature of modern, or "rational domination." According to Weber, rational domination or authority is one in which agent *A* is able to issue a command to agent *B* and agent *B* accepts that command as legitimate and as if it were emanating from his own conscience. The submission to authority therefore requires that the character of individuals are formed in such a way so that they will accept certain commands and not question them, but see them as valid on their face.

Fromm's thesis is that the defective forms of socialization come to infect the character by implanting, so to speak, the external authority into the subject: "In the formation of conscience, however, such authorities as the parents, the church, the state, public opinion are either consciously or unconsciously *accepted as ethical and moral legislators whose laws and sanctions one adopts, thus internalizing them*."[42] The internalization is not simply the result of routinization, however. Rather, Fromm argues that it becomes embedded in the personality because of the alienated form of cultural life that individuals come to be exposed to. It is precisely the pathological forms of culture that motivate the individual to formulate a "pseudo-self," a kind of escape from the instrumentalized, dehumanized world we come to inhabit: "This particular mechanism is the solution that the majority of normal individuals find in modern society. To put it briefly, the individual ceases to be himself; he adopts entirely the kind of personality offered to him by cultural patterns; and he therefore becomes exactly as all others are and as they expect him to be."[43]

Fromm's thesis about the nature of domination and its origins in defective forms of socialization suggests that we must seek to locate the kinds of social relations and logics that constitute defective socialization processes leading to subjects that are ripe for domination and become submissive to it. But when we ask ourselves about the kinds of institutions, the kinds of practices, the kinds of relations that foster this "submissive mind," I think it is important to look at the connection between the socialization processes of education and work as examples of the defective forms of socialization that foster this kind of character in modern societies. First, it is the context of a capitalist economic system that shapes the defective forms of socialization—defective because they fail to realize the potential powers and capacities of individuals. Fromm makes the distinction between two forms of personal power: between "domination" and "potency." The latter is that form of power that the individual is able to realize his capacities as an individual—to achieve power over himself, to become authentically self-determined. This thesis—adopted from a synthesis of Aristotle and Marx—is at the heart of what Fromm terms a "normative humanism," or the metric by which we can understand and judge the social pathologies within society. When individuals *en masse* fail to attain freedom, self-determination, and genuine personal development, then we can speak of a "socially patterned defect."

In the end, a "normative humanism" comes to mean that normative and empirical forms of knowledge come to be dialectically related such that statements that confine themselves to either one or the other fail to grasp the total reality of the human condition. Recall the Hegelian thesis, first elaborated in the *Phenomenology*, that "absolute knowledge" was that form of knowledge that was able to penetrate beneath the sensory and empirical phases of knowledge, but also, and more important, to encompass the whole of the object being comprehended. Rather than isolating itself to mere moments or aspects of any object of inquiry, "speculative (*begreifende*) knowledge" was able to grasp conceptually the totality of any thing, all of its relations, elements, causal factors, and more. The epistemological strategy at the heart of Fromm's social theory therefore sees that the genuine concept of human being must be seen as the dialectic between its *relational* dimension and its dimension of *instinctual drives*. There is no way to isolate any element of human action or existence and privilege it as a defining aspect of the whole; here again, remembering Hegel, we fall into abstraction by losing connection with the whole reality of human life. So with the relationship between critique and of judgment, of knowledge and of evaluation: these are moments in a more substantive, more robust form of social theory that enables us to reveal the mechanisms responsible for human pathologies and, consequently, the very understanding of why such a state is intrinsically wrong and in need of correction. Without this, critical theory would simply degenerate into another empirical social science, unable to guide through reason and through truth claims about the social world a more emancipatory interest.

IV. CAN THERE BE OBJECTIVE VALUES?

From this we can begin to see that Fromm's account of human pathologies is rooted in the socio-relational contexts that shape and develop human subjectivity. Society precedes subjectivity, but the human being exists materially, as a biological entity. The central concern of normative humanism is to be able to make critical judgments about the ways in which specific forms of social life, structures of relations, and so on are able to shape the drives, consciousness, and emotional complex of the individual. The only way to be able to identify a pathology or defect is to be able to know the essence, or nature of human life. "[W]e are not referring to an abstraction arrived at by the way of metaphysical speculations," writes Fromm on this point, "like those of Heidegger and Sartre. We refer to the real conditions of existence common to man *qua* man, so that the essence of each individual is identical with the existence of the species."[44] The problem with capitalism as a social system lies in the various ways that it shapes those relational contexts that come to mutilate the basic drives of the individual, to direct one's energies to ends that are not, in some sense, serving the total needs that humans possess. The imperatives of society become the cauldron of subject-formation, of identity, of character, and subsequent pathologies of the personality. Indeed, the dialectic of subject and object, the very pulse of critical theory, is here placed within a form of knowledge that synthesizes critique and judgment: it is only by understanding those kinds of relations, practices, norms, and so on that can promote healthy subject-formation that we can have a capacity for critical judgment.

The idea of an *objective ethics* is therefore central to Fromm's critical project, and this makes sense since his social theory is predicated on the thesis that human beings require specific kinds of relations and forms of life in order to flourish.[45] Hence, forms of judgment need to be linked to the critical understanding of the ways social conditions distort the processual realization of a free, healthy human subject. What is "objective" here is the fact that these human needs are themselves not subjectively defined but common to the species of humans as a whole. I cannot simply define ethics or value-concepts arbitrarily according to what I think society should look like or what I might want for my own personal welfare, or as the result of conversationally working it out among others through discursive inquiry. Moral concepts, values in general, must be "objective" in the sense that they express needs that are common, universal, generalizable to others.[46] Ethical statements or postulates must therefore be seen in relation to the *objective interests* that the needs of human beings make necessary. But this also means that ethical postulates can obtain an *objective validity* in the sense that we can point to specific and identifiable forms of social structures and relations that can be harmful to the development of human personalities.[47]

This means that I cannot know or determine such interests through the exchange of reasons, as the pragmatist would argue, nor through the simplification of human interests to the dichotomy of "pleasure" versus "pain" as the utilitarian would argue.[48] In contrast, Fromm sees that our values must conform to what we know about the nature of man's essence, as a member of the species, of what it means to be human. He relates this kind of ethical reasoning first to Spinoza and then to Marx. From the former we see that "[t]he objective character of Spinoza's ethics is founded on the objective character of the model of human nature which, though allowing for many individual variations, is in its core the same for all men. Spinoza is radically opposed to authoritarian ethics. To him man is an end-in-himself and not a means for an authority transcending him. Value can be determined only in relation to his real interests, which are freedom and the productive use of his powers."[49] Fromm is attracted to the fact that Spinoza's ethics are grounded in a rational conception of the nature of man. Indeed, although he sees Marx developing this rational concept of man's nature in a more satisfying way, the basic proposition for an objective ethics remains the same: to see valid ethical postulates as those that harmonize with the needs of the human species.

We cannot, therefore, apply utilitarian or deontological forms of ethical reasoning since these concepts would fail to be grounded in the objective characteristics and needs of human beings. Marx, in a footnote from the first volume of *Capital*, makes this argument as well: "To know what is good for a dog, one must investigate the nature of dogs. This nature itself is not itself deducible from the principle of utility. Applying this to Man, he that would criticize all human acts, movements, relations, etc. according to the principle of utility, must first deal with human nature as modified in each historical epoch."[50] Now, this brings me back to the discussion elaborated above concerning the merging of critical knowledge and normative judgment. What Marx and Fromm are saying—and which is deeply indebted to Hegel's philosophical logic—is that to know anything means knowing it within the functional context of a system of causes and relations. I cannot isolate any object—a particle of dust, a fork, a neurotic tendency—without understanding the way it fits into a particular systemic context of causes and relations.[51] And this systemic context cannot be whatever I like it to be, but must be the *actual character of that system*. The nature, and hence proper concept, of any thing is dependent on other concepts: forks on table settings, eating particular foods, and so on. There are right and wrong answers to what makes water boil just as to what a fork actually is in an ontological, as opposed to a crudely material or physical, sense.

Hence, what things are in any ontological sense cannot be prior to the role they play in a system. Now, the crucial move comes when we consider the extent to which the ontology of any thing is attributed to it by us or is an account of the thing itself. The critical view of Hegel contra Kant was that this was precisely the case. On Hegel's view, the correct concepts about the world are those that are the very properties of those things. Logical categories are not subjectively deployed onto reality to constitute knowledge, but are the very categories of things themselves.[52] This takes us straight to the nerve center of critical social theory and its problem with the division between "facts" and "values." The neo-Kantian structure of noncritical theory is such that it will continue to see that the world is somehow constructed by its members; that what is normative is not in any way connected to what things actually are in any real sense. Normative concepts are therefore construed independent of reality, of the facts of the world. But the argument I have been developing here, and which I believe Fromm is advocating as well, maintains that there is an objective, observer-independent ontology proper to human nature, one that is a function of the system of relations that shapes and determines other aspects of human character and thought. We can call these *strong social facts*. This is not the same as *weak social facts* such as the nature of a fork, which is, and indeed must be, observer-dependent and understood only through its relation to other things. Indeed, a fork is what it is only within a context of other things (of the nature of table manners and their development and so on), but the forkness of the fork is not intrinsic to the material object itself since it requires us to attribute meaning to it, to make it what it is.

But the question of normative values that have political consequence comes into play when we consider these strong social facts—that is, those that pertain to the processual development of human beings and their capacities. In this sense, I differ with John Searle's account of social reality and its nature. For Searle, there are "brute facts" of nature that are intrinsic to objects, such as the statement "that is a stone," and those that are "observer relative" in the sense that they would not exist without people attributing meaning to them, as in the statement about a stone "this object is a paperweight." Only in the latter category, according to Searle, can we assign "a vocabulary of success and failure" to objective things. "Thus we can speak of 'malfunction,' 'heart disease,' and better and worse hearts."[53] But this does not seem to me to be the case. A heart's proper and correct function is not something attributed to it by me or anyone else, it is something *intrinsic* to hearts. This is not the case with a stone being used as a paperweight, to be sure (an example of a weak social fact), but it is the case for those objects and functions that are human and constitute human personality and character. As Searle correctly notes, however, "[w]henever the function of X is to Y, then X is *supposed to cause* or otherwise result in Y."[54] There is, on this account, a normative feature to any functional system: hearts can be bad hearts if they do not do what they are *supposed* to do (for example, pump blood to the body to oxygenate its tissues); an engine is a bad engine if it is not able to move the car of which it is a part; and a society can be a bad or sick society to the extent that it does not aid in the cultivation of the capacities and functions of its members. These are not attributable norms, or observer-dependent norms; they are *intrinsic* to those things—without the normative *telos* to define them, they would not manifest their correct functions.

Similarly, the systemic context within which these objects find themselves must also be so defined: a heart that pumps properly but is connected to the rest of the body with defective arteries and capillaries will not be able to perform its proper *function*. Just as important, it simply does not matter whether a person knows that their heart is part of a functional system, or what its role in the body is; what matters is that hearts do what they are required to do to be properly working or to be evaluated as "good" hearts. Strong social facts have this property: that their normative component is intrinsic to their very existence, they are ontologically prior to the ways we might conceive or judge them. As Hegel's argument suggests, it is not simply our concepts that constitute the reality of strong social facts: those facts have a conceptual structure that is inherent within them, a conceptual structure we can penetrate and know through the activity of critique. Weak social facts, however, do not, and they are basically constituted by a collective activity of attribution by members of a given community.

The nature of human beings is an example of a strong social fact. To be human is to be a social creature. Without it, we would lack language, organized thought, access to emotional care, and so on. Human beings have a nature that is intrinsic to them. A biological entity that is *Homo sapiens* cannot realize the implicit capacities and functions he possesses without specific kinds of social relations. Lacking this, the degree of this person's "humanity" would be put into question. Hence, when we speak of what it means to construct a critical theory of society, we are working with the need to understand the ways in which an objective ethics can arise to dispel the ideological and irrational ways in which people legitimate their world. Since critical theory is concerned with the ways that the individual is shaped by the totality of social relations, of how subjectivity, consciousness, the personality of individuals, are all interspersed with the objective traits of the social order of which it is a part, it becomes necessary to be able to secure a normative critique of society, one that is in some way grounded in the life processes of individuals rather than the antifoundationalist, "plurality," or pragmatic conceptions of ethics that have become ascendant in current theory. An objective ethics is therefore concerned with the ways in which society can be evaluated in terms of the relative health or unhealth of its members.

When we make ethical judgments that are valid in an objective sense, we are not only evaluating what is wrong or pathological in our institutions and culture but also simultaneously suggesting the very starting points for transformation and change toward something correct, healthier, and so on. Fromm comes back to this form of reasoning again and again, and it seems that he does so to distinguish a way of conceiving the nature of social life that allows for the capacity of individuals to overcome the defective forms of consciousness and reasoning that prevent them from attaining critical knowledge of their social world. Critical theory, if it is to achieve its basic purpose, is to be able to formulate forms of knowledge that unmask the mechanisms of power and, more important, the means by which compliance to the commands of elites and forms of potent dissent weakened among members of capitalist society. The power of an ethics with objective validity lies in its ability to shatter reification, to base praxis on ethical grounds that are not constantly shifting and held subject to the manipulation of the errors of public deliberation and discourse. In this sense, a radical form of ethical and political judgment emerges, one that can help in the reconstruction of the enterprise of critical theory.

NOTES

1. Karl-Otto Apel, *Towards a Transformation of Philosophy* (London: Routledge and Kegan Paul, 1980), 230.

2. Ibid.

3. Albrecht Wellmer correctly notes the difficulty of this problem when he says that "any attempt to restore the validity of an idea of practical reason in the empirical social sciences in an epoch that has been rendered scientistic, must appear *prima facie* as a sacrilege to the criterion of the rationality of a science which has laboriously enough emancipated itself from the normative modes of thought of *social philosophy* and the *philosophy* of history." "Practical Philosophy and the Theory of Society: On the Problem of the Normative Foundations of a Critical Social Science," in S. Benhabib and F. Dallmayr (eds.), *The Communicative Ethics Controversy* (Cambridge, MA: MIT Press, 1990), 293–329, 295, and *passim*.

4. Amartya Sen has recently tried to make an argument along similar lines for a theory of justice that keeps to these lines in his *The Idea of Justice* (Cambridge, MA: Harvard University Press, 2009).

5. Cf. Robert N. Proctor, *Value-Free Science? Purity and Power in Modern Knowledge* (Cambridge, MA: Harvard University Press, 1991), 99ff.

6. Max Weber, "'Objectivity' in Social Science and Social Policy," in Maurice Natanson (ed.), *Philosophy of the Social Sciences* (New York: Random House, 1963), 358.

7. Ibid., 363.

8. "Normative standards of value can and must be the objects of *dispute* in a discussion of a problem of social policy because the problem lies in the domain of general *cultural* values." Ibid., 362.

9. Ibid., 363.

10. The alternative critique of Weber's views and modern social scientific rationality came from conservatives. Leo Strauss's argument against this trend is convincing: "One evades serious discussion of serious issues by the simple device of passing them off as value problems. One even creates the impression that all important human conflicts are value conflicts, whereas, to say the least, many of these conflicts arise out of men's very agreement regarding values." *What Is Political Philosophy? and Other Studies* (Chicago: University of Chicago Press, 1959), 23. Strauss also holds Weber to account more strongly on this point: "The prohibition against value judgments in social science would lead to the consequence that we are permitted to give a strictly factual description of the overt acts that can be observed in concentration camps and perhaps an equally factual analysis of the motivation of the actors concerned: we would not be permitted to speak of cruelty." *Natural Right and History* (Chicago: University of Chicago Press, 1953), 57.

11. Richard J. Bernstein, *Beyond Objectivism and Relativism: Science, Hermeneutics, and Praxis* (Philadelphia: University of Pennsylvania Press, 1983), 215.

12. Hannah Arendt, *Between Past and Future* (New York: Penguin, 1954), 237.

13. Ibid., 218.

14. This arises from Arendt's move toward Kant's *Kritik der Urteilskraft* as a means of establishing an epistemic ground for political judgment. Kant's purpose in the early sections of that work is to establish the foundations for "taste," for aesthetic judgment that Kant sees as the only means of reconciling subject and object. Arendt's move toward the aesthetic of Kant can be seen as a crucial move toward establishing a theory of political judgment that is more devoid of questions of social fact than even Weber would have conceived. Arendt notes that Kant's purpose was not to justify private tastes, but rather to make judgments that can appeal to common sense, to the world itself, "an objective datum, something common to all its inhabitants." *Between Past and Future*, 219. This should not lead us to believe, however, that she means that values can become objectively valid or true, but rather that they must appeal to the ways that others see and conceive of the world. This forces us out of a private, subjective abstraction from social processes and into an intersubjective abstraction where we rely on the phenomenological relatedness with others rather than on the specific social mechanisms that define, distort, and constrain our individual and cultural development. See my critique of Arendt and her conception of judgment in "Inventing the 'Political': Arendt, Anti-Politics and the Deliberative Turn in Contemporary Political Theory," in G. Smulewicz-Zucker and M. Thompson (eds.), *Radical Intellectuals and the Subversion of Progressive Politics: The Betrayal of Politics* (New York: Palgrave Macmillan, 2015), 69–97.

15. Ibid., 219.

16. For his indebtedness to Arendt, see Jürgen Habermas, *Philosophical-Political Profiles* (Cambridge, MA: MIT Press, 1985).

17. Jürgen Habermas, *The Inclusion of the Other: Studies in Political Theory* (Cambridge, MA: MIT Press, 1998), 42.

18. Also see Alessandro Ferrara, *The Force of the Example: Explorations in the Paradigm of Judgment* (New York: Columbia University Press, 2008) and Albena Azmanova, *The Scandal of Reason: A Critical Theory of Political Judgment* (New York: Columbia University Press, 2012) for more recent, but basically derivative, approaches to the question of judgment.

19. Max Horkheimer, "Traditional and Critical Theory," in *Critical Theory* (New York: Continuum Press, 1971), 210.

20. Ibid.

21. Erich Fromm, *The Sane Society* (New York: Rinehart and Co., 1955), 12.

22. Ibid., 12–13.

23. Ibid., 14.

24. Cf. Michael J. Thompson, "Marxism, Ethics, and the Task of Critical Theory," in M. Thompson (ed.), *Rational Radicalism and Political Theory* (Lanham, MD: Lexington Books, 2011), 161–88.

25. Erich Fromm, *Marx's Concept of Man* (New York: Frederick Ungar, 1961), 59–60. Fromm also notes that "analytical social psychology seeks to understand the instinctual apparatus of a group, its libidinous and largely unconscious behavior, in terms of its socio-economic structure." Erich Fromm, *The Crisis of Psychoanalysis* (New York: Henry Holt, 1970), 144.

26. Erich Fromm, *The Revolution of Hope: Toward a Humanized Technology* (New York: Harper and Row, 1968), 61.

27. Fromm, *The Sane Society*, 15.

28. See particularly Axel Honneth, *The Fragmented World of the Social: Essays in Social and Political Philosophy* (Albany, NY: SUNY Press, 1995), 5ff. These views signify a decisive shift away from the ways that economic life condition and shape subjective action and cognition, a basic premise that Fromm has at the basis of his social theory.

29. For adherents of discourse ethics, this may seem problematic, since social relations, on their view, are essentially communicative. But Fromm suggests that the core problem is that such rational forms of communicative action and discourse are not possible within the force field of capitalist economic life. In this sense, the discursive theoretical position is simply abstract: it tells us nothing about how to correct or include reactionary forms of thought, or power relations grounded in property, or the strong forms of socialization crystallized in hierarchical, legal-rational institutions. A more difficult problem arises, however, when we consider the relation between Fromm's emphasis on human relations and their essential nature for human freedom, development, and health, and Honneth's thesis of the "ethics of recognition." For one thing, both seem to be saying that it is only through humane forms of social relationships that human can develop in a more robust way. But Fromm's thesis is quite distinct in the sense that healthy, recognitive, creative forms of social relations require the removal of specific social and material conditions before that can be realized and even useful. Fromm's roots in Marx means that his social theory is directed at the material forms of life that structure social relations and that these structures are tied historically to the structural-functional logics of capitalist economic life and institutions. Honneth's rejection of Marxism therefore places his social theory in a problematic position because of his rejection of Marx's understanding of the material

dimensions of social relations. There can be recognition in any ethical sense within the sphere of capitalist social relations. For Fromm, on the other hand, Marx plays a more important, nay, a central role in this sense because it is the pathological social relations that will disable the capacity to perform either proper communicative or recognitive acts because these pathologies are rooted in "the whole social organization of man which directs his consciousness in certain directions and blocks him from being aware of certain facts and experiences." Erich Fromm, *Marx's Concept of Man* (New York: Frederick Ungar, 1961), 21.

30. Erich Fromm, *The Crisis of Psychoanalysis* (New York: Henry Holt, 1970), 141.

31. Elsewhere, I have elaborated a Marxian theory of ethics by synthesizing "cognitive" and "evaluative" claims and statements. See my essay, "Philosophical Foundations for a Marxian Ethics," in M. Thompson (ed.), *Constructing Marxist Ethics: Critique, Normativity, Praxis* (Leiden: Brill, 2015), 235–65.

32. For an important, and alternative, analytic view on deriving normative statements from factual statements, see John Searle, "How to Derive an 'Ought' from an 'Is,'" *Philosophical Review* 73, no. 1 (1964): 43–58. Searle claims that a simple statement such as "I hereby promise to pay you, Smith, five dollars" can logically be seen to contain a factual claim from which a normative claim can be derived. Fromm's view, by contrast, or the view that I think we can deduce from his writings, seems to me to be that statements about the nature of human life must contain a normative dimension within them if they are to communicate any kind of valid knowledge about the social world.

33. Fromm, *Marx's Concept of Man*, 62.

34. Karl Marx, *Marx & Engels: Basic Writings on Politics and Philosophy* (New York: Anchor Books, 1959), 244.

35. Erich Fromm, *Man for Himself: An Inquiry into the Psychology of Ethics* (New York: Holt, Rinehart and Winston, 1947), 67.

36. Erich Fromm, *Beyond the Chains of Illusion* (New York: Pocket Books, 1962), 69.

37. Karl Marx, *The German Ideology* (New York: Prometheus Books, 1991), 220.

38. Ibid., 87. Fromm argues that in these arguments by Marx, we see a distinctively Marxian theory of human and social pathologies. *The Crisis of Psychoanalysis*, 62–75.

39. Fromm, *Beyond the Chains of Illusion*, 69.

40. Also influenced by Fromm on this point, see Karen Horney, *Our Inner Conflicts: A Constructive Theory of Neurosis* (New York: Norton, 1945), and *Neurosis and Human Growth: The Struggle toward Self-Realization* (New York: Norton, 1950). More specifically, Horney, like Fromm, sees that "neuroses are brought about by cultural factors—which more specifically meant that neuroses are generated by disturbances in human relationships." *Our Inner Conflicts*, 12. Horney dwells on this latter theme, but ignores the relationship between these "disturbances" and the structural-functional imperatives of the social order of capitalism, something Fromm places at the center of his social theory.

41. Fromm, *Beyond the Chains of Illusion*, 148.

42. Ibid.

43. Erich Fromm, *Escape from Freedom* (New York: Henry Holt, 1941), 185–86.

44. Erich Fromm, *The Anatomy of Human Destructiveness* (New York: Henry Holt, 1973), 27.

45. It should be noted that in seeking to distill a theory of objective ethics from Fromm's work, I distance myself from his more abstract and naïve ideas about social transformation, which I see as largely mistaken, particularly Fromm's ideas about a return to Buddhist values, to a National Council on Conscience, and the like. However, although I agree with Russell Jacoby on this broad point, I see it as mistaken to critique the attempt at constructing an ethics that can serve radical purposes in place of emphasizing instead the sexual character of psychoanalysis. See Jacoby, *Social Amnesia: A Critique of Contemporary Psychology from Adler to Laing* (Boston: Beacon Press, 1975).

46. Fromm notes that "[s]uch value judgments, however, are not mere statements of the likes and dislikes of individuals, for man's properties are intrinsic to the species and thus common to all men." Erich Fromm, *Man for Himself: An Inquiry into the Psychology of Ethics* (New York: Holt, Rinehart and Winston, 1947), 36.

47. Contrast this approach that I am developing here with those that express an "ethical naturalism," which is when "an ethical code emerges within the familiar universe where persons struggle in a material and social context. It functions to expedite the winning of that struggle. Its validity is then to be judged in terms of whether it furthers or impedes the realization of the possibilities opened up by the nature the person has in that context." Milton Fisk, *Ethics and Society: A Marxist Interpretation of Value* (New York: NYU Press, 1980), 23. But this seems problematic, especially when we consider that part of the burden of a radical ethics is not only to be able to chart paths for dissent and struggle but also, and more important, to be able to endow individuals with a set of postulates or a framework for thinking through the veil of ideology and reified consciousness. Hence, Fromm's view seems to me to lead us toward an objective ethics where we can refer back to the essence of socialized human individuality and its various features in order to determine valid ethical principles and postulates.

48. Fromm's critique of Dewey is relevant here: "Like Spinoza, he postulates that objectively valid value propositions can be arrived at by the power of human reason; for him, too, the aim of human life is the growth and development of man *in terms of his nature* and constitution. But his opposition to any fixed ends leads him to relinquish the important position reached by Spinoza: that of a 'model of human nature' as a scientific concept." Fromm, *Man for Himself*, 37–38. The pragmatist, as a consequence, may have allegiance to rational forms of reflection, but by dismissing any kind of foundations for ethical postulates, these claims remain abstract and, in the end, unable to secure the validity of objective ethical claims.

49. Fromm, *Man for Himself*, 36.

50. Karl Marx, *Capital* (New York: Vintage, 1977), 758–59.

51. T. H. Green puts this nicely when he says, "Abstract the many relations from one thing, and there is nothing. They, being many, determine or constitute its definite unity. It is not the case that it first exists in its unity, and then is brought into various

relations. Without the relations it would not exist at all. In like manner the one relation is a unity of the many things. They, in their manifold being, make the one relation." T. H. Green, *Prolegomena to Ethics* (New York: Thomas Y. Crowell, 1969), section 28.

52. Stephen Houlgate makes a similar point when he states that "the words 'concept,' 'judgment,' and 'syllogism' name structures in nature, and so in being itself, not just forms of human understanding and reason. They are, therefore, ontological as well as logical structures—structures of being, as well as categories of thought." *The Opening of Hegel's Logic* (West Lafayette, IN: Purdue University Press, 2006), 116. Also see the excellent discussion by A. Doz, *La logique de Hegel et les problèmes traditionnels de l'ontologie* (Paris: A. Vrin, 1987), 22ff., for a similar view.

53. John Searle, *The Construction of Social Reality* (New York: Free Press, 1995), 15.

54. Ibid., 19.

Part III

RENEWING CRITICAL PHILOSOPHY

Chapter 7

Against the Postmetaphysical Turn
Toward a Critical Social Ontology

My critique of the neo-Idealist paradigm in critical theory requires that I propose some alternative for critical theory to be able to advance and deepen itself as a tradition. My proposition here will be to return to Hegel and Marx to sketch a critical social ontology that can serve as a starting point for this alternative paradigm. Indeed, an essential aspect of the neo-Idealist turn in critical theory has been its turn away from metaphysics and toward a pragmatist conception of social practice. But as I have been arguing, this project, despite its rich academic theoretical production, falls into the trap of mirroring back to us the very social pathologies that constitute and reproduce capitalist modernity. This occurs because the procedural and formalist nature of neo-Idealist theories wrongly posit that critical forms of consciousness and ego-development can be produced from the everyday structures of language, intersubjectivity, and recognition that they see as phylogenetically developed through processes of sociation. The problem has been that the neo-Idealists are unable to decouple these processes of sociation and socialization from the ways that social power and the dominance of elite power actually operate. As I have suggested, we should instead follow the thesis that the social power characteristic of administered society—one based on the imperatives of capital and the centrality of particular forms of production and consumption—is rooted in the forms of consciousness and cultural processes of self-development that neo-Idealists posit as having the intrinsic capacity to critique. But my view has been that if these things, such as language, communication, recognition, and so on, really have this capacity, then critical theory is no longer needed.

This neo-Idealist view is not convincing. In fact, the persistence of theory is needed because these structures, already active and embedded in everyday life, are not only corrupted by social pathologies, thereby weakening their innate critical potential, but also unable to provide a critical perspective distinct from the logics of the prevailing reality. In working off a paradigm based on intersubjectivity and the exchange of reasons, neo-Idealists have not been able to defend against the real problem of epistemic and ethical contingency. Simply put, the intersubjective exchange of reasons and of recognitive relations is presupposed to be able to provide us with rational, critical forms of solidarity and moral norms. What is needed, I maintain here, is a critical theory rooted in a critical social ontology, one that can help secure critical cognition as well as a rational means of diagnosing and comprehending social pathologies and articulating normative propositions. By detaching itself from the ontological questions that Hegel and Marx had pursued, neo-Idealists are unable to secure a rational, universal understanding of the dynamics of a rational social order structured by truly free agents.

In this sense, the real function of theory should be to play a role not dissimilar to what Hegel puts forth as the function of cognition in his *Phenomenology*: we obtain rational (i.e., critical) cognition about the world only by estranging ourselves from it, not by being folded into its immediacy. Only conceptual thought can mediate the object domain, and as concept-users, the central task is to find those concepts that can mediate the world rationally. Marx, too, held to this similar view, for why else would he have placed such an emphasis on the critique of political economy than to seek the proper— that is, rational, concrete concepts—that will reveal the true mechanisms of how the social world actually works? I take this to be a central task of critical theory, but I want to push it one step further. My basic proposition here is that the proper conceptual scheme that can help us mediate the world in a critical sense is to be grounded in a social ontology that can provide us with the content necessary for critical cognition. In this sense, the neo-Idealist strains of critical theory can be corrected by giving them an ontological content, and we can discover in this project a much more comprehensive and more critically engaged form of social critique.

With this in mind, what I would like to propose here is an alternative paradigm for critical theory. I contend that a critical social ontology can provide us with an antireificatory, critical form of cognition that can aid in eroding the thick context of norms and values that constitute social power. Even more, as I have suggested in discussing Fromm's approach to the fact-value split and his idea of a "normative humanism," a critical social ontology will also aid us in diagnosing and assessing the nature of social pathologies that plague subject-formation and cultural forms of life shaped by the dialectics of power and domination. At its core, as I see it, a critical social ontology needs to be able to provide a new space for critical cognition, one that has the ability to provide us with both diagnostic and normative forms of thought unifying them in a single form of cognition. This can be achieved by seeing that thought itself, to be rational and to be critical, needs to be accountable not only to the structures of the world as they empirically exist but also to the world as it could exist *if it were rationally constituted*. But knowing what constitutes this rationality is only properly answerable by grounding critical inquiry in features of human sociality, relatedness, and collective forms of action. But this cannot be reduced to the exchange of reasons, to justificatory discourse, or recognition alone. There is a deeper set of structures that constitute our sociality, and access to these structures is possible through a critical social ontology. In essence, following Hegel's argument in his metaphysics, critique needs to be able to trace the negations of social pathologies back into a structure of being that we can use as the proper space for developing critical reasons. This means understanding the limits of an epistemic approach and embracing the ontological as a sphere for grounding critical cognition, for doing so provides us with a paradigm of thought that can serve to reconcile the positive contributions of the discursive and recognitive strands of contemporary critical theory while avoiding the necessary problems that arise when we pursue them alone. The question is not whether critical theory will have a theory of discourse, of recognition, and so on, or not, but rather within which framework they can usefully be placed.

I. CRITICAL ONTOLOGY AGAINST POSTMETAPHYSICS

The idea that the postmetaphysical turn is also neo-Idealist lies in the false thesis that epistemology—whether conceived in purely Kantian terms or in pragmatist terms—is self-sufficient for an adequate cognitive grasp of the world. The move toward a neopragmatist conception of epistemology has led much of critical theory on a path away from its radical foundations in Hegel and Marx, who saw ontology as a central pathway to a critical comprehension of reality. This pragmatist epistemology is cast as social and intersubjective, but it no longer requires any kind of ontological ground for rational propositions to be stated. It embraces the view that reality can be understood as our own practices and forms of self-understanding mirrored back to us or, as Rolf-Peter Horstmann has argued, "the totality of reality presents itself as the reflex of the way in which we understand ourselves, that is, of the way in which (given certain practices of justification) we are capable of conceptualizing ourselves."[1]

In line with this philosophical vantage point, contemporary critical theory has largely accepted a paradigm of thinking inherited from pragmatism and oriented toward a new form of ethical reasoning. This move—made principally by thinkers such as Karl-Otto Apel, Jürgen Habermas, Axel Honneth, and others of the third generation of critical theory—was made to formulate a theory of practical reason as well as a social-theoretical account of moral learning and cognition that would serve to displace the essentially Marxian foundations of earlier forms of critical theory. According to the latter, capitalism represents a social formation that shapes and structures institutional logics as well as the personality of subjects. This results in a reification of consciousness in which the critical faculties of subjects are rendered sterile in the face of modern forms of domination and dehumanization. Materialism, in this sense, is not a matter of a priority of "matter over consciousness," but rather a theory about the ways that social relations are structured by economic interests and imperatives and that themselves shape cognitive capacities and powers of subjects. Reification is therefore a theory of defective consciousness wherein the subject is unable to grasp the *actual reality* of the objective world (i.e., its essential, dynamic structure) and instead perceives merely its surface characteristics. Reification is therefore a failure to be able to grasp the ontological character of the social world and as a result to be able to judge the deformed practices and institutions that make up capitalist modernity.

But the shift away from a critical theory grounded in Marxian premises was solidified with the move toward the linguistic turn and a "communicative community." Basic to this approach is an understanding of social action and philosophical thinking as "postmetaphysical." According to this view, as Habermas argues, "Modern empirical science and autonomous morality place their confidence solely in the rationality of their own approaches and their procedures—namely, in the method of scientific knowledge or in the abstract point of view under which moral insights are possible."[2] Rationality, therefore, becomes a kind of *formalism*: it is the method rather than the content that determines the extent of rationality of any philosophical approach to reality. We must leave behind any hope to grasp the world in any objectivist or concrete sense and instead choose the path of an antifoundational, situated reason. As Apel further argues defending this philosophical shift, "There exists no super-science which might guarantee the unity of theory and practice through objective analysis. Rather, an ethics is required which provides a mediation between theory and practice by means of a normative principle in the historical situation."[3]

But what is it that can ground such a "normative principle"? In what sense can we close the gap between the analysis of social reality and the critical evaluation of it? The neo-Idealist solution has been to dissolve this question into pragmatic intersubjectivity and, in so doing, make the articulation of norms and values contingent on the discursive and recognitive dimensions of sociality. I would like to call into question this decisive move in critical theory. Specifically, I would like to salvage a form of critical reason from what Habermas and others have relegated to the dustbin of philosophical history. In fact, my thesis here will be that postmetaphysical thinking places us in a situation inferior to that which lies at the heart of Hegel's and Marx's critical-epistemological views. In contrast to the postmetaphysical and anti-foundationalist views held by contemporary critical theory, my thesis here is that we must return to the project of building a critical social ontology that, although abandoned today, can prove a more fruitful path for a critical theory of cognition and judgment. In fact, both Hegel and Marx can show why it is that *metaphysical ideas are required to grasp a truly critical and antireificatory form of practical rationality.* I therefore want to suggest that, against the neo-Idealist strands of contemporary critical theory, we adopt a social-ontological view that places emphasis on the objective structures of human sociality and seek to draw from these basic conceptual premises the kinds of categories required for critical practical rationality.

In contrast to the nonfoundational and postmetaphysical view, I therefore want to propose that critical theory articulate a critical social ontology that will be able to provide foundational claims for cognitive and evaluative forms of thought. I take this view because I am convinced that a rational, radical, and critical theory that holds to an emancipatory theory of society will require access to the immanent rational structure of social life—that is, to the inner potentialities and capacities that human sociality can achieve given the basic shapes or forms that social organization takes. But even more, I think that this is necessary because the neo-Idealists have worked themselves into a decidedly noncritical position. By placing emphasis on the discursive and recognitive capacities of intersubjectivity, they have become unable to secure a nonreified theory of practical reason and cognition in general. Instead, they are unable to secure the realm of a supposedly rational realm of intersubjectivity immune from the effects of reified forms of thought. As a result, without a foundational, objective stance from which to generate critical categories, their theories are far too susceptible to the colonization by the reified categories of the existent reality. Indeed, shattering reification will be possible only to the extent that we are able to formulate an alternative critical model of rationality that can provide a foundation for normative and empirical forms of knowledge; a foundation that can come from understanding the ways that normative and cognitive claims are dialectically sublated into a richer, more critical form of rationality.

But in order to accomplish this, we will need to construct a critical social ontology that can provide for us a basic framework to comprehend social pathologies but also generate normative alternatives to those pathological conditions. My contention is that Hegel and Marx did see that critique required a social-ontological ground from which critical postulates about the social world could be generated. But what has been lost—indeed, what has been purposefully moved away from—is the conviction that an ontology of society is necessary for the project of critique: that we need to establish a framework, a systematic means of being able to judge the reasons that any culture deploys to legitimate its social reality. This means that the question of the relation of social ontology and critical theory is a question of how we can establish a foundation for critical social research as well as a form of critical cognition that can serve to shatter the reification of consciousness. A theory of society that is critical must be able to understand social pathologies, but these can only be properly grasped once we see them as negations of the potential forms of life and negations of the potential ends that social life is capable of achieving. In this sense, social ontology provides us with the conceptual scheme that can underwrite both a project of social research and a normative and emancipatory theory of society.

In what follows, I seek to provide an outline for such a foundation for critical theory through the lens of a *critical social ontology*. My working thesis is that a theory of social ontology can provide us with a foundational framework to build a comprehensive and unified critical theory that can unite the *diagnostic* function of critical theory, or one that seeks to understand and theorize social pathologies—such as alienation, reification, domination, and so on—and the *normative* function of critical theory that should provide us with a means by which we can articulate a critical theory of judgment and thereby provide an emancipatory theory of society as well. In this sense, I want to sketch here a comprehensive critical social ontology that can serve as the ground for dialectically uniting these two aspects of critical theory for the purposes of articulating an impulse for social transformation as the definitive feature of a genuine critical theory of society.

One of the corrosive implications of the "postmetaphysical" and "anti-foundational" turns in philosophy and social theory has been the eclipse of ontology as a necessary component in understanding social critique. In my view, social ontology must serve as a foundation for a renewed critical theory because lacking it, we will fall into the problems that have plagued critical theory at least since the rise of communicative and discourse-based approaches in the 1970s and 1980s—namely, the neo-Idealist trap wherein we are limited to the sphere of intersubjective reason giving and recognitive relations. This neo-Idealist move seals us off from the ontological dimension of reality and therefore cuts off access to the theories of potentiality, actuality, and purposes that can be used to diagnose social pathologies. With the move away from the Hegelian and Marxian foundations of critical theory, recent theorists have dissolved critical questions of social reality into questions of social epistemology. A return to metaphysics—albeit a critical and immanent metaphysics—is therefore needed to return critical theory to its more radical roots because it has the ability to open up for us once again the importance of the ontological in determining and shaping a critical theory of judgment.

II. CONSTRUCTING A CRITICAL SOCIAL ONTOLOGY

To speak of a social ontology is to inquire into the structure of being of social phenomena and society as a totality. Any ontological approach distinguishes between the real existence of an object and its appearance; between the immanent structure of the object and the empirical existence of that object. Another element of social ontology is the relation of parts and wholes: any individual thing must be seen as part of a more organic form of existence in that it derives its relative existence from the totality of which it is a part. Lastly, a social ontology is concerned with the symbolic dimension of how we create social facts; in other words, how it is that forms of collective intentionality are shaped and ordered so as to produce social facts and institutions. What is essential to grasp about any ontological investigation is that social reality cannot be reduced to matter or to its material substrates. Rather, it must be seen to be something more than the physical matter that constitutes it. Thus, a critical social ontology must be able to comprehend the total, real structure of human social life and do so in such a way that it does not reduce sociality to any one of its various features—say, to labor, language, relations, and so on—and thereby be able to serve as the foundational framework for normative-evaluative claims. Hence, my overall thesis here: that a critical social ontology will be able to unite the faculties of critique and judgment.

The postmetaphysical move, by contrast, asks us to ground a critical theory of society in the capacity for rational intersubjective relations—a giving and taking of reasons, of discursive justification, or the recognition of others as a precondition for the development of social rights. But the problem this cannot overcome is the deeper question of reification; in other words, to what extent can we be sure that the exchange of reasons that are deployed, or the kinds of selves that enter into recognitive relations, are in fact not simply reproducing the forms of domination and alienation that constitute capitalist modernity?[4] One salient reason for this is that the structure of language itself is unable to account for the structure of the social world in any normative sense. Indeed, it was Hegel's view that the purpose of phenomenology was not simply a mechanism to provide us with the recognition of others. Rather, what we come to realize through the phenomenological encounter with others is a realization of our interdependence on them. The *Philosophy of Right*, therefore, develops the thesis that increasingly more complex forms of life and interaction—from the family, to civil society, to the "corporations" and ultimately the state—reveal to us the ever-expanding forms of interdependence and that our subjective will must be expanded into a larger frame of reference that takes the common interest into account and, finally, that truly rational, modern institutions objectify and make concrete this reality in their respective logics as well as their ends and purposes. What this means is that

Hegel's search for the universal, the essence of what is rational in human social life, is the realization of this interdependence and our placing it at the center of our subjective wills and our collective understanding of the good life. Hegel's thesis, therefore, seeks to overcome what he saw to be an intrinsic limitation to subjective Idealism—namely, that there was no way to secure concrete, nonrelativistic concepts about the good.[5] Hegel's project is therefore to provide a social ontological understanding of human essence that can provide us with a dialectical synthesis of descriptive and normative categories to judge rationally the social world.

The approach of a critical metaphysics, therefore, needs to be able to link the structures of subjective concepts held *about the world* with those actual structures *in the world*. Hegel's metaphysics is a starting point here because his fundamental aim was to overcome the Kantian dualism of thought and being, to be able to articulate a philosophical system that would be able to breach the chasm between the concepts utilized by us as concept users and the actual way that reason is embedded in the structures of reality. Hegel's metaphysics is therefore an *immanent metaphysics* insofar as it seeks to understand the world rationally according to its own terms, according to the structures, purposes, and ends that essentially constitute it. This interpretation of Hegel's project differs from much of the contemporary interpretations that have taken Klaus Hartmann's interpretation of Hegel's logical system as a scheme of epistemic categories.[6] This has had the result of bringing Hegel's project closer to the Kantian project by seeing his logical categories as features of reason rather than as of the structures of both reality and cognition and, implicitly at least, away from its links with Marx and a more comprehensive ontological approach to social philosophy. Opposing this interpretive move, Stephen Houlgate has argued (correctly, in my view) that "Hegel conceives of his logic as both a logic and a metaphysics or an ontology because he understands the fundamental concepts of thought to be identical in logical structure to the fundamental determinations of being itself."[7] Concepts are therefore not simply subjective categories of thought, they are the very structures of reality itself: the explanatory reasons why things occur, or appear as they are, or work as they do, and so on.[8] This means that critical rationality should search for the essential structures that explain reality, not for epistemic forms of justification with criteria of validity detached from those essential structures. We proceed to this kind of knowledge, it is important to note, not from any essential external vantage point but from our inquiry into the object itself. Hence, the object of inquiry must generate its own categories for comprehension: phenomenology leads us dialectically to ontology.

This is an important corrective to the Kantian-pragmatist move in neo-Idealist theory. For one thing, we now have a more compelling criterion for normative postulates about the world since they must in some sense refer to reality and therefore refer to the rational (explanatory) structure that is that reality.[9] Indeed, Hegel is clear that this is the very nature of reason that moves beyond what is immediate and what is arbitrary and that moves into the realm of essence, of the "inner reality" (*Inneres*) of objects. Rationality cannot be understood as read off of the justifications of others, nor off of the "lifeworld" of experience of the given reality. Hence, in the *Phenomenology* he writes that "here the essence of the thing is not yet complete; it must be known as self not only through the immediacy of its being and its determinateness, but also as *essence* or *inner reality* (*Inneres*)."[10] This essence is not something abstract or disembodied; it is the very immanent structure that produces that thing.[11] Hence, the limits of the intramundane attempt to cultivate critical rationality must fail because it is unable to push into the essential structure of reality, to be able to forge a context for critical judgment. Objective reality and the processual dynamics of that reality is what Hegel is after here as the true object of critical rationality. These immanent structures are not only real by which we can say they are *in* the world but also graspable by thought, by cognition. In constructing a critical ontology we are looking for those reasons that *properly grasp the world*. Essence is therefore not a static thing, or composite of things. It is only properly understood as process: as the process of how a thing can become what it immanently has the potential to be. In this sense, all reality is seen as in tension with its own negation. There are negating factors that can mutilate the realization of the actuality of any thing. Here the dialectic between fact and norm comes into play. Explanatory reason, as long as it is sufficiently critical, is able to grant us access to a kind of reasoning that is, as I suggested in the previous chapter, evaluative-cognitive. This means that rational grasp of the essential structure of any thing must also generate the normative means of its evaluation. There are no ontological categories that stand alone, outside of history, in some Platonic sense, that we can use to diagnose empirical reality. Rather, the immanent structures that make things what they are are also structures that can manifest themselves incompletely in that they present us with deficient appearances of what the essential structure can be in potential.

We should not dismiss this kind of rationale as abstract or in some way mystical and antiscientific. Rather, it constitutes the very essence of the method of critical cognition itself. The unity of fact and value, of cognitive and evaluative forms of knowledge, derives from the thesis that it alone truly comprehends the whole of the object. To say that something does not realize its concept is to say that it possesses some kind of defect that negates that fuller, richer development; it is to posit that there is some kind of contradiction between what something empirically is and what it can potentially be. A pen that is unable to write properly is not an *actual* pen no more than a log is a tree. These empirical realities are not actual (*wirklich*) because they do not manifest the inner structure that makes pens and trees what they are in their fullest sense. When taken as a method of social critique, contradictions within society emerge into cognitive view once we begin to posit the deeper essential structure of what social institutions, indeed, what society itself, has as its purpose. For Hegel and Marx, this was the notion that society was a totality of interdependent persons who cooperatively create their world and come to realize through this act of creation and self-creation the rational essence of their being and the essential nature of things in the world. They become self-conscious of themselves as both relational and interdependent as well as necessarily active in needing to form the world according to reason. Hence, in this basic ontological thesis, we see the limits of neo-Idealist theory: once we analytically separate elements from the whole—discourse, communication, recognition, or whatever—we lose the capacity to see that these are moments within a larger dynamic totality. Their role is not to serve as the foundation for a critical theory but to aid in the cognitive realization of the essential structure of human sociality. They must, in this sense, reveal the ways that the prevailing reality either promotes or negates the kind of equal interdependence that should lead to the universal needs of the community. Individuals are not to be folded into some communal blob, but rather to be reshaped as understanding that a rational, critical individuality is one in which each seeks to make judgments, follow norms, and validate institutions that promote the social freedom that is *worthy of the commitments and practices of rational individuality itself.*[12] The essential thesis here is that only by changing the space of reasons within which we operate by grounding them in the ontological domain can we begin to act differently in the world, change the world according to the dictates of what is rational.

So this second feature of a critical social ontology is that human beings are not simply concept users, they are also beings that actively shape their world, who seek to bring about the rational within the given reality itself. For both Hegel and Marx, what constitutes the essence of human social life is not only their interdependence and the way that individuality is functionally related to the structure of social relations but also that we must achieve the self-consciousness of this essential structure. Our labors, mental and physical, must be collectively organized for the common ends of the community, one purpose of which is the development and cultivation of free individuals who are themselves self-conscious of this sociality as the ground for their own freedom. The key to social criticism, in this sense, is to see that the kind of cognition that liberal-capitalist societies encourage is a narrow, desiccated one that is unable to grasp this deeper ontological, essential reality; it is therefore unable to see that pathologies of the prevailing reality as rooted in distortions of this sociality, as frustrations of the immanent potential of the actualization of a cooperative form of social interdependence that can enable a higher, more developed form of culture and individualism. Human beings are interdependent beings who live and are shaped within a web of relations that foster their essential potentialities, but they are also equally to be seen not as contemplative but as active beings who achieve self-consciousness only through the active self-creation. Of course, for Hegel, activity is largely the work of conceptual thought, whereas for Marx it is human labor, but, in fact, the supposed divide between Hegel and Marx here is not as significant as has traditionally been argued. In truth, Hegel and Marx must be seen as placing emphasis on different elements of this process, not as refuting one another.

But at the heart of the Hegelian position is the thesis developed in the *Phenomenology* that the essential structure of cognition is *Geist*, which means that our ideas about the world and our individuality are all dependent on recognitive relations that grant our thoughts, actions, and intentions their meaning. What Hegel develops in this argument is the notion that our concepts, norms, practices, and self-understanding and self-consciousness are all dependent on the mutual recognition of others of those concepts, norms, and so on that the subject takes to be valid in the world. Agency is social in the sense that it requires for its satisfaction the recognition by others within my ethical community (*Sittlichkeit*) the very ideas and practices that I instantiate.[13] Free agency is therefore the specific kind of agency that is self-conscious of the reasons that underwrite the practices, norms, concepts, commitments, and so on, and that these reasons are *rational* in that they express not simply the mutually held norms of the community that could be arbitrary, but rather that they express *objectively valid reasons* or reflect the actual nature of our sociality.

Here is where the project of the *Phenomenology of Spirit* and the *Science of Logic* can be seen to interpenetrate. Hegel saw not only that the nature of objective *Geist* needed institutions to constitute ethical life but also that there was more to the nature of our social interdependence than mutual recognition of the norms and practices of others in the community. What Hegel's thesis of recognition is providing is the means, a cognitive opening into the realm of our essential nature, of human life itself. The consciousness that views itself as independent comes to the view that this independence is impossible alone; that there is no way to be independent without being dependent on others. But this "dependence" should not be seen as the negation of independence, but its enhancement and fulfillment, its true realization through interdependence. The dialectic of identity and nonidentity that seems at first to be opposed is in fact to be dialectically sublated. In this sense, the relation between independence and dependence, or between A and ~A, therefore is resolved only through a form of cognition that has in view the self-consciousness of social *interdependence*, +A, or a knowledge of self-and-other-relations that grasps a kind of relatedness that is free but also necessary. These kinds of relations would be structured so that our interdependence leads to our mutual self-development; they would be shaped and structured in order to develop and cultivate individuals who are also cognizant that their enhanced form of individuality is a function of the cooperative labor and practices of others within the community. Nevertheless, it would be the individual himself who endorses these relations; there would be no melting of the self into the community. This +A is therefore an enhanced form of cognition, of self-consciousness that grasps this ontological reality of human relatedness and sociality. It would allow the individual to have in view a critical form of judgment that would be able to call into question the purposes and ends of the social institutions, practices, and structures of society. This enhanced form of cognition is not an arbitrary content to consciousness; it is rather the true essence of what it means to be a free agent, a person. As Frederick Beiser describes this move, "What the ego learns through this dialectic is that it cannot satisfy its ideal of independence as an isolated individual but only as one part of a whole."[14] Thus, any form of failed sociality will be one that erodes this essential dependence, that distorts it, that shapes it for ends other than what its essential structure has the capacity to promote: the *Verwirklichung* of the free self and, at the same time, the free community.

Hegel sees that there is a deeper ontological structure of interdependence that should also rationally undergird our plans as agents, and this deeper ontological structure is the very context for free individual agency. Robert Pippin, too, sees that there is more to this social dependence than linguistic and communicative relations: "Hegel is claiming there to be a far deeper level of human dependence than would be claimed by mutual commitment to an ideal communicative exchange, or mutual obligation to a moral law. The content of one's status as an individual and not just the linguistic form of its expression is also taken to reflect such recognitional dependence."[15] But what I am suggesting here is that Pippin's portrait of Hegel's theory of social dependence itself needs to be deepened. Hegel sees this social dependence (I prefer interdependence) as an ontological claim, one that is objective and yet also not reducible to material substrates. It is an ontology of the social that is constituted by us and that also constitutes us. It is an ontology because it is shaped by the kinds of norms and practices that any given community shares and which individuals use in their actions and thoughts. But it is also ontological in that there is a rationally best way to shape those relations. We need a ground, an objective basis for judging which forms of social relatedness, which structures of social cooperation, what kinds of social institutions and processes, and so on, are most consonant with the development and cultivation of free individuality and the kinds of sociality required for that development. Indeed, seen in the light of his metaphysics, it is only when we are able to grasp the essential structure of any thing that we can be said to know it rationally, and the universal feature of our humanity is our sociality. The *Phenomenology* points this out at the level of consciousness and cognition just as the *Philosophy of Right* posits it as the basis for the state and rational laws and institutions. Hegel's social philosophy is therefore meant to bring to consciousness what modern man is able to cognize for the first time: that he is only free to the extent that each is free; that this freedom requires that social dependence be shaped for our mutual benefit, and that the freedom of my own self is dependent on my rational knowledge of the freedom of all others.

Hegel sees in the ontology of mutual interdependence not only a cognitive claim about the true nature of mental states but also a kind of ontological structure of being that constitutes mental states, our material needs (hence the discussion of Adam Smith, James Steuart, and political economy more generally in Hegel's writings), serving to understand the fundamental relations that make our sociality also underwrite a truly free form of agency and self-development. This structure of interdependent relations constitutes the essential reality or ground for our freedom. A modern, free agent will therefore act with the reality of this interdependence as the foundation for judging and acting in the world. He will see that—not unlike Rousseau's general will—that he can only be free once others in his community are free also—that is, once they, too, grasp conceptually this ontology of essential relations. Failed forms of sociality are therefore those that are unable to fulfill or realize this richer context of sociality, unable to grasp it as an Idea, as the source of their norms and practices. It is one reason why Marx's ideas moved to political economy as a central means of understanding the distorted structure of social relations under capital: a distorted structure that expressed itself through the pathologies of alienation, commodity fetishism, the distorted forms of reasoning and consciousness produced by economic logics, and so on. Marx gives richer content to capitalist society that Hegel does, theorizing exploitation, labor, and other aspects of political economy. But what he still shares with Hegel no less than Aristotle is that we are socially dependent on others, that this is an ontological reality that transforms its shape over historical time in an anthropological sense, and that only once we order our concepts, institutions, actions, and plans according to this as a general end for the community will we be able to realize our freedom.

The implications here for critical theory are numerous. Only by promoting the kind of cognition that is self-aware of its essential interdependence on others, that sees this interdependence as active in the way individuals are shaped in a processual sense, can we begin to interrogate the social pathologies that are created when social life is organized according to dependence and control as well as according to exclusion or exploitation. We lack not only recognition and self-esteem but also the cognitive grasp of our essential sociality as the basis for a rational society and a rational self. But this inter-dependence is not an epistemic construct, nor is it a contingent fact of life. Rather, it is the ontological structure of human sociality itself. It embraces more than recognitive relations in that it is part of a thicker reality of production and creation, and it is more than linguistic and communicative in that it requires a deeper grasp of the actual ways in which human beings rely on others without communicative practices. It is also a historical reality in that the forms that this interdependence takes changes over time. Ancient Egyptians differ from modern societies not in their interdependence, but in the form it took: whether it is organized for the good of one, or the good of a few, or the good of all. This social interdependence is therefore the essential structure of social life, and the core riddle of history has been to discover the rational organization of this essential property of our social being.

Hence, dependence, exclusion, exploitation, and so on, are social pathologies because they corrupt the higher potentialities of personal and collective development that are possible if inclusion, cooperation, and interdependence were primary. Any time we sanction social structures, norms, or values that promote or reproduce these kinds of perverted social life, we are disabling the totality of social life from realizing its essence through us. We are, in effect, deconstructing the kind of social solidarity and rich nexus of social relations that will enable the realization of a more rational social order and culture. Particularity thereby comes to dominate individuality: we are colonized by the drives and interests of the atomized self. Hence, recognition, for instance, must be dialectically sublated into the more general structure of the whole: into the ontology of interdependent social relations. In this sense, recognition is not simply a means for the I to evolve into a kind of we-thinking, it is also a means of establishing a critical grasp of social ontology. Far from being a social-psychological mechanism, it is the means by which we grasp the objective ontological essence of human sociality. Stressing the emotive side of interpersonal recognition, Honneth and his followers misconstrue the real power of recognition as a cognitive mechanism. Recognition should lead us to the ontological realm, to a space of critical reasons that are *grounded in the world*.

What a critical theory of society must consistently keep in view is the ontology of human interdependence as the essential structure for higher forms of social being and individual development and freedom. When the structure of social relations are instead distorted by power relations, when they become unequal, or relations of dependence, or when cultural forms encourage a kind of independence of consciousness from social relations and realities, we negate the potentialities that living in social relations ought to be able to grant us. This is no communitarian argument, it rather posits that a richer, more satisfying conception of freedom than that of liberalism is one in which we can be at home in the institutions of our society, and this entails that these institutions are *for us*, that they serve the ends of all of us, and these ends include the promotion of those public goods, social relations, and forms of culture and so on that will cultivate citizens who rationally grasp that these institutions are organized not for a minority, not for reasons we cannot validate, and not for purposes or ends that are not in our complete, universal interest as members of a cooperative community of equals. This insight is at the heart of a critical theory that embraces a social-ontological vantage point.

The attempt to provide ethical postulates or ideas without an ontology of the social must lead to relativism since there is no way to have access to the concrete nature of what society is and, more important, as I will show below, to grasp the purposes that social life should be able to achieve. If we cannot comprehend the deeper purposes and developmental potentialities that social life makes possible for individuals, then we are simply at the mercy of the different language games and discourses that are deployed by prevailing structures of life.[16] Common sense, the logic of the prevailing reality, pushes itself onto the "play of language." The postmetaphysical move is therefore unable to defend against reification and therefore unable to shape a coherent vantage point for critique. If we view the metaphysical in an objective, material sense, we can see that a critical ontology is one that is capable of articulating a critical space of reasons wherein the critique of capitalist society draws on a distinctive form of critical rationality. Indeed, the core thesis here is that a critical capacity for judgment can only most fruitfully be developed by understanding how the predominant, existing reality either facilitates or constrains the kinds of social relations that produce the common goods that provide for our individual and collective development and good. If Hegel is right—as was Rousseau before him and Marx after—that modern man can only be truly free by grasping how his individuality can only be properly and most rationally developed when it is part of a web of interdependent social relations and practices, then we can see how this ontological basis for judgment is opposed to the postmetaphysical view.

This critical rationality is given more potency when we are able to contrast the existence of things with their inner rational essence. This dynamic, dialectical form of cognition seeks to reconstruct the given reality and to provide the kinds of organizational requirements that can lead to a higher realization or "actualization" (*Verwirklichung*) of the object. Hence Marcuse, discussing Hegel's ontological views, argues that it is engaged in "the high task of bringing the existing order of reality into harmony with the truth. The separation of thought from being implies that thought has withdrawn before the onslaught of 'common sense.' If, then, truth is to be attained, the influence of common sense is to be swept away and with it the categories of traditional logic, which are, after all, the philosophical categories of common sense that stabilize and perpetuate a false reality."[17] The critical role of social ontology here is that we are able to contrast the irrational, particularist forms of social life with more rational, universalist forms of life. This means asking about the deeper purposes of social practices, norms, and institutions. It means asking about what the purpose of living and working together actually is. It is the organization, the shaping of our interdependent social relations and our consciousness of this fact, that constitutes the real basis for any critical theory of society. Hence, cognitively grasping this simultaneously grants us the normative-evaluative move necessary for critique. Lacking any ontological ground, we have no way to secure a critical-rational claim. We cannot rely on language, discourse, or recognition in the way that the neo-Idealists do because they provide no objective ground for critical claims. We are instead asked to accept a postmetaphysical form of reasoning that promises that critical rationality will emerge from social practices themselves. Contrary to this, Hegel and Marx saw that we have to contrast real human needs and qualities with false needs and qualities. Social practices on their own will tend to reproduce false needs and ideas since they are given no means of contrasting them with any other form of life.[18]

Indeed, Marx made use of just such an ontological and epistemological move. He sees that normative and cognitive claims—or claims about values and facts—must be dialectically sublated for us to be able to make genuinely critical statements. In other words, truth-claims about the world must capture the actual nature of the world as dynamic and as internally related to other objects and processes. In this sense, a critical truth-claim is one in which we seek to understand the empirical state of any thing by asking about its essential structure and the potentialities of that structure. No object can be reduced to its physical structure, to matter alone, in order to comprehend it. Rather, it must be understood to exist and operate within a systemic context of causes and relations, and this means that *any understanding of a social fact synthesizes empirical and normative claims*: there is no objective ontology of social facts that simply occurs on its own through internal mechanisms and potentialities.[19] The emancipatory aims of a Marxian critical theory are therefore concerned with the extent to which the reification of consciousness can be shattered; this is important because reification is ultimately the obfuscation of the ontological structure of our sociality, of the substantive understanding that all social facts are the emergent property of an essential social-relatedness, a kind of essential structure that, depending on how that structure of relations is shaped and ordered, *expresses* the nature of human freedom.

Hegel and Marx were therefore deeply invested in the project of developing a theoretical means by which we place the comprehension of reality at the center of our cognitive and normative claims. What is essential here is that the social-ontological claims that they both articulate seek to grant us a scheme for rational comprehension and critical judgment: we can not only know what things are by grasping their essential, rational structure but also derive evaluative claims based on the cognitive grasp of the objects; we can therefore obtain critical knowledge of the deformed state of existence by contrasting it with the essential structure and the immanent potentialities of that part of that essential structure. A critical social ontology will therefore have to provide us with a conceptual scheme that will be able to show how certain *essential structures* of human sociality are deformed and mutilated by the forms or shapes of organization it takes on under capitalism. It will need to reveal a deeper, essential rational structure inherent to human sociality that is deeper and richer than the neopragmatist thesis of reason-giving and reason-taking intersubjectivity. Indeed, it will need to grant us access to the kind of essence that will allow us to ground critical statements and claims.

III. CRITICAL ONTOLOGY AND CRITICAL SOCIAL THEORY

Both Hegel and Marx look back to Aristotle, but not for the simple reason that he postulates a social essence to man. Rather, their view is different, since they want to introduce the modern concept of the individual into the Aristotelian structure of thought. What they see in Aristotle's thesis is that substantialist, relational, and processual ontologies already exist as a conceptual scheme for understanding critical judgment. Book I of the *Politics* plays the crucial role of laying out a basic social ontology from which empirical claims about political institutions and practices can be derived and evaluative judgments about these institutions and practices are formed. Aristotle's basic contention is that human beings can only develop to their most complete, perfected form (ἐντελέχεια) within the thick network of diverse social relations that constitutes the *polis*. His social ontology therefore blends the substantialist, relational, and processual dimensions of ontology in order to understand what he sees to be the natural conditions for human growth and development.[20] Later books of the *Politics* are therefore concerned with developing forms of judgment based on what he views as the natural reality of human social life. Hence, he posits that the common interest is an essential value not simply because it rests on a series of moral arguments but also because it is a good that best provides for the natural needs of human beings living together to promote their common life. Hence, the category Aristotle sees as central is one in which an individual has all that he needs because he is part of the richest set of social relations that only complex polis life can provide. He calls this "self-sufficiency" (αὐταρκείας), and it conveys a particular way of understanding social relations. They are to provide each individual with his requisite needs and, in a certain sense, form a kind of relational structure that has as its purpose the self-sufficiency, the capacity to fulfill the needs of

its members. Indeed, since individuals are to be conceived as the ends they
achieve, that these ends require a social-relational context that grants them
the sufficient preconditions for their processual development, then we can
see that Aristotle is seeking to construct an ontology of the social that is both
social-relational and *processual* or dynamic.

Of course, Hegel and Marx diverge from Aristotle's idea that there is
some *natural essence* of human sociality and instead see it as an achievement of human cultural development. The point to stress here, however, is
that unlike Kantian and neo-Kantian approaches to social theory and social
science, they did accept that a social ontology is necessary for the formulation of rationally valid forms of social knowledge as well as for the formulation of critical-evaluative forms of judgment that can promote a rational
society. In the end, we can derive the view that a critical social ontology
has in view a concept of society that is dynamic, relational, processual, and
also constructivist. It possesses these elements synthesized into a totality,
one in which we must see that the degradation of human social life can
be understood as the defective operation of these mechanisms toward the
enrichment of the others. The basic proposition that Hegel introduces into
his ontology of the social—and one that Marx, too, incorporates and that
was derived from the ideas of Rousseau—is that the individual and society
are different dimensions of a singular reality, that this reality is essentially
relational and processual, and that it necessitates certain forms of self-
cognition to be able to guide practical reasoning (and, for Marx, *theoretical*
reflection as well).

Hegel and Marx are not very different on one central thesis: that the
essential structure of human life is interdependent and ought to be organized
according to universal (i.e., rational) human needs. They saw that the relation
between individual and society had to be understood dialectically, that each
was a dimension of the other. The main concern of a critical social ontology,
however, is that we do not proceed to construct an *a priori* set of categories of
the social world. What we need to do is proceed negatively—that is, through
an analysis of the pathologies and thwarted potentialities that any historically bound culture evinces. We cannot remain within a negative dialectic,
as Adorno would have it, but instead must seek to understand that social
pathologies are comprehensible as an inversion of some basic set of needs
and potentials that any social context produces. We must, then, comprehend
the ontology of social reality phenomenologically. Hence, Marx, in the *Economic and Philosophical Manuscripts*, holds:

> [T]he social character is the universal character of the whole movement; as
> society itself produces *man* as *man*, so it is *produced* by him. Activity and mind
> are social in their content as well as in their *origin*; they are *social* activity

and *social* mind. The *human* significance of nature only exists for *social* man, because only in this case is nature a *bond* with other *men*, the basis of his existence for others and of their existence for him. Only then is nature the *basis* of his own *human* experience and a vital element of human reality. The *natural* existence of man has here become his *human* existence and nature itself has become human for him. Thus *society* is the accomplished union of man with nature, the veritable resurrection of nature, the realized naturalism of man and the realized humanism of nature.[21]

Marx's thesis unites the idea that a social ontology possesses relational and processual dimensions, that part of what we can understand as the objective, essential being of human life is that it is necessarily constituted by relations and by processual development from which to construct a theory about the ways that human life—individual and collective—is essentially social. In this sense, thought, language, labor, and so on are all *social products* and therefore are expressions of a fundamental social reality that marks human life as distinctive, as essentially being what it is. The substance of human social reality is therefore, on Marx's view, something objective in nature: it is something that we can understand as relational, processual, and constructivist.

By this, ontology must be understood not as materialist—something that smacks of natural physics and should be dropped as a term—as a kind of reality that can take different forms. Human beings are able to shape their own relations, the processes that shape them, and to construct form of life and meaning according to their needs. But it is only when these attributes of social being are freely determined, the products of genuine self-creation, that we can speak of an emancipated society.[22] The negation of this is what critical theory must seek to diagnose. For the young Marx, it is, in the final analysis, man's interdependence on others that constitutes his *Gattungswesen*, which we can see now as a concept that is essentially ontological in that the substance of man's true being, his *Gattungswesen*, is social-relational, processual-developmental, and constructivist through the activity of labor.[23] These need not be "directly communal," but rather need to be seen *as the ontological reality that underwrites the substance of what it means to be human in its fullest sense*. Individuals are therefore properly understood as social:

Even when I carry out *scientific* work, etc. an activity which I can seldom conduct in direct association with other men, I perform a *social*, because *human*, act. It is not only the material of my activity—such as the language itself which the thinker uses—which is given to me as a social product. *My own existence* is a social activity. For this reason, what I myself produce I produce for society, and with the consciousness of acting as a social being.[24]

Marx seeks to show that this basic social ontology must be the means by which we understand the pathology of alienation that has been made possible by the emergence of private property:

> Private property has made us so stupid and partial that an object is only *ours* when we have it, when it exists for us as capital or when it is directly eaten, drunk, worn, inhabited, etc., in short, *utilized* in some way; although private property itself only conceives these various forms of possession as *means of life*, and the life for which they serve as means is the *life* of *private property*—labor and creation of capital.[25]

The pathological effects of private property are here seen to be the product of the fact that it undermines the crucial social essence of human collective and individual life. Marx here argues that we can understand the negative effects of private property only by comprehending what it is thwarting: namely, the fact that our social reality is a product of a collective kind of agency and that social interdependence and our social relatedness all constitute the source for our own lives.

Private property therefore alienates us from this reality, from the fact that, as an institution, it shreds our sociality into particularistic forms of atomism. It is an institutionalization of a false understanding of human being—one that rests on the liberal conception of human agency and independence that both Hegel and Marx saw as only partial in its conception of human reality. What is central for Marx's critique of capitalism—and one that critical theorists should have at the base of their critical work as well—is that social pathologies are the negation of the essence of the kind of human life that modern forms of social organization can make possible: that the end, the proper *telos* of our labor, our institutions, our forms of life should be to enhance and enrich the common goods that allow for our social and individual development and perfection. The problem with capitalism is therefore that it violates this basic tenet—a tenet that Marx derives from a basic social-ontological account of the potentialities of modern social life. Therefore, even in *Capital*, Marx retains this essential evaluative view when he asks us to imagine as an alternative to capitalist social relations and economic life

> a community of free individuals, carrying on their work with the means of production in common, in which the labor power of all the different individuals is consciously applied as the combined labor power of the community. All the characteristics of Robinson's labor are here repeated, but with this difference: that they are social instead of individual. . . . The total product of our community is a social product.[26]

For Marx, too, the common interest of the community serves as the evaluative mechanism by which the organization of social relations and the purposes or ends of social life are to be gauged. The critique of capitalism achieves its coherence, in this sense, from the social-ontological foundation that Marx lays out, one inherited from Aristotle and Hegel.

IV. SOCIAL ONTOLOGY AND ITS RELATION
TO CRITIQUE AND JUDGMENT

By rethinking Hegel and Marx along the lines of a critical social ontology, we are able to renew the importance of critical cognition, viewing it as a central means of grasping the ways that social life ought to be constructed around the dictates of rational, universal needs and capacities. The importance of how we shape the essential, distinctive feature of human social life and the kinds of individuality that that kind of life would require is the aim of critical cognition. In this way we can see how the various pathologies—such as alienation, reification, exploitation, and so on—that plague modern societies can have a more comprehensive explanation. The diagnostic function of critical theory—in other words, its effort to understand the sources and mechanisms of social pathologies—is here wedded with the normative function, or the intention to understand the proper functioning that should be attributed to social phenomena.

Once we accept that a critical social ontology is in fact a fruitful means of conceptualizing social life, then we can begin to ask how any ontological approach can help reconstruct critical theory toward a more rationally compelling and realist set of ends for social transformation. My next thesis will therefore be that we can derive from this critical social ontology the necessary methodological categories for diagnosing social pathologies as well as positing emancipatory claims against such pathologies. Such a project needs to proceed *negatively*: since there can be no recipe, no ready-made set of prerequisites that we can determine *a priori* for what makes a fully realized or actualized human being or society, we can begin with the pathologies in order to work back to the positive moments. What the negative performs is the task of diagnosing the distortion of some essential feature of our sociality. It leads us to ask how we can re-create a social form so as to solve the pathology. But to do this, we need to have some criteria for which properties grant us fuller, richer forms of development and which do not. We need to be able to contrast the rational with the irrational, to be able to understand what conditions allow for the fuller development of any individual, and this leads us back to the kind of social resources that any society evinces. A society's institutions, both Hegel and Marx seem to be saying, require our commitments only when they serve universal (i.e., rational) ends and purposes; only when we can endorse them as serving the interdependent relations to which I as an individual belong. This is the political element that Aristotle had in view, modified by Hegel: since the purpose of social life is to promote our freedom as rational individuals, we cannot rationally commit ourselves to those institutions, norms, and relations that are organized for the benefit of others and not for our full, complete benefit. The Kantian "kingdom of ends" now possesses content and loses its purely formal character. The enhanced cognition that allows for this kind of critical subjectivity is informed by, or has as its ground, a critical social ontology.

Suffice it to say that the real core hypothesis that structures Marx's critical social science is that there exists a social ontology to human life—that the different shapes that social relations can take *produce different kinds of social being*. We judge these kinds of social being based on the extent to which individuals are able to attain the development of their potentialities. Defective forms of consciousness accompany defective forms of social reality and social relations. Hence, we can see that a social pathology, such as alienation, is only graspable as a defect of a more integrated whole. Human beings are cooperative beings, they develop in and through their relations, and insofar as this ontological structure of human sociality is accepted, any emphasis on partiality, on the particular over the whole, must lead to pathologies—of the individual, of culture, and so on. Alienation is the *negation* of the higher reality that can be achieved by human beings if they were to exist under different social conditions. But this is an inherently ontological vantage point in the sense I have been developing it here in that it requires categories of social being and becoming for it to be rationally understood. As Marcuse notes in his comments on Hegel's metaphysical doctrine, "The human being, to take an instance, finds his proper identity only in those relations that are in effect the negation of his isolated particularity—in his membership in a group or social class whose institutions, organization, and values determine his very individuality."[27]

It also is able to provide us with another important and distinctive feature of critical ontological reasoning: the dialectical sublation of facts and values or, put differently, the capacity to articulate a theory of judgment based on the objective characteristics of any object. For Hegel and Marx, the processual aspect of social ontology requires that we see the essence or truth of things *in process*, as becoming, and the appearance of things as static entities. Society therefore cannot be conceived as an abstract entity. Rather, as Marx correctly notes in the *1844 Manuscripts*, "It is above all necessary to avoid postulating 'society' once again as an abstraction confronting the individual. The individual is the social being. The manifestation of his life—even when it does not appear directly in the form of a communal manifestation, accomplished in association with other men—is therefore a manifestation and affirmation of social life."[28] Rather, the method of Hegel and Marx sought to overcome the distinction between facts and values by showing that the ontological categories of social being themselves contain the criteria for their rational understanding as well as their evaluation.[29] Hence, the empirical observation of any social reality must, according to the critical-ontological view, summon its evaluation. Knowing what alienation is, understanding its deeper structure and cause, requires knowledge of the totality of social life of which it is a part. This means showing how alienation is deformation of self- and other-relations and the kinds of partial existence that results from such social forms.

Human beings, therefore, cannot achieve freedom, for instance, simply through the blind mechanisms of becoming, but rather require a self-consciousness of that freedom, that their rational faculties must be self-directed for them to be free and fully developed. But this kind of rationality cannot be grasped alone, through solipsism, but rather entails that we come to conceptual awareness of our related interdependence on others for our own individuality to be developed. We therefore need to ask whether the ways that the organization or shape of these social relations that shape me and in which I participate either thwart or enhance this distinctive kind of individuality. This requires that I interrogate the forms of consciousness, the forms of collective intentionality that my culture employs to construct social norms and facts and whether these norms, practices, institutions, and so on enhance or thwart this socialized kind of individuality. This means the critique of my social world and my judgment of it are unified.

V. THE RELATION BETWEEN CRITICAL ONTOLOGY AND CRITICAL COGNITION

As I have sought to show up to this point, the importance of ontology is to demonstrate the untenability of the thesis that epistemology is self-sufficient to grasp and understand the social world and to generate a rational ethical life. My alternative thesis has been that we should understand a critical cognition as functionally related to the kind of critical social ontology that I have been pursuing here. It means that the very problem of cognition under capitalism—that of reification—should be understood not, as Axel Honneth has recently sought to reconstruct it, as a failure of recognition, or as Rahel Jaeggi's recent attempt to reconstruct alienation as a failure of social relations, but rather as a *failure to cognize, to be able to grasp the fuller purposes and ends that society ought to be able to realize.* It means a failure to understand that the purpose of living in society is the production and enrichment of its members—that this kind of common interest is one that is a best fit for the kind of substantive, relational, and processual realities that constitute a fully developed form of sociality. Indeed, just as the project of social critique should seek to explore the negations of this richer form of social purpose, so our form of ethical reflection, or moral cognition, can only become truly critical once we are able to impose this alternative ontological-conceptual scheme onto the prevailing reality. Only once we are able to do this can we seek to explode reification and shatter its capacity to hamper cognition from grasping the social totality.

I would now like to return to the primacy of reification as a problem of critical theory and show how it is intrinsically related to a critical social ontology. My thesis here will be that critical cognition requires a critical social ontology as a foundation for critique of judgment. The reason for this, as I have been suggesting, is that the reification is the inability to perceive the rational structure of social being—its deeper purposes and its rational structure. It is an inability to cognize that the correct purposes of living within society are for the enhancement and enrichment of common goods, for the nitrification of all of its members. Reification is the cognitive incapacity to perceive this reality—a failure not of recognition but of the cognitive grasp that the purposes of social life are essentially common in terms of their ends. Lukács suggests that the very act of labor makes this evident to its participants, that all that is needed is a slight cognitive reorientation to see that social reality is produced through collective means and that capitalist social relations are a deformation of this deeper rational truth. Lukács's thesis of reification is therefore that reified consciousness is unable to perceive the essentially cooperative and interdependent nature of human social life. Modern society has made available to human beings for the first time a truly universal kind of cooperative life, one in which the common interest of all as well as the full development of the individual is possible not only in material terms but also in terms of the moral and intellectual resources of our culture. The key is to wipe away the false forms of knowing that prevent us from seeing this and from using it as the basis of a new, more emancipatory form of praxis. Capitalism is therefore not simply a mechanism of inequality and domination but also the negation of a rational, free, human society.

If what I have been suggesting thus far is even conditionally accepted, then we must admit that an ontology of society is only of use to the extent to which it is accessible by the *cognition of subjects*. Hegel's approach to this is phenomenological. He sees that it is through everyday experience that we can come to grasp the essential structure of human freedom. This occurs, as he lays it out in the "master-slave dialectic" in the *Phenomenology*, once rational subjects recognize that their own individual freedom is dependent on the other. Hence, what we come to grasp phenomenologically is not simply a concrete "other" through the process of recognition, but rather the structure of sociality itself upon which I and others depend. The "I that is the we and the we that is the I" is meant to distinguish an enhanced form of cognition in which individuals come to see their embeddedness in a broader system of social relations and dependencies, and their freedom as realizable only within a set of such relations in which these interdependencies are uniformly cared for and nourished by the society as a whole. The universal can only realize itself once individuals come to realize their essential interdependence on others—this is something that institutions such as the modern family, the free market, and corporations are supposed to help subjects perceive.

Marx is different in that he *sees theoretical knowledge* as a necessary precondition to grasp modern social processes affected by capitalism. We cannot rely on the phenomenological dimensions of consciousness in everyday life to be able to grasp the whole. Hence, *Capital* is an effort in de-reification: an attempt to set critical ideas against an all-encompassing, distorted reality. Since capitalism has transformed social relations to such an extent, it is no longer possible for mere intersubjectivity alone to accomplish the task of comprehending the whole. Furthermore, since the ontology of society exists in such a way so as to possess both a reality principle and a potentiality principle, the neo-Idealist and neopragmatist moves are unable to secure a critique of the norms and "constitutive rules" of collective intentionality that are themselves generated by the social relations and established purposes that have been set by class-based society. Rather, the commodity form has so shaped modern subjectivity that we need to come to terms with the objective processes inherent in the logic of commodity production in order to grasp the organizing principle of capitalist society. In the end, the problem of reification pointed to by Lukács relates to this as well since only by overcoming the immediacy of the commodity form can workers finally see reality for what it is: process, as social relations that have been distorted by capital, but the extraction of surplus, and therefore that they live in a social world that is based on extraction, domination, and the thwarting of the general, common interest of society *as a whole*.[30] This therefore becomes the essence of the emancipatory interest that is derived from a critical social ontology.

A critical social ontology, therefore, is able to introduce us to categories of social life that are essential for a critical and indeed radical confrontation with modern liberal-capitalist society. It places critical theory back at the center of a struggle against irrational social institutions, helps dissolve the false forms of cognition, the false needs and wants, and the distorted forms of subjectivity that such a society evokes and cultivates. Once we are able to grasp conceptually the view that social reality is a collective product, a cooperative expression of human agency—only then can we begin to glimpse what an emancipated society would look like. Once we see that the institutions and products of society should have as their central purpose our collective benefit, and that this collective benefit is the very precondition for a truly free individuality, we can see that critical theory offers us more than mere social criticism. Only by transforming the forms of cognition that we use to understand our world can we begin self-consciously to re-create forms of life to according to the demands of reason. Self-development as a common good, as the emergent property of a society shaped by relations of interdependence, therefore as values, can then confront the prevailing ideas about the deeper purposes living in society. But this kind of rational society cannot be achieved on its own, through some mechanism embedded in history. It requires that critical thinking grasp the pathologies of the present and construct an alternative vantage point to grasp the essential purposes of social and individual life. Hence, critical theory still retains its salience in helping to reconstruct the requisite capacities of critique and judgment that must be employed for the ends of social transformation. Perhaps when we rethink the purpose of critical theory along these lines, the political implications that it entails, we will see that the project of critical theory remains at the center of the rational project to create a cooperative, free society of equals.

NOTES

1. Rolf-Peter Horstmann, "Substance, Subject and Infinity: A Case Study of the Role of Logic in Hegel's System," in Katerina Deligiorgi (ed.), *Hegel: New Directions* (London: Acumen Press, 2006), 70.

2. Jürgen Habermas, *Postmetaphysical Thinking: Philosophical Essays* (Cambridge, MA: MIT Press, 1992), 35.

3. Karl-Otto Apel, *Towards a Transformation of Philosophy* (London: Routledge and Kegan Paul, 1980), 232.

4. Horstmann therefore rightly questions this postmetaphysical move: "It is also extremely difficult to see how this approach can avoid the sort of epistemic relativism that Hegel himself clearly repudiated: the view not only that our knowledge claims can only be justified contextually, but also that the states of affairs to which those knowledge claims refer, what Hegel calls the 'other' of the concept, can be dissolved entirely into certain epochally or culturally dependent conceptual constellations." "Substance, Subject and Infinity," 70.

5. As Charles Taylor explains on this point, "The demands of reason are thus that men live in state articulated according to the Concept, and that they relate to it not just as individuals whose interests are served by this collectively established machinery, but more essentially as participants in a larger life. And this larger life deserves their ultimate allegiance because it is the expression of the very foundation of things, the Concept. Freedom has been given a very concrete content indeed." *Hegel* (Cambridge: Cambridge University Press, 1975), 374.

6. Klaus Hartmann, "Hegel: A Non-Metaphysical View," in Alasdair MacIntyre (ed.), *Hegel: A Collection of Critical Essays* (Notre Dame: University of Notre Dame Press, 1976), 101–24. Also see Béatrice Longuenesse, *Hegel's Critique of Metaphysics* (New York: Cambridge University Press, 2007).

7. Stephen Houlgate, "Hegel's Logic," in Frederick C. Beiser (ed.), *The Cambridge Companion to Hegel and Nineteenth-Century Philosophy* (New York: Cambridge University Press, 2008), 118. Houlgate further contends that "[t]his is true of all the categories analysed in the *Science of Logic*. The logical structure of the concept of 'something'—a concept that *we* must employ—is at the same time the logic structure of whatever *is* something in the world." Ibid.

8. James Kreines has recently proposed interpreting Hegel's metaphysics as setting forth a distinctive form of "explanatory reason." Kreines correctly counterposes this to the epistemic project of exchanging reasons: "The point is to single out the idea of the *explanatory* reason (the why or because) as opposed to *epistemic* reasons (as, for example, where we have the practice of asking for reasons, in the sense of justifications, for claims one has made)." James Kreines, *Reason in the World: Hegel's Metaphysics and Its Philosophical Appeal* (New York: Oxford University Press, 2015), 8.

9. Kreines reiterates this by arguing that, for Hegel, "the reasons that explain why things are as they are and do what they do are always found in immanent 'concepts' (*Begriffe*), akin to immanent universals or kinds (*Gattungen*)." Ibid., 22. This is a methodological point that points toward a deeper form of knowledge than the communicative and merely intersubjective conception of reason and action.

10. G. W. F. Hegel, *Phänomenologie des Geistes* (Frankfurt: Suhrkamp, 1970), 578.

11. Stanley Rosen argues that when Hegel employs the concept of essence, "he is referring to ontological truth in two closely related senses. First: he means that truth is a property of states of affairs or processes of actuality. Second: not only is the 'property' in question not a linguistic predicate or the name of a determinate structural feature of things, but it is the underlying process by which formal structure is produced." *The Idea of Hegel's Science of Logic* (Chicago: University of Chicago Press, 2014), 236.

12. See the important discussion by Allen Wood, *Hegel's Ethical Thought* (New York: Cambridge University Press, 1990), 195–218.

13. Robert Pippin notes on this aspect of Hegel's theory of social recognition and agency that "clearly what is driving his argument is, can be nothing other than, a social status, and a social status exists by being taken to exist by members of some community. A priest, a knight, a statesman, a citizen, are not, that is, natural kinds. One exists as such a kind by being treated as one, according to the rules of that community. And the radicality of Hegel's suggestion is that we treat being a concrete subject of a life, a free being, the same way. It is in this sense that being an individual already presupposes a complex recognitional status." "Recognition and Reconciliation: Actualized Agency in Hegel's Jena *Phenomenology*," in Deligiorgi (ed.), *Hegel: New Directions*, 125–42, 133.

14. Frederick Beiser, *Hegel* (New York: Routledge, 2005), 185.

15. Pippin, "Recognition and Reconciliation," 137–38.

16. The error here seems to me to be that we cannot expect any concrete grasp of social reality to come from language games, but from a conceptual scheme that grants us access to the structure of the objective world. Hilary Putnam's project of constructing an ethics without an ontology therefore relies on this sort of language constructivism. As a result, he advocates for a "pragmatic pluralism," which is little more than a conceptual relativism: "Pragmatic pluralism does not require us to find mysterious and supersensible objects *behind* our language games; the truth can be told in language games that we actually play when language is working, and the inflations that philosophers have added to those language games are examples, as Wittgenstein said—using a rather pragmatist turn of phrase—of 'the engine idling.'" *Ethics without Ontology* (Cambridge, MA: Harvard University Press, 2004), 22. The fundamental error here is that a critical social ontology does not look for "supersensible" or "mysterious" objects, but rather the *immanent logics and rational structures inherent within concrete forms of social life*.

17. Herbert Marcuse, *Reason and Revolution: Hegel and the Rise of Social Theory* (Boston: Beacon Press, 1960), 123.

18. Erich Fromm notes on this problem, "Only on the basis of a specific concept of man's nature can Marx make the difference between true and false needs of man. Purely subjectively, the false needs are experienced as being as urgent and real as the true needs, and from a purely subjective viewpoint, there could not be a criterion for the distinction." *Marx's Concept of Man* (New York: Frederick Ungar, 1961), 62.

19. This interpretation of Marx's critical ontology therefore differs from the critical realist position that is more tuned to issues in natural science rather than social facts. On this view, "the generative mechanism may come to be established as real in the course of the ongoing activity of science." Roy Bhaskar, *A Realist Theory of Science* (London: Verso Books, 1975), 45 and *passim*. The problem with the critical realist position is that it fails to take into account the ways that social facts are couched in cognitive mechanisms, values, and practices and not as objectively distinct mechanisms generating reality.

20. Aristotle is still a substantialist, but his social ontology absorbs the relational and processual elements of ontology into the very definition of substance itself since the term *substance* is used to translate οὐσια, or "essential being." Nevertheless, Aristotle is explicit in his sublation of the three kinds of ontology, as in Book I of his *Politics* when he argues that "τέλος γὰρ αὕτη ἐκείνον, ἡ δὲ φύσις τέλος ἐστίν, οἷον γὰρ ἕκαστόν ἐστι τῆς γενέσεως τελεσθείσης, ταύτην φαμὲν τὴν φύσιν εἶναι ἑκάστου, ὥσπερ ἀνθρώπου, ἵππου, οἰκίας." *Politics*, 1252b, 33. This sentence shows how Aristotle sees the seamless relation between substantialist, relational, and processual aspects of ontology in his conceptualization of human sociality.

21. Karl Marx, *Economic and Philosophical Manuscripts* in Erich Fromm, *Marx's Concept of Man*, 129.

22. Erich Fromm therefore notes regarding this vision in the young Marx, "First, man produces in an associated, not competitive way; he produces rationally and in an unalienated way, which means that he brings production under his control, instead of being ruled by it as by some blind power." *Marx's Concept of Man*, 60.

23. Lukács seeks to build a comprehensive social ontology on the basis of labor as "teleological positing," or the capacity to shape nature in line with preconceived mental plans. See his *Ontology of Social Being*, vol. 3, *Labor*, 29–63. For an interesting discussion of Marx's concept of *Gattungswesen* and human relations of dependence, see Michael Quante, "Das gegenständliche Gattungswesen. Bemerkungen zum intrinsischen Wert menchlischer Dependenz," in R. Jaeggi and D. Loick (eds.), *Nach Marx. Philosophie, Kritik, Praxis* (Frankfurt: Suhrkamp, 2013), 69–88.

24. Marx, *Economic and Philosophical Manuscripts*, 130. Cf. the discussion by Jean Hyppolite, *Studies on Marx and Hegel* (New York: Harper Torchbooks, 1969), 127ff.

25. Marx, *Economic and Philosophical Manuscripts*, 132.

26. Karl Marx, *Capital*, vol. 1 (New York: Vintage, 1977), 78.

27. Marcuse, *Reason and Revolution*, 124.

28. Marx, *Economic and Philosophical Manuscripts*, 130.

29. Elsewhere, I have explored this theme in more depth. See my paper "Philosophical Foundations for a Marxian Ethics," in M. Thompson (ed.), *Constructing Marxist Ethics: Critique, Normativity, Praxis* (Leiden: Brill, 2015), 235–65.

30. Lukács notes, "By becoming aware of the commodity relationship the proletariat can only become conscious of itself as the object of the economic process. For the commodity *is* produced and even the worker in his quality as commodity, as an immediate producer is at best a mechanical driving wheel in the machine. But if the reification of capital is dissolved into an unbroken process of its production and reproduction, it is possible for the proletariat to discover that it is itself the *subject* of this process even though it is in chains and is for the time being unconscious of the fact. As soon, therefore, as the ready-made, immediate reality is abandoned the question arises: 'Does a worker in a cotton factory produce merely cotton textiles? No, he produces capital. He produces values which serve afresh to command his labor and by means of it to create new values.'" *History and Class Consciousness* (Cambridge: MIT Press, 1971), 180–81. This is a distinctively ontological kind of reasoning in that the critique of the process is approached not from the material involved but the kinds of meaning and relations to which the material (in this case, wool) belongs. Capital, again, is not a thing, but a process, a set of specific relations relating things in specific ways, as well as a congealed set of norms, practices, and concepts that organize subjective reasoning as well as cultural and social structures and reality itself.

Bibliography

Adorno, T. W. 1973. *Negative Dialectics*. New York: Continuum.

Adorno, T. W. 1991a. "Culture and Administration," in *Adorno: The Culture Industry: Selected Essays on Mass Culture*. New York: Routledge.

Adorno, T. W. 1991b. "The Culture Industry Reconsidered," in *Adorno: The Culture Industry: Selected Essays on Mass Culture*. New York: Routledge.

Adorno, T. W. 1994. "Subject and Object," in Andrew Arato and Eike Gebhardt (eds.), *The Essential Frankfurt School Reader*. New York: Continuum, 497–512.

Adorno, T. W. 1998a. *Aesthetic Theory*. Minneapolis: University of Minnesota Press.

Adorno, T. W. 1998b. *Critical Models: Interventions and Catchwords*. New York: Columbia University Press.

Adorno, T. W. and Max Horkheimer. 1995. *Dialectic of Enlightenment*. New York: Continuum..

Althusser, Louis. 1971. *Lenin and Philosophy and Other Essays*. New York: Monthly Review Press.

Amariglio, J., S. Resnick, and R. Wolff. 1988. "Class, Power, and Culture," in C. Nelson and L. Grossberg (eds.), *Marxism and the Interpretation of Culture*. Urbana: University of Illinois Press.

Apel, Karl-Otto. 1980. *Towards a Transformation of Philosophy*. London: Routledge and Kegan Paul.

Arendt, Hannah. 1954. *Between Past and Future*. New York: Penguin.

Aristotle. 1957. *Politics*. Oxford: Clarendon Press.

Athens, Lonnie. 2002. "'Domination': The Blind Spot in Mead's Analysis of the Social Act." *Journal of Classical Sociology* 2: 25–42.

Athens, Lonnie. 2010. "Human Subordination from a Radical Interactionist's Perspective." *Journal for the Theory of Social Behaviour* 40, no. 3: 339–68.

Athens, Lonnie. 2012. "Mead's Analysis of Social Conflict: A Radical Interactionist's Critique." *American Sociologist* 43: 428–47.

Azmanova, Albena. 2012. *The Scandal of Reason: A Critical Theory of Political Judgment*. New York: Columbia University Press.

Barker, David C. and James D. Tinnick. 2006. "Competing Visions of Parental Roles and Ideological Constraint." *American Political Science Review* 100, no. 2: 249–63.

Beckert, J. 2010. "Institutional Isomorphism Revisited: Convergence and Divergence in Institutional Change." *Sociological Theory* 28, no. 2: 150–66.

Beiser, Frederick. 2005. *Hegel*. New York: Routledge.

Bergesen, A. 1993. "The Rise of Semiotic Marxism." *Sociological Perspectives* 36, no. 1: 1–22.

Bernstein, Richard J. 1983. *Beyond Objectivism and Relativism: Science, Hermeneutics, and Praxis*. Philadelphia: University of Pennsylvania Press.

Bernstein, Richard J. 1991. *The New Constellation: The Ethical-Political Horizons of Modernity/Postmodernity*. Cambridge, MA: MIT Press.

Bernstein, Richard J. 2010. *The Pragmatic Turn*. Cambridge: Polity Press.

Bhaskar, Roy. 1975. *A Realist Theory of Science*. London: Verso Books.

Block, James. 2002. *A Nation of Agents: The American Path to a Modern Self and Society*. Cambridge, MA: Harvard University Press.

Block, James. 2012. *The Crucible of Consent*. Cambridge, MA: Harvard University Press.

Boehme, Eric. 2011. "Embodiment as Resistance: Evaluating Stephen Bronner's Contributions to Critical Theory," in Michael J. Thompson (ed.), *Rational Radicalism and Political Theory: Essays in Honor of Stephen Eric Bronner*. Lanham, MD: Lexington Books.

Borman, David A. 2009. "Labour, Exchange and Recognition: Marx Contra Honneth." *Philosophy and Social Criticism* 35, no. 8: 935–59.

Bourdieu, Pierre. 1990. *The Logic of Practice*. Cambridge: Polity Press.

Bourdieu, Pierre. 1991. *Language and Symbolic Power*. Cambridge, MA: Harvard University Press.

Brandom, Robert B. 2009. *Reason in Philosophy: Animating Ideas*. Cambridge, MA: Harvard University Press.

Bronner, Stephen Eric. 1992. *Moments of Decision*. New York: Routledge.

Bronner, Stephen Eric. 2004. *Reclaiming the Enlightenment*. New York: Columbia University Press.

Brudney, Daniel. 2010. "Producing for Others," in Hans-Christoph Schmidt am Busch and Christopher Zurn (eds.), *The Philosophy of Recognition: Historical and Contemporary Perspectives*. Lanham, MD: Lexington Books, 151–88.

Bubner, Rüdiger. 2003. *The Innovations of Idealism*. New York: Cambridge University Press.

Buchwalter, Andrew. 2012. *Dialectics, Politics, and the Contemporary Value of Hegel's Practical Philosophy*. New York: Routledge.

Carpenter, D. 2001. *The Forging of Bureaucratic Autonomy: Reputations, Networks, and Policy Innovation in Executive Agencies, 1862–1928*. Princeton, NJ: Princeton University Press.

Celikates, Robin. 2009. "Recognition, System Justification and Reconstructive Critique," in Christian Lazzeri and Soraya Nour (eds.), *Reconnaisance, identité et intégration sociale*. Paris: Presses Universitaires de Paris Ouest, 82–93.

Cohen, G. A. 1978. *Karl Marx's Theory of History: A Defence*. Oxford: Oxford University Press.

Cruikshank, Barbara. 1996. "Revolutions Within: Self-Government and Self-Esteem," in Andrew Barry, Thomas Osborne, and Nikolas Rose (eds.), *Foucault and Political Reason: Liberalism, Neo-Liberalism, and Rationalities of Government*. Chicago: University of Chicago Press.

Dahms, Harry. 1997. "Theory in Weberian Marxism: Patterns of Critical Social Theory in Lukács and Habermas." *Sociological Theory* 15, no. 3: 181–214.

Dahrendorf, Rolf. 1958. "Out of Utopia: Towards a Re-Orientation of Sociological Analysis." *American Journal of Sociology* 64: 115–27.

Dahrendorf, Rolf. 1959. *Class and Class Conflict in Industrial Society*. Stanford, CA: Stanford University Press.

Dannemann, Rüdiger. 1987. *Das Prinzip Verdinglichung. Studie zur Philosophie Georg Lukács*. Frankfurt: Sendler Verlag.

de Boer, Karin. 2013. "Beyond Recognition? Critical Reflections on Honneth's Reading of Hegel's *Philosophy of Right*." *International Journal of Philosophical Studies* 21, no. 4: 534–58.

Dean, Mitchell. 1999. *Governmentality: Power and Rule in Modern Society*. London: Sage.

Dennett, Daniel. 1987. *The Intentional Stance*. Cambridge, MA: MIT Press.

Dent, Nicholas. 1988. *Rousseau: An Introduction to His Psychological, Social and Political Theory*. Oxford: Basil Blackwell.

Deranty, Jean-Philippe. 2013. "Marx, Honneth, and the Tasks of a Contemporary Critical Theory." *Ethical Theory and Moral Practice* 16, no. 2: 745–58.

Dews, Peter. 1987. *Logics of Disintegration: Post-Structuralist Thought and the Claims of Critical Theory*. London: Verso.

DiMaggio, Paul and Woody Powell. 1983. "The Iron Cage Revisited: Institutional Isomorphism and Collective Rationality in Organizational Fields." *American Sociological Review* 48, no. 2: 147–60.

Doz, André. 1987. *La logique de Hegel et les problèmes traditionnels de l'ontologie*. Paris: A. Vrin.

Dufour, Frédéric Guillaume and Éric Pineault. 2009. "Quelle théorie du capitalisme pour quelle théorie de la reconnaissance?" *Politique et Sociétés* 28, no. 3: 75–99.

Durkheim, Emile. 1938. *The Rules of Sociological Method*. New York: Free Press.

Durkheim, Emile. 1983. *Pragmatism and Sociology*. Cambridge: Cambridge University Press.

Feenberg, Andrew. 2014. *The Philosophy of Praxis: Marx, Lukács and the Frankfurt School*. London: Verso.

Ferrara, Alessandro. 2008. *The Force of the Example: Explorations in the Paradigm of Judgment*. New York: Columbia University Press.

Fisk, Milton. 1980. *Ethics and Society: A Marxist Interpretation of Value*. New York: NYU Press.

Forst, Rainer. 2012. *The Right to Justification: Elements of a Constructivist Theory of Justice*. New York: Columbia University Press.

Forst, Rainer. 2014. *Justification and Critique: Toward a Critical Theory of Politics*. Cambridge: Polity Press.

Foucault, Michel. 2004. *Naissance de la biopolitique: Cours au Collège de France (1978–1979)*. Paris: Gallimard & Seuil.

Freud, Sigmund. 1959. *Group Psychology and the Analysis of the Ego*. New York: Norton.

Fromm, Erich. 1941. *Escape from Freedom*. New York: Henry Holt.

Fromm, Erich. 1947. *Man for Himself: An Inquiry into the Psychology of Ethics*. New York: Holt, Rinehart and Winston.

Fromm, Erich. 1955. *The Sane Society*. New York: Rinehart and Co.

Fromm, Erich. 1961. *Marx's Concept of Man*. New York: Frederick Ungar.

Fromm, Erich. 1962. *Beyond the Chains of Illusion*. New York: Pocket Books.

Fromm, Erich. 1968. *The Revolution of Hope: Toward a Humanized Technology*. New York: Harper and Row.

Fromm, Erich. 1970. *The Crisis of Psychoanalysis*. New York: Henry Holt.

Fromm, Erich. 1973. *The Anatomy of Human Destructiveness*. New York: Henry Holt.

Galbraith, John Kenneth. 1967. *The New Industrial State*. Boston: Houghton Mifflin.

Giddens, Anthony. 1986. *The Constitution of Society: Outline of the Theory of Structuration*. Berkeley: University of California Press.

Godelier, Maurice. 1986. *The Mental and the Material: Thought, Economy and Society*. London: Verso.

Goff, Tom W. 1980. *Marx and Mead: Contributions to a Sociology of Knowledge*. London: Routledge and Kegan Paul.

Goldman, Lucien. 1973. *The Human Sciences and Philosophy*. London: Jonathan Cape.

Gorz, André. 1989. *Critique of Economic Reason*. London: Verso.

Green, T. H. 1969. *Prolegomena to Ethics*. New York: Thomas Y. Crowell.

Haber, Stéphane. 2007. "Recognition, Justice and Social Pathologies in Axel Honneth's Recent Writings." *Revista Ciencia Politica* 27, no. 2: 159–70.

Habermas, Jürgen. 1971. *Knowledge and Human Interests*. Boston: Beacon Press.

Habermas, Jürgen. 1973. *Legitimation Crisis*, trans. Thomas McCarthy. Boston: Beacon Press.

Habermas, Jürgen. 1976. *Zur Rekonstruktion des Historischen Materialismus*. Frankfurt: Suhrkamp.

Habermas, Jürgen. 1984. *The Theory of Communicative Action*, vol. 1, trans. Thomas McCarthy. Boston: Beacon Press.

Habermas, Jürgen. 1985. *Philosophical-Political Profiles*. Cambridge, MA: MIT Press.

Habermas, Jürgen. 1987. *The Theory of Communicative Action*, vol. 2, trans. Thomas McCarthy. Boston: Beacon Press.

Habermas, Jürgen. 1988. *On the Logic of the Social Sciences*, trans. Shierry Weber Nicholsen and Jerry A. Stark. Cambridge, MA: MIT Press.

Habermas, Jürgen. 1992. *Postmetaphysical Thinking: Philosophical Essays*. Cambridge, MA: MIT Press.

Habermas, Jürgen. 1998. *The Inclusion of the Other: Studies in Political Theory*. Cambridge, MA: MIT Press.

Hartmann, Klaus. 1976. "Hegel: A Non-Metaphysical View," in Alasdair MacIntyre (ed.), *Hegel: A Collection of Critical Essays*. Notre Dame, IN: University of Notre Dame Press.

Harvey, David. 2005. *A Brief History of Neoliberalism.* New York: Oxford University Press.

Haslanger, Sally. 2012. *Resisting Reality: Social Construction and Social Critique.* New York: Oxford University Press.

Haslanger, Sally (forthcoming). "What Is (Social) Structural Explanation?" *Philosophical Studies.*

Hegel, G. W. F. 1970. *Phänomenologie des Geistes.* Frankfurt: Suhrkamp.

Hegel, G. W. F. 1977. *The Difference between Fichte's and Schelling's System of Philosophy.* Albany, NY: SUNY Press.

Hegel, G. W. F. 1995. *Lectures on Natural Right and Political Science.* Berkeley, CA: University of California Press.

Hetherington, Marc J. and Jonathan D. Weiler. 2009. *Authoritarianism and Polarization in American Politics.* New York: Cambridge University Press.

Holmwood, John. 2008. "From 1968 to 1951: How Habermas Transformed Marx into Parsons." *Czech Sociological Review* 69, no. 5: 923–43.

Honneth, Axel. 1995. *The Fragmented World of the Social: Essays in Social and Political Philosophy.* Albany, NY: SUNY Press.

Honneth, Axel. 1996. *The Struggle for Recognition: The Moral Grammar of Social Conflicts.* Cambridge, MA: MIT Press.

Honneth, Axel. 2007. *Disrespect: On the Normative Foundations of Critical Theory.* Cambridge: Polity Press.

Honneth, Axel. 2008. *Reification: A New Look at an Old Idea.* New York: Oxford University Press.

Honneth, Axel. 2010a. *Das Ich im Wir. Studien zur Anerkennungstheorie.* Frankfurt: Suhrkamp.

Honneth, Axel. 2010b. *The Pathologies of Individual Freedom: Hegel's Social Theory.* Princeton, NJ: Princeton University Press.

Honneth, Axel. 2011. *Das Recht der Freiheit. Grundriß einer demokratischen Sittlichkeit.* Frankfurt: Suhrkamp.

Horkheimer, Max. 1971a. "Authority and the Family," in *Critical Theory: Selected Essays.* New York: Continuum, 47–128.

Horkheimer, Max. 1971b. "Traditional and Critical Theory," in *Critical Theory: Selected Essays.* New York: Continuum.

Horkheimer, Max. 1974 [1947]. *Eclipse of Reason.* New York: Continuum Press.

Horney, Karen. 1945. *Our Inner Conflicts: A Constructive Theory of Neurosis.* New York: Norton.

Horney, Karen. 1950. *Neurosis and Human Growth: The Struggle toward Self-Realization.* New York: Norton.

Horstmann, Rolf-Peter. 2006. "Substance, Subject and Infinity: A Case Study of the Role of Logic in Hegel's System," in Katerina Deligiorgi (ed.), *Hegel: New Directions.* London: Acumen Press.

Houlgate, Stephen. 2006. *The Opening of Hegel's Logic.* West Lafayette, IN: Purdue University Press.

Houlgate, Stephen. 2008. "Hegel's Logic," in Frederick C. Beiser (ed.), *The Cambridge Companion to Hegel and Nineteenth-Century Philosophy.* New York: Cambridge University Press, 111–34.

Houlgate, Stephen. 2009. "Phenomenology and *De Re* Interpretation: A Critique of Brandom's Reading of Hegel." *International Journal of Philosophical Studies* 17, no. 1: 29–47.

Hyppolite, Jean. 1969. *Studies on Marx and Hegel*. New York: Harper Torchbooks.

Ingram, David. 1987. *Habermas and the Dialectic of Reason*. New Haven, CT: Yale University Press.

Jacoby, Russell. 1975. *Social Amnesia: A Critique of Contemporary Psychology from Adler to Laing*. Boston: Beacon Press.

Jaeggi, Rahel. 2005. *Entfremdung. Zur Aktualität eines sozialphilosophischen Problems*. Frankfurt: Campus Verlag.

Jakubowksi, Franz. 1976. *Ideology and Superstructure in Historical Materialism*. London: Allison and Busby.

Jost, John T., Mahzarin R. Banaji, and Brian Nosek. 2004. "A Decade of System Justification Theory: Accumulated Evidence of Conscious and Unconscious Bolstering of the Status Quo." *Political Psychology* 25, no. 6: 881–919.

Kalyvas, Andreas. 1999. "Critical Theory at the Crossroads: Comments on Axel Honneth's Theory of Recognition." *European Journal of Social Theory* 2, no. 1: 99–108.

Kavoulakos, Konstantinos. 2011. "Back to History? Reinterpreting Lukács' Early Marxist Work in Light of the Antinomies of Contemporary Critical Theory," in M. Thompson (ed.), *Georg Lukács Reconsidered: Critical Essays in Politics, Philosophy and Aesthetics*. New York: Continuum, 151–71.

Kögler, Hans Herbert. 1997. "Alienation as Epistemological Source: Reflexivity and Social Background after Mannheim and Bourdieu." *Social Epistemology* 11, no. 2: 141–64.

Kosman, Aryeh. 2013. *The Activity of Being: An Essay on Aristotle's Ontology*. Cambridge, MA: Harvard University Press.

Kreines, James. 2015. *Reason in the World: Hegel's Metaphysics and Its Philosophical Appeal*. New York: Oxford University Press.

Lakoff, George. 2002. *Moral Politics: How Liberals and Conservatives Think*. Chicago: University of Chicago Press.

Lau, Chong-Fuk. 2006. "Language and Metaphysics: The Dialectics of Hegel's Speculative Proposition," in Jere O'Neill Surber (ed.), *Hegel and Language*. Albany, NY: SUNY Press, 55–74.

Little, Daniel. 1986. *The Scientific Marx*. Minneapolis: University of Minnesota Press.

Longuenesse, Béatrice. 2007. *Hegel's Critique of Metaphysics*. New York: Cambridge University Press.

Lovett, Frank. 2010. *A General Theory of Domination and Justice*. New York: Oxford University Press.

Luhmann, Niklas. 1995. *Social Systems*. Stanford, CA: Stanford University Press.

Luhmann, Niklas and Jürgen Habermas. 1971. *Theorie der Gesellschaft oder Sozialtechnologie. Was leistet die Systemforschung?* Frankfurt: Suhrkamp.

Lukács, Georg. 1971. *History and Class Consciousness*. Cambridge, MA: MIT Press.

Marcuse, Herbert. 1960. *Reason and Revolution: Hegel and the Rise of Social Theory*. Boston: Beacon Press.

Marcuse, Herbert. 1964. *One-Dimensional Man: Studies in the Ideology of Advanced Industrial Society.* Boston: Beacon Press.

Marcuse, Herbert. 1970. "The Obsolescence of the Freudian Concept of Man," in *Five Lectures.* Boston, MA: Beacon Press, 44–61.

Marcuse, Herbert. 1972. "A Study on Authority," in *Studies in Critical Philosophy.* Boston: Beacon Press.

Marx, Karl. 1959. *Marx & Engels: Basic Writings on Politics and Philosophy.* New York: Anchor Books.

Marx, Karl. 1971. *Zur Kritik der Politischen Ökonomie,* in *Marx-Engels Werke,* vol. 13. Berlin: Dietz Verlag.

Marx, Karl. 1973. *Grundrisse.* London: Penguin Books.

Marx, Karl. 1977. *Capital,* vol. 1. New York: Vintage.

Marx, Karl. 1991. *The German Ideology.* New York: Prometheus Books.

Maynor, John. 2003. *Republicanism in the Modern World.* Cambridge: Polity.

McMurtry, John. 1978. *The Structure of Marx's World-View.* Princeton, NJ: Princeton University Press.

McNay, Lois. 2008. *Against Recognition.* Cambridge: Polity Press.

Meister, Robert. 1990. *Political Identity: Thinking through Marx.* Oxford: Basil Blackwell.

Mendieta, Eduardo. 2002. *The Adventures of Transcendental Philosophy.* Lanham, MD: Rowman & Littlefield.

Mészáros, István. 2010. *Social Structure and Forms of Consciousness,* vol. 1. New York: Monthly Review Press.

Myrdal, Gunnar. 1969. *Objectivity in Social Research.* New York: Random House.

Park, Robert. 1952 [1934]. "Dominance," in Everett Hughes (ed.), *Human Communities.* New York: Free Press, 159–64.

Parsons, Talcott. 1951. *The Social System.* Glencoe, IL: Free Press.

Parsons, Talcott. 1960. *Structure and Process in Modern Societies.* Glencoe, IL: Free Press.

Parsons, Talcott. 1968 [1937]. *The Structure of Social Action.* New York: Free Press.

Parsons, Talcott. 1969. *Politics and Social Structure.* New York: Free Press.

Parsons, Talcott. 1991. "The Place of Ultimate Values in Sociological Theory," in Charles Camic (ed.), *Talcott Parsons: The Early Essays.* Chicago: University of Chicago Press, 231–58.

Parsons, Talcott and Edward Shils (eds.). 1951. *Toward a General Theory of Action.* Cambridge, MA: Harvard University Press.

Pettit, Philip. 1997. *Republicanism: A Theory of Freedom and Government.* New York: Oxford University Press.

Piccone, Paul. 2008. "Artificial Negativity as a Bureaucratic Tool?" in Gary Ulmen (ed.), *Confronting the Crisis: Writings of Paul Piccone.* New York: Telos Press.

Pineault, Éric. 2008. "Quelle théorie critique des structures sociales du capitalisme avancé?" *Cahiers de recherche sociologiques* 45: 111–30.

Pippin, Robert. 2006. "Recognition and Reconciliation: Actualized Agency in Hegel's Jena *Phenomenology,*" in Katerina Deligiorgi, *Hegel: New Directions.* London: Acumen, 125–42.

Pippin, Robert. 2008. *Hegel's Practical Philosophy: Rational Agency as Ethical Life*. New York: Cambridge University Press.

Piven, Frances Fox and Richard Cloward. 1993. *Regulating the Poor: The Functions of Public Welfare*. New York: Vintage.

Plekhanov, G. 1992. *Fundamental Problems of Marxism*. New York: International Publishers.

Polanyi, Karl. 1971. *The Great Transformation*. Boston: Beacon Press.

Postone, Moishe. 1993. *Time, Labor, and Social Domination: A Reinterpretation of Marx's Critical Theory*. New York: Cambridge University Press.

Postone, Moishe. 2004. "Critique, State, and Economy," in Fred Rush (ed.), *The Cambridge Companion to Critical Theory*. New York: Cambridge University Press, 165–93.

Proctor, Robert N. 1991. *Value-Free Science? Purity and Power in Modern Knowledge*. Cambridge, MA: Harvard University Press.

Putnam, Hilary. 2004. *Ethics without Ontology*. Cambridge, MA: Harvard University Press.

Quante, Michael. 2011. "Recognition as the Social Grammar of Species Being in Marx," in Heikki Ikäheimo and Arto Laitinen (eds.), *Recognition and Social Ontology*. Leiden: Brill, 239–70.

Quante, Michael. 2013. "Das gegenständliche Gattungswesen. Bemerkungen zum intrinsischen Wert menschlicher Dependenz," in Rahel Jaeggi and Daniel Loick (eds.), *Nach Marx. Philosophie, Kritik, Praxis*. Frankfurt: Suhrkamp, 69–86.

Rader, Melvin. 1979. *Marx's Interpretation of History*. New York: Oxford University Press.

Redding, Paul. 1996. *Hegel's Hermeneutics*. Ithaca, NY: Cornell University Press.

Rienstra, Byron and Derek Hook. 2006. "Weakening Habermas: The Undoing of Communicative Rationality." *Politikon* 33, no. 3: 313–39.

Rockmore, Tom. 1992. *Irrationalism: Lukács and the Marxist View of Reason*. Philadelphia: Temple University Press.

Rockmore, Tom. 2015. "Habermas, Critical Theory and Political Economy," in G. Smulewicz-Zucker and M. Thompson (eds.), *Radical Intellectuals and the Subversion of Progressive Politics: The Betrayal of Politics*. New York: Palgrave Macmillan, 191–210.

Rosen, Michael. 1996. *On Voluntary Servitude: False Consciousness and the Theory of Ideology*. Cambridge, MA: Harvard University Press.

Rosen, Stanley. 2014. *The Idea of Hegel's Science of Logic*. Chicago: University of Chicago Press.

Rousseau, Jean-Jacques. 1964. *Discours sur l'origine et les fondements de l'inégalité parmi les hommes*, in Bernard Gagnebin and Marcel Raymond (eds.), *Œuvres Complètes*, vol. 3. Paris: Éditions Gallimard.

Sahlins, Marshall. 1976. *Culture and Practical Reason*. Chicago: University of Chicago Press.

Schnädelbach, Herbert. 1986. "Transformation der Kritischen Theorie," in Axel Honneth and Hans Joas (eds.), *Kommunikatives Handeln. Beiträge zu Jürgen Habermas' »Theorie des kommunikativen Handelns«*. Frankfurt: Suhrkamp, 15–34.

Searle, John. 1964. "How to Derive an 'Ought' from an 'Is.'" *Philosophical Review* 73, no. 1: 43–58.

Searle, John. 1983. *Intentionality: An Essay in the Philosophy of Mind*. New York: Cambridge University Press.

Searle, John. 1995. *The Construction of Social Reality*. New York: Free Press.

Searle, John. 2007. *Freedom and Neurobiology: Reflections on Free Will, Language, and Political Power*. New York: Columbia University Press.

Searle, John. 2010. *Making Sense of the Social World: The Structure of Human Civilization*. New York: Oxford University Press.

Sellars, Wilfred. 2007. *In the Space of Reasons: Selected Essays of Wilfred Sellars*. Cambridge, MA: Harvard University Press.

Sen, Amartya. 2009. *The Idea of Justice*. Cambridge, MA: Harvard University Press.

Sève, Lucien. 1978. *Man in Marxist Theory and the Psychology of Personality*. Sussex: Harvester Press.

Sidanius, Jim and Felicia Pratto. 1999. *Social Dominance: An Intergroup Theory of Social Hierarchy and Oppression*. New York: Cambridge University Press.

Sidanius, Jim, Felicia Pratto, Colette van Laar, and Shana Levin. 2004. "Social Dominance Theory: Its Agenda and Method." *Political Psychology* 25, no. 6: 845–80.

Skinner, Quentin. 2008. "Freedom as the Absence of Domination," in C. Laborde and J. Maynor (eds.), *Republicanism and Political Theory*. Oxford: Blackwell.

Sklar, Martin. 1988. *The Corporate Reconstruction of American Capitalism, 1890–1916: The Market, the Law, and Politics*. Cambridge: Cambridge University Press.

Skowronek, Stephen. 1982. *Building a New American State: The Expansion of National Administrative Capacities, 1877–1920*. Cambridge: Cambridge University Press.

Smith, Steven B. 1984. "Considerations on Marx's Base and Superstructure." *Social Science Quarterly* 65, no. 4: 940–54.

Stahl, Titus. 2011. "Verdinglichung als pathologie zweiter ordnung." *Deutsche Zeitschrift für Philosophie* 59, no. 5: 731–46.

Stahl, Titus. 2015. "Praxis und Totalität: Lukács' *Ontologie des gesellschaftlichen Seins* im Lichte aktueller sozialontologischer Debatten." *Jahrbuch der Internationalen Georg-Lukács-Gesellschaft* 14/15: 123–50.

Stein, Maurice R. 1960. *The Eclipse of Community: An Interpretation of American Studies*. New York: Harper Torchbooks.

Strauss, Leo. 1953. *Natural Right and History*. Chicago: University of Chicago Press.

Strauss, Leo. 1959. *What Is Political Philosophy? and Other Studies*. Chicago: University of Chicago Press.

Streeck, Wolfgang. 2009. *Re-Forming Capitalism: Institutional Change in the German Political Economy*. New York: Oxford University Press.

Surber, Jere Paul. 1975. "Hegel's Speculative Sentence." *Hegel-Studien* 10: 210–30.

Taylor, Charles. 1975. *Hegel*. Cambridge: Cambridge University Press.

Taylor, Charles. 1995. *Philosophical Arguments*. Cambridge, MA: Harvard University Press.

Therborn, Göran. 1978. *What Does the Ruling Class Do When It Rules?* London: Verso.

Thompson, Michael J. 2011. "Marxism, Ethics, and the Task of Critical Theory," in M. Thompson (ed.), *Rational Radicalism and Political Theory*. Lanham, MD: Lexington Books, 161–88.

Thompson, Michael J. 2013a. "Alienation as Atrophied Moral Cognition and Its Implications for Political Behavior." *Journal for the Theory of Social Behaviour* 43, no. 3: 301–21.

Thompson, Michael J. 2013b. "A Functionalist Theory of Social Domination." *Journal of Political Power* 6, no. 2: 179–99.

Thompson, Michael J. 2013c. "Reconstructing Republican Freedom: A Critique of the Neo-Republican Concept of Freedom as Non-Domination." *Philosophy and Social Criticism* 39, no. 3: 277–98.

Thompson, Michael J. 2015a. "Capitalism as Deficient Modernity: Hegel against the Modern Economy," in Andrew Buchwalter (ed.), *Hegel and Capitalism*. Albany, NY: SUNY Press, 117–32.

Thompson, Michael J. 2015b. "False Consciousness Reconsidered: A Theory of Defective Social Cognition." *Critical Sociology* 41, no 3: 449–61.

Thompson, Michael J. 2015c. "Inventing the 'Political': Arendt, Anti-Politics and the Deliberative Turn in Contemporary Political Theory," in G. Smulewicz-Zucker and M. Thompson (eds.), *Radical Intellectuals and the Subversion of Progressive Politics: The Betrayal of Politics*. New York: Palgrave Macmillan, 69–97.

Thompson, Michael J. 2015d. "Philosophical Foundations for a Marxian Ethics," in M. Thompson (ed.), *Constructing Marxist Ethics: Critique, Normativity, Praxis*. Leiden: Brill, 235–65.

Thompson, Michael J. 2015e. "The Wrath of Thrasymachus: Value Irrationality and the Failures of Deliberative Democracy." *Theoria: A Journal of Social and Political Theory* 62, no. 2: 33–58.

Trachtenberg, Zev M. 1993. *Making Citizens: Rousseau's Political Theory of Culture*. New York: Routledge.

Tuomela, Raimo. 2013. *Social Ontology: Collective Intentionality and Group Agents*. New York: Oxford University Press.

Tyler, Tom R. 1997. "The Psychology of Legitimacy: A Relational Perspective on Voluntary Deference to Authorities." *Personality and Social Psychology Review* 1, no. 4: 323–45.

Tyler, Tom R. and E. Allen Lind. 1992. "A Relational Model of Authority in Groups." *Advances in Experimental Social Psychology* 25: 115–91.

Wacquant, Loic. 1985. "Heuristic Models in Marxism." *Social Forces* 64, no. 1: 17–45.

Weber, Max. 1963. "'Objectivity' in Social Science and Social Policy," in Maurice Natanson (ed.), *Philosophy of the Social Sciences*. New York: Random House.

Weber, Max. 1972 [1922]. *Wirtschaft und Gesellschaft*. Tübingen: J. C. B. Mohr/ Paul Siebeck.

Weissman, David. 2000. *A Social Ontology*. New Haven, CT: Yale University Press.

Wellmer, Albrecht. 1990. "Practical Philosophy and the Theory of Society: On the Problem of the Normative Foundations of a Critical Social Science," in S. Benhabib and F. Dallmayr (eds.), *The Communicative Ethics Controversy*. Cambridge, MA: MIT Press, 293–329.

Whitebook, Joel. 2001. "Mutual Recognition and the Work of the Negative," in William Rehg and James Bohman (eds.), *Pluralism and the Pragmatic Turn: The Transformation of Critical Theory*. Cambridge, MA: MIT Press, 257–92.

Williams, Robert R. 1997. *Hegel's Ethics of Recognition*. Berkeley: University of California Press.

Wittgenstein, Ludwig. 1968. *Philosophical Investigations*. Oxford: Basil Blackwell.

Wood, Allen. 1990. *Hegel's Ethical Thought*. New York: Cambridge University Press.

Wrong, Dennis. 2002. *Power: Its Forms, Bases, and Uses*. New Brunswick, NJ: Transaction.

Zurn, Christopher. 2005. "Recognition, Redistribution, and Democracy: Dilemmas of Honneth's Critical Social Theory." *European Journal of Philosophy* 13, no. 1: 89–126.

Index

About the Author

Michael J. Thompson is associate professor of political theory in the Department of Political Science, William Paterson University.